G. W. F. Hegel

ENCYCLOPEDIA OF THE PHILOSOPHICAL SCIENCES IN OUTLINE

and Critical Writings

The German Library: Volume 24
Volkmar Sander, General Editor

G. W. F. Hegel

ENCYCLOPEDIA OF THE PHILOSOPHICAL SCIENCES IN OUTLINE

AND CRITICAL WRITINGS

Edited by Ernst Behler

CONTINUUM · NEW YORK

1990
The Continuum Publishing Company
370 Lexington Avenue, New York, NY 10017

The German Library
is published in cooperation with Deutsches Haus,
New York University.
This volume has been supported by a grant from
Deutscher Akademischer Austauschdienst.

Printed in the United States of America

Library of Congress Cataloging-in-Publication Data

Hegel, Georg Wilhelm Friedrich, 1770–1831.
 [Selections. English. 1990]
 Encyclopedia of the philosophical sciences in outline, and critical
writings / G.W.F. Hegel ; edited by Ernst Behler.
 p.   cm. — (The German library ; v. 24)
First work is a translation of: Enzyklopädie der philosophischen
Wissenschaften.
 Includes bibliographical references.
 Contents: Preface to the system of science / translated by
A. V. Miller — Encyclopedia of the philosophical sciences in outline
/ translated by Steven A. Taubeneck — Solger's posthumous writings
and correspondence / translated by Diana I. Behler.
 ISBN 0-8264-0339-5. — ISBN 0-8264-0340-9 (pbk.)
 1. Philosophy. I. Behler, Ernst, 1928–   . II. Miller, Arnold
V. III. Taubeneck, Steven A. IV. Behler, Diana. V. Title.
VI. Series.
B2908   1990
193—dc20   90-34418
                                                   CIP

Grateful acknowledgment is made to Oxford University Press for permission to
reprint "Preface: On Scientific Cognition." © Oxford University Press 1977.
Reprinted from Hegel's *Phenomenology of Spirit* translated by A V Miller
(1977) by permission of Oxford University Press.

Contents

SOLGER'S POSTHUMOUS WRITINGS AND CORRESPONDENCE
Translated by Diana I. Behler   265

Introduction

The course of transcendental philosophy from about 1780 to 1830, as it unfolds in the texts of volumes 13 (Immanuel Kant, *Philosophical Writings*), 23 (Fichte, Jacobi, and Schelling, *Philosophy of German Idealism*), and the present volume in The German Library, seems to suggest that with Hegel, we are approaching the culmination of this development and its ultimate expression. There is a strong warning in the introduction to volume 23 against such a teleological conception, which would devaluate Kant, Fichte, Schelling, and many others to mere steppingstones on the way to Hegel. Given the truly colossal dimensions of Hegel's philosophy of spirit, however, its powerful realization down to specific branches such as logic, philosophy of law, philosophy of religion, or aesthetics, and the broad historical contours in which this system is executed, we can hardly refrain from assuming this view of Hegel. This impression seems to be confirmed by the strong impact his thought has had over leading minds in many parts of the world up until our own time. The alliance with Marxism also gave this philosophy an additional appearance of political power. Considering the historical consciousness, inextricably linked with Hegelian thought, such an inveterate enemy of speculative thinking as Nietzsche recognized the overwhelming influence of Hegelianism, even upon himself, by describing this philosophy almost in terms of a natural force when he said: "We Germans are Hegelians even if there never had been any Hegel, insofar as we (unlike all Latins) instinctively attribute a deeper meaning and greater value to becoming and development than to what 'is'; we hardly believe in the justification of the concept of 'being.' "[1]

Yet we realize that with these remarks we are building a monument for Hegel that would inevitably relegate him to the past. Phrases typical for such distancing and discarding intent characterize Hegel as the philosopher who furnished decisive motifs of thought for two centuries, who was perhaps one of the most influential figures in the history of humankind, whose unequaled power of thought is manifest in the fact that it inspired dialectical materialism as well as conservative theories of the state. Under the impact of these remarks, Hegel soon appears as a curiosity of a part of history which is no longer our own. Heine already depicted this feeling toward Hegel as a segment of a closed-off, bygone part of history as early as 1826 in his image of a dream of an intoxicated God who had stolen away from the carousing assembly of his fellow Gods and lain down to sleep on a lonely star. Here, dream images took shape and began to form a madly lurid, but harmoniously sensible sequence comprising our historical past. Heine said: "the Iliad, the battle of Marathon, Moses, the Medicean Venus, the Strassburg cathedral, the French Revolution, Hegel, steamships, etc., are excellent individual ideas in this creative divine dream."[2] Hegel himself had an acute feeling of standing at the watershed of time, of enunciating the principles of a world historical epoch to which there was no return.

There are good reasons for the reader of the late twentieth century to approach Hegel with this distancing view. Hegel's notion of philosophy as a scientific system in which truth actually exists and is at home will appear peculiar and odd today. At one point Hegel declares it as his highest goal to transform philosophy from a mere "love of knowing" to the actual knowing of truth[3]—as if such transformation were possible. The subdivisions of that system appeared to Hegel not as convenient and dispensable schemes of organization, but as categories of truth formulating ontological relationships. The whole structure of this system of truth smacks of a strong Eurocentric, yes, Germanocentric bias. Hegel's bias can also be sensed in his rationalistic concept of philosophy, which disdainfully treats literature, the arts, religion, every other form of human experience but the philosophical as something that has not sufficiently lifted itself up to the height of the idea, to his notion of philosophy. Not even the other sciences are exempted from his scorn. Heraldry is looked down at from his philosophy of the spirit, but also anthropology, even history, and we might add pharmacology, theoretical physics, statistics, and many other forms of investigation to that list. At a professional meeting of 1850, a congress of classicists took issue with Hegel, who had blemished their discipline for not being a science but only a conglomerate, an aggregate of knowledge.[4] What appears to be most foreign to our manner of thinking, however, is Hegel's stubborn maintenance of reason as the sole dominating principle in the intellectual world—an attitude that could appropriately be called his totalitarianism of reason.

These reservations toward Hegel only increase if we move into the specifics of his texts. If we look for his literary taste, we notice a narrow predilection for the traditional, the familiar, combined with an incriminating censoring of everything avant-gardist, new, or un-established. His opinions about Tieck, Hoffmann, Novalis, Kleist, *Lucinde,* or romantic irony are sufficient examples for that attitude. Hegel is of course the author of a three-volume course on aesthetics. The importance of this work for literature, however, is minor, and for the theory of literature it is not much more than a "relapse into older rationalist attitudes and concepts."[5] Hegel certainly favored the French Revolution. Whenever political upheavals or simply un-rest in his own country occurred, however, his attitude was quite different. With unrelenting scorn he opposed representative democ-racy, universal suffrage, even constitutional monarchy, and as the philosopher of the state, maintained the same supremacy of the central absolute state over all realms of public and private life as he did with the principle of reason over all other forms of human experience in his philosophy of spirit. All this comes forth in a style of prose that has justly been called "Himalayan" and which one likes to describe as grandiose only in order to consign it all the more securely to the past.

Hegel's philosophy of spirit has, on the other hand, always tran-scended the confines of the historical epoch it seemed to express and through its effects entertained the most active interrelationship with the future up into our present time. As far as the apparent final form of this philosophy is concerned, we could easily turn this impression around by considering philosophy, in a genuinely Hegelian spirit, as the consciousness of its time and thereby project the realization of the true philosophy of spirit into the future of the world. Nietzsche sensed in Hegel's historical approach to truth far-reaching potential when he surmised that the fall of the human subject might well belong to its consequences. He expected that under the impact of this thought we would eventually no longer be inclined "to concede that our human logic is logic as such or the only kind of logic (we would rather persuade ourselves that it is merely a special case and perhaps one of the oddest and most stupid cases)."[6] The modern and postmodern appropriation of Hegel is entirely in accordance with the principles of his philosophy and has indeed been an essential and lasting feature of its history. This reception of Hegel can be noticed in the focus on special, sometimes minute instances within this immensely structured thought process, in the isolation of particularly intriguing moments of thought from this infinitely enchained system, such as the melancholy of the sad type of consciousness, the tragedy of the great world historical personalities, or what is known as the dialectic of master and slave. Alexandre Kojève has shown in brilliant lectures how to actualize Hegel from such instances and how to appropriate his philosophy to the interests of one's own time.[7] In these instances, the Himalayan character of Hegel's prose writing seems to disappear in favor of an almost poetic power and freshness of language. Richard Rorty finds this literary quality in Hegel's entire attitude as a philosopher, but especially in his dealing with previous philosophers. Long before Nietzsche, according to Rorty, Hegel exercised the transformation of philosophy into a literary genre when he treated previous philosophers like abbreviations of a particular vocabulary, conducted the philosophical critique of them by putting other philosophers with new vocabularies in their place, and considered a decision between these various vocabularies as a matter of perspective.[8]

The present volume attempts to convey some of these impressions, which have become part of the Hegel image. The volume is also intended to show on the basis of three characteristic texts how Hegel's philosophy gained the position in history it has enjoyed since its inception. That was mainly due to the author's unrelenting work on the individual parts of his system, his constant "laboring on the concept." Otto Pöggeler remarked correctly:

> Hegel won his time over to him not only because he revised in solitary work the attempt at a new founding of philosophy constantly anew, but also because he turned to the concrete work in the individual disciplines such as philosophy of law, aesthetics, and philosophy of

religion. Even for those who attempted to go beyond idealistic philosophy, Hegel's philosophy became the authoritative "world philosophy," namely the self-understanding of an expired epoch.[9]

The results of these efforts in terms of doctrines, contents of learning, instruction, and so forth, were of course soon outdone by the
rise of the individual academic disciplines during the nineteenth
century, which also set an end to speculative philosophy as such.
What remained, however, was the manner of thinking, the conceptual effort, the affirmation and maintenance of philosophy in
the intellectual environment of the post-Revolutionary period, as
well as the exemplary character this effort provided for succeeding
attempts.

To appreciate this effort, we have to recognize that the stable
system of rationalism and the Enlightenment with its belief in
absolute norms that are accessible to the human mind had been
shaken by the time of Hegel's appearance on the philosophical
scene. This had not only taken place through the event of the
Revolution, but also through perhaps more profound experiences
dominant in the late eighteenth century of which the Revolution is
only a partial expression. To name them at random, these are the
experiences of individualism, subjectivity, concreteness, playfulness,
rococo, irrationality, cynicism, and, in general, of an encounter with
the world that cannot be subjected to a pregiven lawfulness, but
which has the structure of the unforeseen, of openness to new
possibilities, of history. Rousseau, Blake, and Schlegel are expressions of this experience of the world.

Hegel did not encounter this attitude in a European framework
but from the confines of his German environment, originally in the
atmosphere of a Tübingen theological seminar. Yet even within these
limits, he could experience this new perception of the world in its
most sophisticated—although most abstract—form as a replace-
ment of being by obligation (the "Ought"), of original constitution
by final purpose, of "this is" by "this shall be." This is the common
core of the philosophies of Kant and Fichte. Fichte even proclaimed
it to be the central aim of his philosophy to substitute for the
concept of static being that of an infinite becoming. If we look back
at the Nietzsche quote given at the beginning of this introduction
about the dissolution of the concept of being into that of becoming
and development, we seem to be at the root of Hegelianism. We

would have to modify this statement, however, by adding that it was not Hegel's goal to dissolve meaning into an unidentified, anonymous process of becoming, but to safeguard structures of meaning, structures of becoming, structures of being through his relentless "laboring on the concept." While giving full recognition to the historicity of all events, Hegel attempted to disentangle their meaning beyond an ephemeral appearance, their relevance for a general purpose, and their place within the system of the philosophy of spirit.

Some examples from Hegel's historical lectures can best illustrate this attitude. In his *The Philosophy of History,* Hegel presents the ancient Egyptian world as "shut up within the limits of particular conceptions," as almost "imbruted in them." Yet truth, spirit, consciousness came forth at least as a problem, as an enigma. This appears to be evident from the inscription in the sanctuary of the Goddess Neith at Sais: "I am that which is, that which was, and that which will be; no one has lifted my veil."[10] From this inscription we gather already that the solution of the riddle, the answer to the problem is "that which is clear to itself." This becomes indeed the meaning of the inscription at Apollo's temple in Delphi: "Man, know thyself!" Hegel comments: "In this dictum is not intended a self-recognition that regards the specialties of one's own weaknesses and defects: it is not the individual that is admonished to become acquainted with his idiosyncrasy, but humanity *in general* is summoned to self-knowledge" (546). In a more philosophical sense, however, it was Anaxagoras in the Greek world who was the first to enunciate that *nous,* understanding in general, or reason governed the world. That was not to be understood in the sense of a "self-conscious reason" or a "spirit as such" ruling the world from outside, but more in analogy to the movements of the solar system which take place according to unchangeable laws implicit, like reason, in their movements (11). In Hegel's own time, the idea of law in the sense of right asserted its authority during the French Revolution when the notion of "Reason embodied in Laws" founded a constitution on which all future legislation was to be based. Hegel commented: "Never since the sun had stood in the firmament and the planets revolved around it had one perceived that man's existence centers in his head, i.e., in thought, inspired by which he builds up the world of reality. Anaxagoras had been the first to say that nous governs the world; but not until now had man advanced to the recognition of the principle that thought ought to govern spiritual reality. This was accordingly a glorious mental dawn" (447).

In a broader perspective, Hegel saw the level to which nous, logos, spirit had advanced during all these centuries as reason and thought, based on the assumption that everything else in the world exhibits the same type of reason that the human subject possesses (439). Accordingly, science had become the experience of the world. Descartes had introduced the general reign of the subject (440). Reason was called all that which had been deduced from consciousness—"the laws of nature and the substance of what is right and good"—and the name Enlightenment was given to the "recognition of the validity of these laws" (441). Yet this form of reasoning and thought was "abstract" and general for Hegel and could not satisfy the "living spirit, the concrete human soul" (442). Here began the task of Kant, Fichte, Schelling, and, finally, of Hegel himself in the sense of an absolute knowledge that comprises the general and the concrete, the systematical and the historical. "This formally absolute principle brings us to *the last stage in history, our world, our own time*"—with these words Hegel used to announce the approaching of this moment in his lectures on *The Philosophy of History* (442) or on *The History of Philosophy*.[11] In similar fashion he traced the enhancement of consciousness to the final goal of absolute knowledge in his systematic lectures on *The Science of Logic* or on *The System of Philosophy*.[12] This thought process also forms the framework in the lectures on the *Encyclopedia of the Philosophical Sciences in Outline*.

"This magnificent Hegelian synthesis has dissolved"—with this compact statement Charles Taylor introduced the concluding chapter of his influential *Hegel*, in which he attempted to answer the question about Hegel's continuing relevance, Hegel's importance for us today.[13] To substantiate his claim, Taylor pointed to the obvious fact that members of modern society would hardly see history as the "unfolding of spirit" (545), or he argued that in 1975 perhaps no one any longer believed Hegel's "central ontological thesis that the universe is posited by a spirit whose essence is rational necessity" (538). The decisive question for all critical dealing with Hegel, that is, "how his thought can remain important while his conclusions are quite abandoned" (539), was answered by Taylor with an assumption, however, which now appears at least as outworn as Hegel's vision of a world reconciled to the spirit. He advanced the opinion that Hegel's synthesis had been "anthropologized," or "transferred from *Geist* to man" (546). This move had of course already been made by the Young Hegelians, but Taylor went beyond these earlier attempts and also beyond the protest against Hegel articulated by Kierkegaard, Marx, and the late Schelling. Still feeling the validity of the romantic aspiration toward "freedom as self-dependence," toward "freedom as total self-creation," he saw in Hegel the most successful corrective of that desire, in that his philosophy provided a model of how "to situate subjectivity by relating it to our life as embodied and social beings" (570). Taylor consequently proclaimed this "situated subjectivity" and "embodied subjectivity," or rather the search for it in response to the "claims of absolute freedom" and "expressivist protest" against any strictures and embodiments, as the most relevant aspect in Hegel's thought today (571). And it seems that in spite of its reference to anthropology and subjectivity, his answer, or at least a central motif in it, still guides a good deal of the present occupation with Hegel.

The critique of the ontological or metaphysical foundations of this thought has become much more intense in today's critique and not only relates to Hegel's notion of the unfolding spirit, but extends to his presupposition of the subject, to his notions of rationality, meaning, and logic, as well as to all that these principles imply. Removing the truth-value from the construct of Hegel's system but letting it stand as an interesting invention of the human mind, Lyotard has characterized the Hegelian philosophy as one of the great "metanarratives," as the prototype of those comprehensive and foundational discourses of modern history which provide an umbrella of ultimate sense and meaning for all details of human knowledge and activity.[14] For the more literary oriented reader, such criticism awakens with all its vigilance when one reads Hegel's discriminations of romantic irony, which reveal not only a lack of humor, his inability to laugh (Bataille), but also an incapability of any form of self-criticism, self-annihilation, of suspending one's own foundations. "Suppose that he deceived himself"—this type of Nietzschean criticism animates today's reading of Hegel. Derrida appears as one of these readers when he comments:

The necessity of *logical* continuity is the decision or interpretative milieu of all Hegelian interpretations. In interpreting negativity as labor, in betting for discourse, meaning, history, etc., Hegel has bet against play, against chance. He has blinded himself to the possibility of his own bet, to the fact that the conscientious suspension of play . . . was itself a phase of play; and to the fact that play *includes* the work of meaning or the meaning of work, and includes them not in terms of *knowledge,* but in terms of *inscription:* meaning is a function of play, is inscribed in a certain place in the configuration of a meaningless play.[15]

This attitude seems to point out that which continues to be relevant in Hegel, his importance for us today. If one used Benedetto Croce's formula of *What is living and what is dead of the philosophy of Hegel?*[16] in order to circumscribe that portion of relevance, we certainly would no longer hold on to Hegel's philosophy of spirit by letting his logic and philosophy of nature go, as Croce did, but declare all three parts of this system obsolete and thoroughly dead. This declaration would be total and not only also include the sketches and outlines of the "early" Hegel, but even his dialectics. For such a radicalized critique of Hegel could not satisfy itself by keeping the instrument of his thought, his "methodology" in stock while dismissing all contents, all doctrines, all results obtained through it. In a reverse consideration, however, we would regard all three sections of this system as eminently alive because for a type of thinking that essentially has turned into a critique of philosophy, into self-criticism of philosophy, Hegel's system is still one of the most formidable edifices of thought with which a philosophy in the state of its self-overcoming has to cope and against which it has to prove itself. Again, this attitude would extend to dialectics, although not in the sense of believing in dialectics, but in that of denying its validity while critically examining it, operating with it. This total affirmation of Hegel through his complete denial, however, would be self-critical enough to know that Hegel's oeuvre cannot be comprised in toto, neither in denial nor in affirmation, and that it is one of those texts that constantly shows itself anew to different generations.

E. B.

Notes

1. Friedrich Nietzsche, *The Gay Science*, trans. Walter Kaufmann (New York: Random House, 1974), p. 306 (Aph. 357).
2. Heinrich Heine, Sämtliche Schriften, ed. Klaus Briegleb (München: Carl Hanser, 1969), vol. 3, p. 253 (*Das Buch Le Grand*, ch. III).
3. See below, p. xxii.
4. *Philologie und Hermeneutik im 19. Jahrhundert*, ed. Helmut Flashar, Karlfried Gründer, and Axel Horstmann (Göttingen: Vandenhoeck and Ruprecht, 1979), p. 24.
5. René Wellek, *A History of Modern Criticism: 1750–1950*, vol. 2: *The Romantic Age* (New Haven: Yale University Press, 1955), p. 320.
6. Friedrich Nietzsche, *The Gay Science*, p. 306 (Aph. 357).
7. Alexandre Kojève, *Introduction to the Reading of Hegel: Lectures on the Phenomenology of Spirit*, trans. James H. Nichols (New York: Basic Books, 1969).
8. Richard Rorty, *Contingency, Irony, and Solidarity* (Cambridge: Cambridge University Press, 1989), pp. 78–79.
9. *Hegel. Einführung in seine Philosophie*, ed. Otto Pöggeler (München: Karl Alber, 1977), p. 22.
10. G. W. F. Hegel, *The Philosophy of History*, trans. C. J. Friedrich (New York: Dover, 1956), p. 220. Subsequent references to this edition are cited in parentheses with page number in the text.
11. G. W. F. Hegel, *The History of Philosophy*, trans. E. S. Haldane and Frances H. Simson (New York: The Humanities Press, 1955), p. 546: "To this point the World Spirit has come. . . ."
12. *The Logic of Hegel*, trans. William Wallace (Oxford: Oxford University Press, 1892); *Hegel's Philosophy of Nature*, trans. A. V. Miller (Oxford: Oxford University Press, 1970); *Hegel's Philosophy of Mind*, trans. William Wallace and A. V. Miller (Oxford: Oxford University Press, 1971). This is the translation of Hegel's late three-volume lecture course on the *Encyclopedia of Philosophy*, a considerably enlarged version of the early

Heidelberg *Encyclopedia of the Philosophical Sciences,* and also entitled *The System of Philosophy.* For a translation of Hegel's *Science of Logic* see *Hegel's Science of Logic,* trans. A. V. Miller (New York: Humanities Press, 1989). This is a reprint of the 1969 translation of this text.

13. Charles Taylor, *Hegel* (Cambridge: Cambridge University Press, 1975), p. 537. Subsequent references to this edition are cited in parentheses with page number in the text.

14. Jean-François Lyotard, *The Postmodern Condition: A Report on Knowledge,* trans. Geoff Bennington and Brian Massumi (Minneapolis: University of Minnesota Press, 1984).

15. Jacques Derrida, "From Restricted to General Economy: A Hegelianism without Reserve," *Writing and Difference,* trans. Alan Bass (Chicago: University of Chicago Press, 1978), p. 260.

16. Benedetto Croce, *What Is Living and What Is Dead of the Philosophy of Hegel,* trans. Douglas Ainslie (London: Macmillan, 1915).

Note on the Texts

The three texts chosen for this volume represent major aspects of Hegel's thought and interest. The first is usually, but erroneously, known as the introduction to Hegel's *Phenomenology of Spirit* because it appeared as a preface in this work when Hegel published it in 1807. However, the *Phenomenology* was not conceived by its author as an individual book but as the introductory volume to the presentation of his philosophical system in the habitual tripartite scheme of (1) The Science of Logic, (2) Philosophy of Nature, and (3) Philosophy of Spirit. The *Phenomenology* occupied a particular position in this projected system of philosophy in that it had more of an introductory, piloting, propaedeutic relationship to it. Hegel designated the *Phenomenology* as the "first part" of his system of philosophy, and its function obviously was to describe the "history of consciousness," the pathway of the Spirit, until the moment for a formulation of the system of philosophy had come. Yet by choosing such a concrete starting point, Hegel entangled himself in the insoluble problem of a true "beginning" in philosophy and consequently did not pursue this theme any further. In his *Encyclopedia* of 1817 he said self-critically about this attempt:

> Earlier, in the *Phenomenology of Spirit,* I have treated the scientific history of consciousness as the first part of philosophy, since it was meant to precede pure science and to generate its concept. At the same time, however, consciousness and its history, like every other philosophical science, are not an absolute beginning, but an element in the circle of philosophy.[1]

At that time, as well as in the later editions of his *Encyclopedia,* Hegel saw the beginning of philosophy, because of a lack of a circumscribable subject matter and the indeterminable nature of free thought, as constantly receding, as a "circle of circles" in which each circle (logic, philosophy of nature, philosophy of spirit) breaches through its own periphery and infringes upon the others.[2]

The *Phenomenology* thereby assumed more and more the status of an individual work. Yet the preface attached to it clearly relates to the original conception of the system of philosophy and the introductory journey to it. Hegel said in this preface: "The true shape in which truth exists can only be the scientific system of truth. To help bring philosophy closer to the form of science, to the goal where it can lay aside the title '*love* of knowing' and be *actual* knowing—that is what I have set myself to do" (3). He saw his time as the beginning of a new period, the essence of which was the movement toward a scientific system of philosophy, and said:

> Besides, it is not difficult to see that ours is a birth-time and a period of transition to a new era. Spirit has broken with the world it has hitherto inhabited and imagined, and is of a mind to submerge it in the past, and in the labor of its own transformation. Spirit is indeed never at rest but always engaged in moving forward. But just as the first breath drawn by a child after its long, quiet nourishment, breaks the gradualness of merely quantitative growth—there is a qualitative leap, and the child is born—so likewise the Spirit in its formation matures slowly and quietly into its new shape, dissolving bit by bit the structure of its previous world, whose tottering state is only hinted at by isolated symptoms. (6)

The preface conveys something of the grandiose contours in which Hegel thought about his philosophy.

In a certain way one could maintain that Hegel never carried out this system of philosophy in which his thought was so absolutely centered but furnished only parts of it. Yet we have at least "outlines" of the system, and the first of these outlines has been chosen for this volume. This is Hegel's *Encyclopedia of the Philosophical Sciences in Outline,* a text he published in 1817 as a guide for his students at Heidelberg University. In 1827, then at Berlin University, Hegel published an enlarged version of this outline, almost twice its size, and in 1830, one year before his death, a third version appeared, again considerably augmented. The work now had expanded to three volumes, according to its three subdivisions, and in some of

Hegel's collected works assumed the title *The System of Philosophy*. Yet the original *Encyclopedia*, because of its brevity, condensation of thought, and freshness of ideas has always kept a special place among Hegel's writings, although Steven Taubeneck's translation is the first appearance of the text in English. The *Encyclopedia* became the basic book of Hegel's philosophy, and Hegel used it not only when he gave lecture courses on his system of philosophy, but also when he lectured on individual parts of it like Logic, Philosophy of Nature, and Philosophy of Spirit, or even when he lectured on sections of these parts such as Philosophy of Law, Philosophy of Religion, and so on. As Hegel said himself in the introduction to the text, the title *Encyclopedia of the Philosophical Sciences in Outline* should suggest "partly the scope of the whole, and partly the intent to leave the details for oral delivery" (47).

In order to understand the relationship of the term *Encyclopedia* to the original project of a *System of Philosophy*, one has to distinguish carefully between Hegel's notion of encyclopedia and the traditional notion of encyclopedia in the sense of a sum of all knowledge. The most famous realization of an encyclopedia before Hegel was undoubtedly the *Encyclopédie ou Dictionnaire raisonné, des sciences, des arts et des métiers,* which Diderot and d'Alembert published from 1751 to 1772 in 35 sumptuous volumes. All previous attempts at encyclopedic knowledge in classical antiquity (εγκυκλιος παιδεια, *encyclios disciplina*), the Middle Ages (Vincent de Beauvais, *Speculum historiale, naturale, doctrinale, et morale,* 1260), the Renaissance (*disciplina orbicularis quam Encyclopaedia Graeci vocant*), or the modern age by Francis Bacon (*De dignitate et augmentis scientiarum,* 1623), Leibniz *(Characteristica universalis),* and in the encyclopedias of the early eighteenth century (Chambers) were outdone by this work, which combined a systematic thrust with the most ramified knowledge of details. The systematic character of this encyclopedia is often overlooked because of the mechanical arrangement of the facts according to the order of the alphabet. It is maintained, however, through the "enchainment of knowledge," through references among the articles according to Bacon's division of the human mind into memory, imagination, and reason, and through d'Alembert's introductory essay establishing the genealogy and filiation of all our knowledge.

In contrast to this encyclopedia of all sciences and arts, Hegel's encyclopedia focuses on one particular branch of knowledge, philosophy, and develops an exhaustive as well as detailed treatment of this discipline. In this attitude Hegel followed a particular tendency of the late eighteenth and beginning nineteenth century, which can be characterized as establishing encyclopedias of special disciplines such as an encyclopedia of law, an encyclopedia of theology, an encyclopedia of archeology, and so forth. The famous Hellenist F. A. Wolf worked at that time on an encyclopedia of classical philology that was meant to provide a model for the interpretative, the hermeneutic disciplines. It was also habitual in Germany to present such universal views of individual disciplines in comprehensive lecture courses at the university. These projects were indeed closely connected with the curriculum at the universities and contributed to the self-understanding of the university and of higher education in general by reflecting on the particular nature of individual branches of knowledge. When Hegel was asked in 1812 by the Bavarian Ministry of Education to present a statement on how to teach philosophy as a propaedeutic discipline at high schools, he wrote:

> The encyclopedia, as it is meant to be philosophical, precludes the literary encyclopedia which is anyhow insubstantial and worthless for the youth. The encyclopedia can contain nothing but the general content of philosophy, that is, the basic concepts and principles of its particular branches which I count as three main ones: 1. logic, 2. philosophy of nature, 3. philosophy of spirit. All other sciences, considered as non-philosophical, belong in their origins to these and should be considered in the encyclopedia, because it is philosophical, only according to these origins.[3]

As is obvious from these remarks, the encyclopedia was closely related to general education, and Hegel believed that philosophy, not literature, provided the best model for general education. The one who most strongly promoted the literary type of general education and advocated that the principles of knowledge could best be gained through the encyclopedia of literature, was Friedrich Schlegel, who in this regard again formed the direct opposite to Hegel.[4]

A feature of the encyclopedia in Hegel's sense not to be overlooked is its character of an outline. Hegel said in the introduction to the third edition of his *Encyclopedia:* "As *Encyclopedia* science is not presented in the detailed development of its specification, but limited to the origins and the basic concepts of the particular sciences" (vol. 8, ¶ 16, p. 60). Yet the "lessened rigor of scientific method" implied in this procedure does not mean that the "logical connection" could be neglected (vol. 8, ¶ 3, p. 44). In the first edition, Hegel designated his encyclopedia as an "outline" and a "manual" (p.47), whereas in the second he speaks of a "reading-book," which "through oral presentation should receive its necessary explanations." Through the voice of the lecturer the encyclopedia was supposed to attain a vivid enactment, although we have to add that Hegel's reputation as a lecturer was quite poor. To see a lively element in these texts, one also should consider that Hegel reworked them until the end of his life and constantly gave them new shape. In this structure, his *Encyclopedia* has become the basis and synopsis of the extraordinarily influential lectures of Hegel.

When Hegel presented his *Encyclopedia* as the summary of a particular discipline, we have of course to consider which discipline he is dealing with, that is, a fundamental discipline that claims to contain the principles of all other disciplines within itself. Hegel formulates this thought in ¶ 10 of our text where he says: "What is true in any one science is so through and by virtue of philosophy, whose encyclopedia thus comprises all true sciences" (53). The other, ordinary encyclopedia is distinguished from this philosophical one in that it is only an assemblage, an aggregation of knowledge that has occurred in more or less accidental fashion and in an empirical manner and where one also finds disciplines "which bear the names of sciences but are otherwise only collations of bits of information" (53). Next to disciplines of a merely "aggregational" character such as classical philology, Hegel's encyclopedia excludes those that have "arbitrariness" as their basis, for example, heraldry. Other disciplines such as jurisprudence are considered only insofar as they reach through their "rational basis and origin" into philosophy. As far as their "empirical distinctiveness and reality" are concerned, they are irrelevant for the encyclopedic project. The same applies to natural sciences such as natural history, geography, and medicine, which ramify into specialites governed by "external chance and play, not by reason." Hegel even counts history among these disciplines, since it resides in "contingencies and in the field of arbitrariness." Also those expressions of philosophy founded on "anthropology, facts of consciousness, inner intuition, or external experience" do not belong to the sphere of a philosophical encyclopedia (vol. 8, ¶ 16, pp. 61–62).

The most distinguishing mark of Hegel's encyclopedia is without a doubt its rigorously systematic character. Already in his early writing *On the Difference of the Fichtean and Schellingian System of Philosophy* of 1801, he said with a certain disdain for Fichte's claim to have a system without, however, ever carrying it out: "That philosophizing which does not construct itself as a system is a permanent escape from limitations, is more of a struggling of reason for freedom than a pure self-recognition of freedom which is certain and conscious of itself." If this systematic drive ever came to realization in Hegel's writings, it was mostly in his encyclopedias that it manifested itself, although more in the form of an outline, a manual, a reading-book. However, to gain a notion of Hegel's grand conception of philosophy, one has to take his *Encyclopedia* into account, and in order to orient oneself in this enormously multifarious edifice, no text is more suited than the first edition of this work.

Hegel's long essay on Solger has been translated into English as one of his rare pieces in literary criticism and the theory of literature and also as a type of writing that reveals aspects usually unknown and lacking in the common image of the philosopher. This is obvious, first of all, in the casual, almost conversational style of communication, as well as in Hegel's interest in individual features such as Solger's personal appearance and professional career. Solger was by no means a close friend or disciple of Hegel. Hegel mentioned him occasionally in his earlier writings and lectures, such as in his *Philosophy of Law,* and associated him with the notion of irony as Friedrich Schlegel had brought it up. Such association was usually disastrous in the eyes of Hegel, but he exculpated Solger by declaring that Solger adhered "primarily only to the side of the actually dialectical" in irony, "to the animating pulse of a speculative consideration."[5] As Hegel formulated it in his lectures on *Aesthetics,* Solger, out of a truly speculative desire, grasped the "dialectical moment of the idea," what Hegel called "infinite absolute negativity," and clung to this negativity. For Hegel, this negativity, as important as it may be, is of course "only *one element* and not, as Solger will have it, the whole Idea."[6] Yet in real life Solger was neither an "ironic artist" for Hegel, nor was his profound sense for genuine works of art of an "ironical nature" (64–65). With this attitude, Solger had gained Hegel's respect.

Solger had studied philosophy with Fichte and Schelling at Jena University and in the wake of Schelling had become one of the prominent aestheticians, a philosopher of art at a time in Germany when each book fair brought new volumes and handbooks on aesthetics. He taught philosophy and aesthetics at the University of Frankfurt on the Oder until that university was dissolved in 1811. Solger then moved to the University of Berlin where he died on October 25, 1819, an early death. He had requested and supported Hegel's appointment at Berlin University in 1818 and wrote to Tieck on April 26, 1818: "I admire Hegel very much and agree with him in many parts most remarkably." The two worked together at the same university for only one year, and their relationship was more collegial than personal, more distant than close, more silent than communicative. Solger remained a philosopher of romanticism and thereby intellectually removed from Hegel, although, as René Wellek observed, he was "hardly a romanticist in the ordinary sense." Wellek adds: "Rather, with his philosophy of irony, his dialectical union of opposites, his emphasis on the concrete presence of beauty, his tragedy of reconciliation, he belongs to the group of critics who favor a fundamentally symbolic view of art as imagination."[7]

To review the edition of Solger's posthumous writings and correspondence that Ludwig Tieck and Friedrich von Raumer had edited in 1826 was a welcome opportunity for Hegel to reexamine after so many years the romantic school and the romantic period of literature that had occupied him in his early writings, especially in his *Phenomenology*. Hegel says at the beginning of the review that a "great many literary phenomena and opinions which belong to the spirit of this time pass before our eyes in this correspondence" (235) and that "we see ourselves transferred into the midst of the view of one of the remarkable epochs" of German literature (237). Hegel gives us his frank opinion about the main representatives of the romantic movement. His Solger Review is also one of the rare texts in which he occasionally speaks about his own writings, the *Phenomenology* as well as his *Logic*. He talks about Goethe, the purpose of philosophy, Socrates, religion, and a great number of subject matters without, however, subjecting them to the rigorously systematic pursuit that usually marks his writings. The impression is one of listening to Hegel in a relaxed conversation. The assumption is perhaps not wrong that Hegel engaged in this long digression into Solger's posthumous writings and correspondence because it offered him a last opportunity to speak about irony and to qualify his position on a subject matter toward which his attitude had been unbendingly hostile and negative. To be sure, Hegel does not yield and give irony a more positive evaluation. The Solger Review remains one of his merciless incriminations of that romantic attitude that appears to have annoyed him more than anything else in the world. Yet he makes efforts to accept at least a certain type of irony, Solger's irony, and to describe it as reconcilable with the life of the Idea, although even that type is basically wrong and one-sided for him. A few examples from Hegel's earlier writings should illustrate this attitude.

One of the classical instances is Hegel's introduction to his *Lectures on Aesthetics*. Irony is presented in these passages "as this concentration of the *ego* in itself, for which all bonds are snapped and which can live only in the bliss of self-enjoyment." Hegel adds: "This irony was invented by Friedrich von Schlegel, and many others have babbled about it or are now babbling about it again." He says:

> The ironical, as the individuality of genius, lies in the self-destruction of the noble, great, and excellent; and so the objective art-formations too will have to display only the principle of absolute subjectivity, by showing forth what has worth and dignity for mankind as null in its self-destruction. This then implies that not only is there to be no seriousness about law, morals, and truth, but that there is nothing in what is lofty and best, since, in its appearance in individuals, characters, and actions, it contradicts and destroys itself and so is ironical about itself.

Solger is exempted from this verdict because he was not, as Hegel puts it, "content, like the others, with a superficial philosophical culture." So he probed "the depths of the philosophical Idea," although he only experienced the negative side of it. His life was broken off too soon "to permit him to grasp the concrete development of the philosophical Idea." Tieck and the other romantics, however, always insist on the importance of irony. Yet when they come to making judgments on great works of art, for instance on *Romeo and Juliet,* we are deceived and "hear no more about irony." (*Aesthetics: Lectures on Fine Art.* vol. 1, pp. 64–69.)

The most comprehensive statement on this subject matter, except for the Solger Review, occurs in Hegel's *Philosophy of Right* in a long footnote to ¶ 140 of this text. This instance deserves complete reproduction as a parallel to essential passages in the Solger Review and also as a pertinent example of Hegel's thinking about romanticism, irony, and Solger.

My colleague, the late Professor Solger, adopted the word "irony" which Friedrich Schlegel brought into use at a comparatively early period of his literary career and enhanced to equivalence with the said principle of subjectivity knowing itself as supreme. But Solger's finer mind was above such an exaggeration; he had philosophic insight and so seized upon, emphasized, and retained only that part of Schlegel's view which was dialectic in the strict sense, i.e. dialectic as the pulsating drive of speculative inquiry. His last publication, a solid piece of work, a thorough *Critique of the Lectures by August Wilhelm Schlegel on Dramatic Art and Literature*,[8] I find somewhat obscure, however, and I cannot agree with the argument which he develops. "True irony," he says, "arises from the view that so long as man lives in this present world, it is only in this world that he can fulfill his appointed task no matter how elevated a sense we give to this expression. Any hope we may have of transcending finite ends is a foolish and empty conceit. Even the highest is existent for our conduct only in a shape that is limited and finite." Rightly understood, this is Platonic doctrine, and a true remark in rejection of what he has referred to earlier, the empty striving towards the (abstract) infinite. But to say that the highest is existent in a limited and finite shape, like the ethical order (and that order is in essence actual life and action), is very different from saying that the highest thing is a *finite* end. The outward shape, the form of finitude, in no way deprives the content of ethical life of its substantiality and the infinity inherent within it. Solger continues: "And just for this reason the highest is in *us* as negligible as the lowest and perishes of necessity with us and our nugatory thoughts and feelings. The highest is truly existent in God alone, and as it perishes in us it is transfigured into something divine, a divinity in which we would have had no share but for its immediate presence revealed in the very disappearance of our actuality; now the mood to which this process directly comes home in human affairs is tragic irony." The arbitrary name "irony" would be of no importance, but there is an obscurity here when it is said that it is "the highest" which perishes with our nothingness and that it is in the disappearance of our actuality that the divine is first revealed; e.g. again: "We see heroes beginning to wonder whether they have erred in the noblest and finest elements of their feelings and sentiments, not only in regard to their successful issue, but also to their source and their worth; indeed, what elevates us is the destruction of the best itself." (The *just* destruction of utter scoundrels and criminals who flaunt their villainy—the hero of a modern tragedy, *Die Schuld,*[9] is one—has an interest for criminal law, but none at all for art proper which is what is in question here.) The *tragic* destruction of figures whose ethical life is on the highest plane can interest and elevate us and reconcile us to its occurrence only insofar as they come on the scene in opposition to one another together with equally justified but different ethical powers which have come into collision through misfortune, because the result is that then these figures acquire guilt through their opposition to an ethical law. Out of this situation there arises the right and wrong of both parties and therefore the true ethical Idea, which, purified and in triumph over this one-sidedness, is thereby reconciled in *us.* Accordingly, it is not the highest in us which perishes; we are elevated not by the destruction of the best but by the triumph of the true. This it is which constitutes the true, purely ethical, interest of ancient tragedy (in romantic tragedy the character of the interest undergoes a certain modification). All this I have worked out in detail in my *Phenomenology of Spirit.*[10] But the ethical Idea is actual and present in the world of social institutions without the misfortune of tragic clashes and the destruction of individuals overcome by this misfortune. And this Idea's (the highest's) revelation of itself in its actuality as anything but a nullity is what the external embodiment of ethical life, the state, purposes and effects, and what the ethical self-consciousness possesses, intuits, and knows in the state and that the thinking mind comprehends there. (*Hegel's Philosophy of Right,* pp. 101–2.)

The *Preface to the System of Science* is taken from the English edition of the *Phenomenology of Spirit* by G. W. F. Hegel. *Translated by A. V. Miller with Analysis of the Text and Foreword by J. N. Findlay* (Oxford: Oxford University Press, 1977). The text has been presented in this volume with the permission of Oxford University Press. Style and spelling of this edition have been preserved.

Hegel's *Encyclopedia of the Philosophical Sciences in Outline* has never been translated into English before.[11] Steven A. Taubeneck assumed the task to make this text available in English. The translation is based on the first edition of this text as it is reproduced in photostatic reprint in volume 6 of the *Jubiläumsausgabe* (Georg Wilhelm Friedrich Hegel, *Sämtliche Werke.* 20 volumes. Edited by Hermann Glockner. Stuttgart: Frommann-Holzboog, 1968), pp. 1–310.

Hegel's *Review of Solger's Posthumous Writings and Correspondence* appears here for the first time in English translation and certainly is a text not too widely known among Hegel experts.[12] Diana I. Behler assumed the translation with the intention of providing a broader textual basis for the study of the philosopher in the English-speaking world. The basis for the translation is the original text as it appeared in photostatic reprint in volume 20 of the *Jubiläumsausgabe* (Georg Wilhelm Friedrich Hegel, *Sämtliche Werke*. 20 volumes. Edited by Hermann Glockner. Stuttgart: Frommann-Holzboog, 1968), vol. 20, pp. 132–202.

I should like to thank Professor Otto Pöggeler, Director of the Hegel-Archives at Bochum University, and Dr. Walter Jaeschke, Director of the Schleiermacher Forschungsstelle in Berlin, who were so kind as to advise me when I selected the texts for this volume and encouraged me to choose the *Encyclopedia* (Jaeschke) and the Solger Review (Pöggeler). My work on this volume was supported by a grant from the Graduate School of the University of Washington.

E. B.

Notes to the Text

1. G. W. F. Hegel, *Encyclopedia of the Philosophical Sciences in Outline* ¶ 36, p. 65. Subsequent references to this edition are cited in parentheses with page number in the text.

2. G. W. F. Hegel, *Enzyklopädie der philosophischen Wissenschaften* (1830), ¶ 15, p. 60, in: G. W. F. Hegel, *Werke,* 20 volumes (Frankfurt: Suhrkamp Taschenbuch, 1986), vol. 8. Subsequent references to this edition are cited in parentheses with volume and page number in the text.

3. G. W. F. Hegel, *Nürnberger Schriften,* ed. Johannes Hoffmeister (Leipzig: F. Meiner, 1938), p. 439.

4. Friedrich Schlegel, *Wissenschaft der europäischen Literatur,* in: *Kritische Friedrich Schlegel Ausgabe,* vol. 11 (Paderborn: F. Schöringh, 1958), pp. 3–15.

5. *Hegel's Philosophy of Right,* trans. T. M. Knox (Oxford: Oxford University Press, 1942), pp. 101–2.

6. G. W. F. Hegel, *Aesthetics. Lectures on Fine Art,* trans. T. M. Knox (Oxford: Oxford University Press, 1975), pp. 64–69.

7. René Wellek, *A History of Modern Criticism: 1750–1950.* vol. 2: *The Romantic Age* (New Haven: Yale University Press, 1955), p. 303.

8. *Wiener Jahrbuch,* vol. 7, pp. 90 ff.

9. *Die Schuld (The Guilt).* A play by Adolf Müllner (1774–1829).

10. G. W. F. Hegel, *Phenomenology of Spirit,* trans. A. V. Miller (Oxford: Oxford University Press, 1977), pp. 364 ff.

11. Daniel Breazeale, Helmut Schneider, and James H. Wilkinson, "English Translations of Hegel: An Annotated Bibliography," Aletheia. An International Journal of Philosophy 3 (1979), pp. 47–52. This is a revised version of the Hegel section in "English Translations of Fichte, Schelling, and Hegel: An Annotated Bibliography," by Daniel Breazeale in Idealistic Studies 6, 3 (1976), pp. 279–97. No. 34.0 lists the *Encyclopedia of Philosophy.* Trans. and annotated by Gustav Emil Mueller, which is characterized as "purportedly a translation of the Enzyklopädie der philo-

sophischen Wissenschaften (1817, 1827, 1830), actually a selective summary, at most a paraphrase." The grand English translation of the three sections of Hegel's *Encyclopedia* is of course the Oxford translation of *The Logic of Hegel* (trans. William Wallace) of 1892, *Hegel's Philosophy of Nature* (trans. A. V. Miller) of 1970, and *Hegel's Philosophy of Mind* (trans. William Wallace and A. V. Miller) of 1971. But these are translations of the late voluminous versions of Hegel's *Encyclopedia,* with considerable additions by Leopold von Henning and K. L. Michelet, which are a world apart from the early Heidelberg text of 1817 which is presented here for the first time in English.

12. There is no trace of a translation of this review in the bibliography mentioned in the previous note, and there are not many mentionings of this text in the English or German literature on Hegel either. One exception is of course Otto Pöggeler, *Hegels Kritik der Romantik* (Bonn: Bouvier 1956), who devotes considerable attention to this particular text. The Italian translation with an introductory essay by Giovanna Pinna appeared in the spring of 1990: G. W. F. Hegel, *Due scritti berlinesi su Solger e Humboldt,* trans. Giovanna Pinna (Naples: Lignori Editore, 1990).

PREFACE TO THE SYSTEM OF PHILOSOPHY

I t is customary to preface a work with an explanation of the author's aim, why he wrote the book, and the relationship in which he believes it to stand to other earlier or contemporary treatises on the same subject. In the case of a philosophical work, however, such an explanation seems not only superfluous but, in view of the nature of the subject matter, even inappropriate and misleading. For whatever might appropriately be said about philosophy in a preface—say a historical *statement* of the main drift and the point of view, the general content and results, a string of random assertions and assurances about truth—none of this can be accepted as the way in which to expound philosophical truth. Also, since philosophy moves essentially in the element of universality, which includes within itself the particular, it might seem that here more than in any of the other sciences the subject matter itself, and even in its complete nature, were expressed in the aim and the final results, the execution being by contrast really the unessential factor. On the other hand, in the ordinary view of anatomy, for instance (say, the knowledge of the parts of the body regarded as inanimate), we are quite sure that we do not as yet possess the subject matter itself, the content of this science, but must in addition exert ourselves to know the particulars. Further, in the case of such an aggregate of information, which has no right to bear the name of Science, an opening

1

talk about aim and other such generalities is usually conducted in the same historical and uncomprehending way in which the content itself (these nerves, muscles, etc.) is spoken of. In the case of philosophy, on the other hand, this would give rise to the incongruity that along with the employment of such a method its inability to grasp the truth would also be demonstrated.

Furthermore, the very attempt to define how a philosophical work is supposed to be connected with other efforts to deal with the same subject matter drags in an extraneous concern, and what is really important for the cognition of the truth is obscured. The more conventional opinion gets fixated on the antithesis of truth and falsity, the more it tends to expect a given philosophical system to be either accepted or contradicted; and hence it finds only acceptance or rejection. It does not comprehend the diversity of philosophical systems as the progressive unfolding of truth, but rather sees in it simple disagreements. The bud disappears in the bursting-forth of the blossom, and one might say that the former is refuted by the latter; similarly, when the fruit appears, the blossom is shown up in its turn as a false manifestation of the plant, and the fruit now emerges as the truth of it instead. These forms are not just distinguished from one another, they also supplant one another as mutually incompatible. Yet at the same time their fluid nature makes them moments of an organic unity in which they not only do not conflict, but in which each is as necessary as the other; and this mutual necessity alone constitutes the life of the whole. But he who rejects a philosophical system [i.e., the new philosopher] does not usually comprehend what he is doing in this way; and he who grasps the contradiction between them [i.e., the historian of philosophy] does not, as a general rule, know how to free it from its one-sidedness, or maintain it in its freedom by recognizing the reciprocally necessary moments that take shape as a conflict and seeming incompatiblility.

Demanding and supplying these [superficial] explanations passes readily enough as a concern with what is essential. Where could the inner meaning of a philosophical work find fuller expression than in its aims and results, and how could these be more exactly known than by distinguishing them from everything else the age brings forth in this sphere? Yet when this activity is taken for more than the mere beginnings of cognition, when it is allowed to pass for actual cognition, then it should be reckoned as no more than a device for evading the real issue [*die Sache selbst*], a way of creating an impression of hard work and serious commitment to the problem, while actually sparing oneself both. For the real issue is not exhausted by stating it as an aim, but by carrying it out, nor is the result the actual whole, but rather the result together with the process through which it came about. The aim by itself is a lifeless universal, just as the guiding tendency is a mere drive that as yet lacks an actual existence; and the bare result is the corpse which has left the guiding tendency behind it. Similarly, the specific difference of a thing is rather its limit; it is where the thing stops, or it is what the thing is not. This concern with aim or results, with differentiating and passing judgment on various thinkers is therefore an easier task than it might seem. For instead of getting involved in the real issue, this kind of activity is always away beyond it; instead of tarrying with it, and losing itself in it, this kind of knowing is forever grasping at something new; it remains essentially preoccupied with itself instead of being preoccupied with the real issue and surrendering to it. To judge a thing that has substance and solid worth is quite easy, to comprehend it is much harder, and to blend judgment and comprehension in a definitive description is the hardest thing of all.

Culture and its laborious emergence from the immediacy of substantial life must always begin by getting acquainted with *general* principles and points of view, so as at first to work up to a *general conception* [*Gedanke*] of the real issue, as well as learning to support and refute the general conception with reasons; then to apprehend the rich and concrete abundance [of life] by differential classification; and finally to give accurate instruction and pass serious judgment upon it. From its very beginning, culture must leave room for the earnestness of life in its concrete richness; this leads the way to an experience of the real issue. And even when the real issue has been penetrated to its depths by serious speculative effort, this kind of knowing and judging will still retain its appropriate place in ordinary conversation.

The true shape in which truth exists can only be the scientific system of such truth. To help bring philosophy closer to the form of Science, to the goal where it can lay aside the title "*love* of knowing" and be *actual* knowing—that is what I have set myself to do. The inner necessity that knowing should be Science lies in its nature, and only the systematic exposition of philosophy itself provides it. But the *external* necessity, so far as it is grasped in a general way, setting aside accidental matters of person and motivation, is the same as the inner, or in other words it lies in the shape in which time sets forth the sequential existence of its moments. To show that now is the time for philosophy to be raised to the status of a Science would therefore be the only true justification of any effort that has this aim, for to do so would demonstrate the necessity of the aim, would indeed at the same time be the accomplishing of it.

To lay down that the true shape of truth is scientific—or, what is the same thing, to maintain that truth has only the Notion as the element of its existence—seems, I know, to contradict a view which is in our time as prevalent as it is pretentious, and to go against what that view implies. Some explanation therefore seems called for, even though it must for the present be no more than a bare assertion, like the view that it contradicts. If, namely, the True exists only in what, or better *as* what, is cometimes called intuition, sometimes immediate knowledge of the Absolute, religion or being—not at the center of divine love but the being of the divine love itself—then what is required in the exposition of philosophy is, from this viewpoint, rather the opposite of the form of the Notion. For the Absolute is not supposed to be comprehended, it is to be felt and intuited; not the Notion of the Absolute, but the feeling and intuition of it, must govern what is said, and must be expressed by it.

If we apprehend a demand of this kind in its broader context, and view it as it appears at the stage which self-conscious Spirit has presently reached, it is clear that Spirit has now got beyond the substantial life it formerly led in the element of thought, that it is beyond the immediacy of faith, beyond the satisfaction and security of the certainty that consciousness then had, of its reconciliation with the essential being, and of that being's universal presence both within and without. It has not only gone beyond all this into the other extreme of an insubstantial reflection of itself into itself, but beyond that too. Spirit has not only lost its essential life; it is also conscious of this loss, and of the finitude that is its own content. Turning away from the empty husks, and confessing that it lies in wickedness, it reviles itself for so doing, and now demands from philosophy, not so much *knowledge* of what it *is,* as the recovery through its agency of that lost sense of solid and substantial being.

Philosophy is to meet this need, not by opening up the fast-locked nature of substance, and raising this to self-consciousness, not by bringing consciousness out of its chaos back to an order based on thought, nor to the simplicity of the Notion, but rather by running together what thought has put asunder, by suppressing the differentiations of the Notion and restoring the *feeling* of essential being: in short, by providing edification rather than insight. The "beautiful," the "holy," the "eternal," "religion," and "love" are the bait required to arouse the desire to bite; not the Notion, but ecstasy, not the cold march of necessity in the thing itself, but the ferment of enthusiasm, these are supposed to be what sustains and continually extends the wealth of substance.

In keeping with this demand is the strenuous, almost overzealous and frenzied effort to tear men away from their preoccupation with the sensuous, from their ordinary, private [*einzelne*] affairs, and to direct their gaze to the stars; as if they had forgotten all about the divine, and were ready like worms to content themselves with dirt and water. Formerly they had a heaven adorned with a vast wealth of thoughts and imagery. The meaning of all that is, hung on the thread of light by which it was linked to that heaven. Instead of dwelling in this world's presence, men looked beyond it, following this thread to an otherworldly presence, so to speak. The eye of the Spirit had to be forcibly turned and held fast to the things of this world; and it has taken a long time before the lucidity which only heavenly things used to have could penetrate the dullness and confusion in which the sense of worldly things was enveloped, and so make attention to the here and now as such, attention to what has been called "experience," an interesting and valid enterprise. Now we seem to need just the opposite: sense is so fast rooted in earthly things that it requires just as much force to raise it. The Spirit shows itself as so impoverished that, like a wanderer in the desert craving for a mere mouthful of water, it seems to crave for its refreshment only the bare feeling of the divine in general. By the little which now satisfies Spirit, we can measure the extent of its loss.

This modest complacency in receiving, or this sparingness in giving, does not, however, befit Science. Whoever seeks mere edification, and whoever wants to shroud in a mist the manifold variety of his earthly existence and of thought, in order to pursue the indeterminate enjoyment of this indeterminate divinity, may look where he likes to find all this. He will find ample opportunity to dream up something for himself. But philosophy must beware of the wish to be edifying.

Still less must this complacency which abjures Science claim that such rapturous haziness is superior to Science. This prophetic talk supposes that it is staying right in the center and in the depths, looks disdainfully at determinateness (*Horos*), and deliberately holds aloof from Notion and Necessity as products of that reflection which is at home only in the finite. But just as there is an empty breadth, so too there is an empty depth; and just as there is an extension of substance that pours forth as a finite multiplicity without the force to hold the multiplicity together, so there is an intensity without content, one that holds itself in as a sheer force without spread, and this is in no way distinguishable from superficiality. The power of Spirit is only as great as its expression, its depth only as deep as it dares to spread out and lose itself in its exposition. Moreover, when this nonconceptual, substantial knowledge professes to have sunk the idiosyncrasy of the self in essential being, and to philosophize in a true and holy manner, it hides the truth from itself: by spurning measure and definition, instead of being devoted to God, it merely gives free rein both to the contingency of the content within it, and to its own caprice. Such minds, when they give themselves up to the uncontrolled ferment of [the divine] substance, imagine that, by drawing a veil over self-consciousness and surrendering understanding they become the beloved of God to whom He gives wisdom in sleep; and hence what they in fact receive, and bring to birth in their sleep, is nothing but dreams.

Besides, it is not difficult to see that ours is a birth-time and a period of transition to a new era. Spirit has broken with the world it has hitherto inhabited and imagined, and is of a mind to submerge it in the past, and in the labor of its own transformation. Spirit is indeed never at rest but always engaged in moving forward. But just as the first breath drawn by a child after its long, quiet nourishment breaks the gradualness of merely quantitative growth—there is a qualitative leap, and the child is born—so likewise the Spirit in its formation matures slowly and quietly into its new shape, dissolving bit by bit the structure of its previous world, whose tottering state is only hinted at by isolated symptoms. The frivolity and boredom which unsettle the established order, the vague foreboding of something unknown, these are the heralds of approaching change. The gradual crumbling that left unaltered the face of the whole is cut short by a sunburst which, in one flash, illuminates the features of the new world.

But this new world is no more a complete actuality than is a newborn child; it is essential to bear this in mind. It comes on the scene for the first time in its immediacy or its Notion. Just as little as a building is finished when its foundation has been laid, so little is the achieved Notion of the whole the whole itself. When we wish to see an oak with its massive trunk and spreading branches and foliage, we are not content to be shown an acorn instead. So too, Science, the crown of a world of Spirit, is not complete in its beginnings. The onset of the new spirit is the product of a wide-spread upheaval in various forms of culture, the prize at the end of a complicated, tortuous path and of just as variegated and strenuous an effort. It is the whole which, having traversed its content in time and space, has returned into itself, and is the resultant *simple Notion* of the whole. But the actuality of this simple whole consists in those various shapes and forms which have become its moments, and which will now develop and take shape afresh, this time in their new element, in their newly acquired meaning.

While the initial appearance of the new world is, to begin with, only the whole veiled in its *simplicity,* or the general foundation of the whole, the wealth of previous existence is still present to con-sciousness in memory. Consciousness misses in the newly emerging shape its former range and specificity of content, and even more the articulation of form whereby distinctions are securely defined, and stand arrayed in their fixed relations. Without such articulation, Science lacks universal intelligibility, and gives the appearance of being the esoteric possession of a few individuals: an esoteric posses-sion, since it is as yet present only in its Notion or in its inwardness; of a few individuals, since its undiffused manifestation makes its existence something singular. Only what is completely determined is at once esoteric, comprehensible, and capable of being learned and appropriated by all. The intelligible form of Science is the way open and equally accessible to everyone, and consciousness as it ap-proaches Science justly demands that it be able to attain to rational knowledge by way of the ordinary understanding; for the under-standing is thought, the pure "I" as such; and what is intelligible is what is already familiar and common to Science and the unscientific consciousness alike, the latter through its having afforded direct access to the former.

Science in its early stages, when it has attained neither to completness of detail nor perfection of form, is vulnerable to criticism. But it would be as unjust for such criticism to strike at the very heart of Science, as it is untenable to refuse to honor the demand for its further development. This polarization seems to be the Gordian knot with which scientific culture is at present struggling, and which it still does not properly understand. One side boasts of its wealth of material and intelligibility, the other side at least scorns this intelligibility, and flaunts its immediate rationality and divinity. Even if the former side is reduced to silence, whether by the force of truth alone or by the blustering of the other, and even if, in respect of fundamentals, it feels itself outmatched, it is by no means satisfied regarding the said demands; for they are justified, but not fulfilled. Its silence stems only half from the triumph of its opponent, and half from the boredom and indifference which tend to result from the continual awakening of expectations through unfulfilled promises.

As for content, the other side make it easy enough for themselves at times to display a great expanse of it. They appropriate a lot of already familiar and well-ordered material; by focusing on rare and exotic instances they give the impression that they have hold of everything else which scientific knowledge had already embraced in its scope, and that they are also in command of such material as is as yet unordered. It thus appears that everything has been subjected to the absolute Idea, which therefore seems to be cognized in everything and to have matured into an expanded science. But a closer inspection shows that this expansion has not come about through one and the same principle having spontaneously assumed different shapes, but rather through the shapeless repetition of one and the same formula, only externally applied to diverse materials, thereby obtaining merely a boring show of diversity. The Idea, which is of course true enough on its own account, remains in effect always in its primitive condition, if its development involves nothing more than this sort of repetition of the same formula. When the knowing subject goes around applying this single inert form to whatever it encounters, and dipping the material into this placid element from outside, this is no more the fulfilment of what is needed, i.e., a self-originating, self-differentiating wealth of shapes, than any arbitrary insights into the content. Rather it is a monochromatic formalism which only arrives at the differentiation of its material since this has been already provided and is by now familiar.

Yet this formalism maintains that such monotony and abstract universality are the Absolute, and we are assured that dissatisfaction with it indicates the inability to master the absolute standpoint and to keep hold of it. Time was when the bare possibility of imagining something differently was sufficient to refute an idea, and this bare possibility, this general thought, also had the entire positive value of an actual cognition. Nowadays we see all value ascribed to the universal Idea in this nonactual form, and the undoing of all distinct, determinate entities (or rather the hurling of them all into the abyss of vacuity without further development or any justification) is allowed to pass muster as the speculative mode of treatment. Dealing with something from the perspective of the Absolute consists merely in declaring that, although one has been speaking of it just now as something definite, yet in the Absolute, the A = A, there is nothing of the kind, for there all is one. To pit this single insight, that in the Absolute everything is the same, against the full body of articulated cognition, which at least seeks and demands such fulfilment, to palm off its Absolute as the night in which, as the saying goes, all cows are black—this is cognition naïvely reduced to vacuity. The formalism which recent philosophy denounces and despises, only to see it reappear in its midst, will not vanish from Science, however much its inadequacy may be recognized and felt, till the cognizing of absolute actuality has become entirely clear as to its own nature. Since the presentation of a general idea in outline, before any attempt to follow it out in detail, makes the latter attempt easier to grasp, it may be useful at this point to give a rough idea of it, at the same time taking the opportunity to get rid of certain habits of thought which impede philosophical cognition.

In my view, which can be justified only by the exposition of the system itself, everything turns on grasping and expressing the True, not only as *Substance,* but equally as *Subject.* At the same time, it is to be observed that substantiality embraces the universal, or the *immediacy of knowledge* itself, as well as that which is *being* or immediacy *for* knowledge. If the conception of God as the one

Substance shocked the age in which it was proclaimed, the reason for this was on the one hand an instinctive awareness that, in this definition, self-consciousness was only submerged and not preserved. On the other hand, the opposite view, which clings to thought as thought, to *universality* as such, is the very same simplicity, is undifferentiated, unmoved substantiality. And if, thirdly, thought does unite itself with the being of Substance, and apprehends immediacy or intuition as thinking, the question is still whether this intellectual intuition does not again fall back into inert simplicity, and does not depict actuality itself in a nonactual manner.

Further, the living Substance is being which is in truth *Subject*, or, what is the same, is in truth actual only in so far as it is the movement of positing itself, or is the mediation of its self-othering with itself. This Substance is, as Subject, pure, *simple negativity*, and is for this very reason the bifurcation of the simple; it is the doubling which sets up opposition, and then again the negation of this indifferent diversity and of its antithesis [the immediate simplicity]. Only this self-*restoring* sameness, or this reflection in otherness within itself—not an *original* or *immediate* unity as such—is the True. It is the process of its own becoming, the circle that presupposes its end as its goal, having its end also as its beginning; and only by being worked out to its end, is it actual.

Thus the life of God and divine cognition may well be spoken of as a disporting of Love with itself; but this idea sinks into mere edification, and even insipidity, if it lacks the seriousness, the suffering, the patience, and the labor of the negative. *In itself*, that life is indeed one of untroubled equality and unity with itself, for which otherness and alienation, and the overcoming of alienation, are not serious matters. But this *in-itself* is abstract universality, in which the nature of the divine life *to be for itself*, and so too the self-movement of the form, are altogether left out of account. If the form is declared to be the same as the essence, then it is ipso facto a mistake to suppose that cognition can be satisfied with the in-itself or the essence, but can get along without the form—that the absolute principle or absolute intuition makes the working-out of the former, or the development of the latter, superfluous. Just because the form is as essential to the essence as the essence is to itself, the divine essence is not to be conceived and expressed merely as essence, i.e., as immediate substance or pure self-contemplation of the divine, but likewise as *form,* and in the whole wealth of the developed form. Only then is it conceived and expressed as an actuality.

The True is the whole. But the whole is nothing other than the essence consummating itself through its development. Of the Absolute it must be said that is is essentially a *result,* that only in the *end* is it what it truly is; and that precisely in this consists its nature, viz., to be actual, subject, the spontaneous becoming of itself. Though it may seem contradictory that the Absolute should be conceived essentially as a result, it needs little pondering to set this show of contradiction in its true light. The beginning, the principle, or the Absolute, as at first immediately enunciated, is only the universal. Just as when I say "*all* animals," this expression cannot pass for a zoology, so it is equally plain that the words, "the Divine," "the Absolute," "the Eternal," etc., do not express what is contained in them; and only such words, in fact, do express the intuition as something immediate. Whatever is more than such a word, even the transition to a mere proposition, contains a *becoming-other* that has to be taken back, or is a mediation. But it is just this that is rejected with horror, as if absolute cognition were being surrendered when more is made of mediation than in simply saying that it is nothing absolute, and is completely absent in the Absolute.

But this abhorrence in fact stems from ignorance of the nature of mediation, and of absolute cognition itself. For mediation is nothing beyond self-moving selfsameness, or is reflection into self, the moment of the "I" which is for itself pure negativity or, when reduced to its pure abstraction, *simple becoming.* The "I," or becoming in general, this mediation, on account of its simple nature, is just immediacy in the process of becoming, and is the immediate itself. Reason is, therefore, misunderstood when reflection is excluded from the True, and is not grasped as a positive moment of the Absolute. It is reflection that makes the True a result, but it is equally reflection that overcomes the antithesis between the process of its becoming and the result, for this becoming is also simple, and therefore not different from the form of the True which shows itself as *simple* in its result; the process of becoming is rather just this return into simplicity. Though the embryo is indeed *in itself* a human being, it is not so *for itself;* this it only is as cultivated Reason, which has *made* itself into what it is *in itself.* And that is when it for the first time is actual. But this result is itself a simple immediacy, for it is self-conscious freedom at peace with itself, which has not set the antithesis on one side and left it lying there, but has been reconciled with it.

What has just been said can also be expressed by saying that Reason is *purposive activity*. The exaltation of a supposed Nature over a misconceived thinking, and especially the rejection of external teleology, has brought the form of purpose in general into discredit. Still, in the sense in which Aristotle, too, defines Nature as purposive activity, purpose is what is immediate and *at rest*, the unmoved which is also *self-moving*, and as such is Subject. Its power to move, taken abstractly, is *being-for-self* or pure negativity. The result is the same as the beginning, only because the *beginning* is the *purpose;* in other words, the actual is the same as its Notion only because the immediate, as purpose, contains the self or pure actuality within itself. The realized purpose, or the existent actuality, is movement and unfolded becoming; but it is just this unrest that is the self; and the self is like that immediacy and simplicity of the beginning because it is the result, that which has returned into itself, the latter being similarly just the self. And the self is the sameness and simplicity that relates itself to itself.

The need to represent the Absolute as *Subject* has found expression in the propositions: *God* is the eternal, the moral world-order, love, and so on. In such propositions the True is only posited *immediately* as Subject, but is not presented as the movement of reflecting itself into itself. In a proposition of this kind one begins with the word "God." This by itself is a meaningless sound, a mere name; it is only the predicate that says *what God is,* gives Him content and meaning. Only in the end of the proposition does the empty beginning become actual knowledge. This being so, it is not clear why one does not speak merely of the eternal, of the moral world-order, and so on, or, as the ancients did, of pure notions like "being," "the One," and so on, in short, of that which gives the meaning without adding the *meaningless* sound as well. But it is just this word that indicates that what is posited is not a being [i.e., something that merely *is*], or essence, or a universal in general, but rather something that is reflected into itself, a Subject. But at the same time this is only anticipated. The Subject is assumed as a fixed point to which, as their support, the predicates are affixed by a movement belonging to the knower of this Subject, and which is not regarded as belonging to the fixed point itself; yet it is only through this movement that the content could be represented as Subject. The way in which this movement has been brought about is such that it cannot belong to the fixed point; yet, after this point has been presupposed, the nature of the movement cannot really be other than what it is, it can only be external. Hence, the mere anticipation that the Absolute is Subject is not only *not* the actuality of this Notion, but it even makes the actuality impossible; for the anticipation posits the subject as an inert point, whereas the actuality is self-movement.

Among the various consequences that follow from what has just been said, this one in particular can be stressed, that knowledge is only actual, and can only be expounded, as Science or as *system;* and furthermore, that a so-called basic proposition or principle of philosophy, if true, is also false, just because it is *only* a principle. It is, therefore, easy to refute it. The refutation consists in pointing out its defect; and it is defective because it is only the universal or principle, only the beginning. If the refutation is thorough, it is derived and developed from the principle itself, not accomplished by counterassertions and random thoughts from outside. The refutation would, therefore, properly consist in the further development of the principle, and in thus remedying the defectiveness, if it did not mistakenly pay attention solely to its *negative* action, without awareness of its progress and result on their *positive* side too—The genuinely *positive* exposition of the beginning is thus also, conversely, just as much a negative attitude towards it, viz., towards its initially one-sided form of being *immediate* or *purpose.* It can therefore be taken equally well as a refutation of the principle that constitutes the *basis* of the system, but it is more correct to regard it as a demonstration that the *basis* or principle of the system is, in fact, only its *beginning.*

That the True is actual only as system, or that Substance is essentially Subject, is expressed in the representation of the Absolute as *Spirit*—the most sublime Notion and the one which belongs to the modern age and its religion. The spiritual alone is the *actual;* it is essence, or that which has *being in itself;* it is that which *relates itself to itself* and is *determinate,* it is *other-being* and *being-for-self,* and in this determinateness, or in its self-externality, abides within itself; in other words, it is *in and for itself.*—But this being-in-and-for-itself is at first only for us, or *in itself,* it is spiritual *Substance.* It must also be this *for itself,* it must be the knowledge of the spiritual, and the knowledge of itself as Spirit, i.e., it must be an *object* to itself, but just as immediately a sublated object, reflected into itself. It is *for itself* only for *us,* in so far as its spiritual content is generated by itself. But in so far as it is also for itself for its own self, this self-generation, the pure Notion, is for it the objective element in which it has its existence, and it is in this way, in its existence for itself, an object reflected into itself. The Spirit that, so developed, knows itself as Spirit, is *Science;* Science is its actuality and the realm which it builds for itself in its own element.

Pure self-recognition in absolute otherness, this Aether *as such,* is the ground and soil of Science or *knowledge in general.* The beginning of philosophy presupposes or requires that consciousness should dwell in this *element.* But this element itself achieves its own perfection and transparency only through the movement of its becoming. It is pure spirituality as the *universal* that has the form of simple immediacy. This simple being in its *existential* form is the soil [of Science], it is thinking which has its being in Spirit alone. Because this element, this immediacy of Spirit, is the very substance of Spirit, it is the *transfigured essence,* reflection which is itself simple, and which is for itself immediacy as such, *being* that is reflected into itself. Science on its part requires that self-consciousness should have raised itself into this Aether in order to be able to live—and [actually] to live—with Science and in Science. Conversely, the individual has the right to demand that Science should at least provide him with the ladder to this standpoint, should show him this standpoint within himself. His right is based on his absolute independence, which he is conscious of possessing in every phase of his knowledge; for in each one, whether recognized by Science or not, and whatever the content may be, the individual is the absolute form, i.e., he is the *immediate certainty* of himself and, if this expression be preferred, he is therefore unconditioned *being.* The standpoint of consciousness which knows objects in their antithesis to itself, and itself in antithesis to them, is for Science the antithesis of its own standpoint. The situation in which consciousness knows itself to be at home is for Science one marked by the absence of Spirit. Conversely, the element of Science is for consciousness a remote beyond in which it no longer possesses itself.

Each of these two aspects [of self-conscious Spirit] appears to the other as the inversion of truth. When natural consciousness entrusts itself straightway to Science, it makes an attempt, induced by it knows not what, to walk on its head too, just this once; the compulsion to assume this unwonted posture and to go about in it is a violence it is expected to do to itself, all unprepared and seemingly without necessity. Let Science be in its own self what it may, relatively to immediate self-consciousness it presents itself in an inverted posture; or, because this self-consciousness has the principle of its actual existence in the certainty of itself, Science appears to it not to be actual, since self-consciousness exists on its own account outside of Science. Science must therefore unite this element of self-certainty with itself, or rather show *that* and *how* this element belongs to it. So long as Science lacks this *actual* dimension, it is only the content as the *in-itself*, the *purpose* that is as yet still something *inward*, not yet Spirit, but only spiritual Substance. This *in-itself* has to express itself outwardly and become *for itself*, and this means simply that it has to posit self-consciousness as one with itself.

It is this coming-to-be of *Science as such* or of *knowledge*, that is described in this *Phenomenology* of Spirit. Knowledge in its first phase, or *immediate Spirit*, is the nonspiritual, i.e., *sense-consciousness*. In order to become genuine knowledge, to beget the element of Science which is the pure Notion of Science itself, it must travel a long way and work its passage. This process of coming-to-be (considering the content and patterns it will display therein) will not be what is commonly understood by an initiation of the unscientific consciousness into Science; it will also be quite different from the "foundation" of Science; least of all will it be like the rapturous enthusiasm which, like a shot from a pistol, begins straight away with absolute knowledge, and makes short work of other standpoints by declaring that it takes no notice of them.

The task of leading the individual from his uneducated standpoint to knowledge had to be seen in its universal sense, just as it was the universal individual, self-conscious Spirit, whose formative education had to be studied. As regards the relation between them, every movement, as it gains concrete form and a shape of its own, displays itself in the universal individual. The single individual is incomplete Spirit, a concrete shape in whose whole existence *one* determinateness predominates, the others being present only in blurred outline. In a Spirit that is more advanced than another, the lower concrete existence has been reduced to an inconspicuous moment; what used to be the important thing is now but a trace; its pattern is shrouded to become a mere shadowy outline. The individual whose substance is the more advanced Spirit runs through this past just as one who takes up a higher science goes through the preparatory studies he has long since absorbed, in order to bring their content to mind: he recalls them to the inward eye, but has no lasting interest in them. The single individual must also pass through the formative stages of universal Spirit so far as their content is concerned, but as shapes which Spirit has already left behind, as stages on a way that has been made level with toil. Thus, as far as factual information is concerned, we find that what in former ages engaged the attention of men of mature mind, has been reduced to the level of facts, exercises, and even games for children; and, in the child's progress through school, we shall recognize the history of the cultural development of the world traced, as it were, in a silhouette. This past existence is the already acquired property of universal Spirit which constitutes the Substance of the individual, and hence appears externally to him as his inorganic nature. In this respect formative education, regarded from the side of the individual, consists in his acquiring what thus lies at hand, devouring his inorganic nature, and taking possession of it for himself. But, regarded from the side of universal Spirit as substance, this is nothing but its own acquisition of self-consciousness, the bringing-about of its own becoming and reflection into itself.

Science sets forth this formative process in all its detail and necessity, exposing the mature configuration of everything which has already been reduced to a moment and property of Spirit. The goal is Spirit's insight into what knowing is. Impatience demands the impossible, to wit, the attainment of the end without the means. But the *length* of this path has to be endured, because, for one thing, each moment is necessary; and further, each moment has to be *lingered* over, because each is itself a complete individual shape, and one is only viewed in absolute perspective when its determinateness is regarded as a concrete whole, or the whole is regarded as uniquely qualified by that determination. Since the Substance of the individual, the World-Spirit itself, has had the patience to pass through these shapes over the long passage of time, and to take upon itself the enormous labor of world-history, in which it embodied in each shape as much of its entire content as that shape was capable of holding, and since it could not have attained consciousness of itself by any lesser effort, the individual certainly cannot by the nature of the case comprehend his own substance more easily. Yet, at the same time, he does have less trouble, since all this has already been *implicitly* accomplished; the content is already the actuality reduced to a possibility, its immediacy overcome, and the embodied shape reduced to abbreviated, simple determinations of thought. It is no longer existence in the form of *being-in-itself*—neither still in the original form [of an abstract concept], nor submerged in existence—but is now the *recollected in-itself*, ready for conversion into the form of *being-for-self*. How this is done must now be described more precisely.

We take up the movement of the whole from the point where the sublation of *existence* as such is no longer necessary; what remains to be done, and what requires a higher level of cultural reorientation, is to represent and to get acquainted with these forms. The existence that has been taken back into the Substance has only been *immediately* transposed into the element of the self through that first negation. Hence this acquired property still has the same character of uncomprehended immediacy, of passive indifference, as existence itself; existence has thus merely passed over into *figurative representation*. At the same time it is thus something *familiar,* something which the existent Spirit is finished and done with, so that it is no longer active or really interested in it. Although the activity that has finished with existence is itself only the movement of the particular Spirit, the Spirit that does not comprehend itself, [genuine] knowing, on the other hand, is directed against the representation thus formed, against this [mere] familiarity; knowing is the activity of the *universal self,* the concern of *thinking.*

Quite generally, the familiar, just because it is familiar, is not cognitively understood. The commonest way in which we deceive either ourselves or others about understanding is by assuming something as familiar, and accepting it on that account; with all its pros and cons, such knowing never gets anywhere, and it knows not why. Subject and object, God, Nature, Understanding, sensibility, and so on, are uncritically taken for granted as familiar, established as valid, and made into fixed points for starting and stopping. While these remain unmoved, the knowing activity goes back and forth between them, thus moving only on their surface. Apprehending and testing likewise consist in seeing whether everybody's impression of the matter coincides with what is asserted about these fixed points, whether it seems that way to him or not.

The *analysis* of an idea, as it used to be carried out, was, in fact, nothing else than ridding it of the form in which it had become familiar. To break an idea up into its original elements is to return to its moments, which at least do not have the form of the given idea, but rather consitute the immediate property of the self. This analysis, to be sure, only arrives at *thoughts* which are themselves familiar, fixed, and inert determinations. But what is thus *separated* and nonactual is an essential moment; for it is only because the concrete does divide itself, and make itself into something nonactual, that it is self-moving. The activity of dissolution is the power and work of the *Understanding,* the most astonishing and mightiest of powers, or rather the absolute power. The circle that remains self-enclosed and, like substance, holds its moments together, is an immediate relationship, one therefore which has nothing astonishing about it. But that an accident as such, detached from what circumscribes it, what is bound and is actual only in its context with others, should attain an existence of its own and a separate freedom—this is the tremendous power of the negative; it is the energy of thought, of the pure "I." Death, if that is what we want to call this nonactuality, is of all things the most dreadful, and to hold fast what is dead requires the greatest strength. Lacking strength, Beauty hates the Understanding for asking of her what it cannot do. But the life of Spirit is not the life that shrinks from death and keeps itself untouched by devastation, but rather the life that endures it and maintains itself in it. It wins its truth only when, in utter dismemberment, it finds itself. It is this power, not as something positive, which closes its eyes to the negative, as when we say of something that it is nothing or is false, and then, having done with it, turn away and pass on to something else; on the contrary, Spirit is this power only by looking the negative in the face, and tarrying with it. This tarrying with the negative is the magical power that converts it into being. This power is identical with what we earlier called the Subject, which by giving determinateness an existence in its own element supersedes abstract immediacy, i.e., the immediacy which barely is, and thus is authentic substance: that being or immediacy whose mediation is not outside of it but which is this mediation itself.

The fact that the object represented becomes the property of pure self-consciousness, its elevation to universality in general, is only one aspect of formative education, not its fulfillment—The manner of study in ancient times differed from that of the modern age in that the former was the proper and complete formation of the natural consciousness. Putting itself to the test at every point of its existence, and philosophizing about everything it came across, it made itself into a universality that was active through and through. In modern times, however, the individual finds the abstract form ready-made; the effort to grasp and appropriate it is more the direct driving-forth of what is within and the truncated generation of the universal than it is the emergence of the latter from the concrete variety of existence. Hence the task nowadays consists not so much in purging the individual of an immediate, sensuous mode of apprehension, and making him into a substance that is an object of thought and that thinks, but rather in just the opposite, in freeing determinate thoughts from their fixity so as to give actuality to the universal, and impart to it spiritual life. But it is far harder to bring fixed thoughts into a fluid state than to do so with sensuous existence. The reason for this was given above: fixed thoughts have the "I," the power of the negative, or pure actuality, for the substance and element of their existence, whereas sensuous determinations have only powerless abstract immediacy, or being as such. Thoughts become fluid when pure thinking, this inner *immediacy,* recognizes itself as a moment, or when the pure certainty of self abstracts from itself—not by leaving itself out, or setting itself aside, but by giving up the *fixity* of its self-positing, by giving up not only the fixity of the pure concrete, which the "I" itself is, in contrast with its differentiated content, but also the fixity of the differentiated moments which, posited in the element of pure thinking, share the unconditioned nature of the "I." Through this movement the pure thoughts become *Notions,* and are only now what they are in truth, self-movements, circles, spiritual essences, which is what their substance is.

This movement of pure essences constitutes the nature of scientific method in general. Regarded as the connectedness of their content it is the necessary expansion of that content into an organic whole. Through this movement the path by which the Notion of knowledge is reached becomes likewise a necessary and complete process of becoming; so that this preparatory path ceases to be a casual philosophizing that fastens on to this or that object, relationship, or thought that happens to pop up in the imperfect consciousness, or tries to base the truth on the pros and cons, the inferences and consequences, of rigidly defined thoughts. Instead, this pathway, through the movement of the Notion, will encompass the entire sphere of secular consciousness in its necessary development.

Further, an exposition of this kind constitutes the *first* part of Science, because the existence of Spirit qua primary is nothing but the immediate or the beginning—but not yet its return into itself. The *element of immediate existence* is therefore what distinguishes this part of Science from the others. The statement of this distinction leads us into a discussion of some fixed ideas which usually crop up in this connection.

The immediate existence of Spirit, *consciousness*, contains the two moments of knowing and the objectivity negative to knowing. Since it is in this element [of consciousness] that Spirit develops itself and explicates its moments, these moments contain that antithesis, and they all appear as shapes of consciousness. The Science of this pathway is the Science of the *experience* which consciousness goes through; the substance and its movement are viewed as the object of consciousness. Consciousness knows and comprehends only what falls within its experience; for what is contained in this is nothing but spiritual substance, and this, too, as *object* of the self. But Spirit becomes object because it is just this movement of becoming an *other to itself*, i.e., becoming an *object to itself*, and of suspending this otherness. And experience is the name we give to just this movement, in which the immediate, the unexperienced, i.e., the abstract, whether it be of sensuous [but still unsensed] being, or only thought of as simple, becomes alienated from itself and then returns to itself from this alienation, and is only then revealed for the first time in its actuality and truth, just as it then has become a property of consciousness also.

The disparity which exists in consciousness between the "I" and the substance which is its object is the distinction between them, the *negative* in general. This can be regarded as the *defect* of both, though it is their soul, or that which moves them. That is why some of the ancients conceived the *void* as the principle of motion, for they rightly saw the moving principle as the *negative*, though they did not as yet grasp that the negative is the self. Now, although this negative appears at first as a disparity between the "I" and its object, it is just as much the disparity of the substance with itself. Thus what seems to happen outside of it, to be an activity directed against it, is really its own doing, and Substance shows itself to be essentially Subject. When it has shown this completely, Spirit has made its existence identical with its essence; it has itself for its object just as it is, and the abstract element of immediacy, and of the separation of knowing and truth, is overcome. Being is then absolutely mediated; it is a substantial content which is just as immediately the property of the "I," it is self-like or the Notion.

With this, the Phenomenology of Spirit is concluded. What Spirit prepares for itself in it, is the element of [true] knowing. In this element the moments of Spirit now spread themselves out in that *form of simplicity* which knows its object as its own self. They no longer fall apart into the antithesis of being and knowing, but remain in the simple oneness of knowing; they are the True in the form of the True, and their difference is only the difference of content. Their movement, which organizes itself in this element into a whole, is *Logic* or *speculative philosophy*.

Now, because the system of the experience of Spirit embraces only the *appearance* of Spirit, the advance from this system to the Science of the *True* in its *true shape* seems to be merely negative, and one might wish to be spared the negative as something false, and demand to be led to the truth without more ado. Why bother with the false?—The view already discussed, namely, that we should begin with Science straight away, is to be answered at this point by examining the nature of the negative in general regarded as what is *false*. This is a topic regarding which established ideas notably obstruct the approach to truth. It will give us occasion to speak of mathematical cognition, which unphilosophical knowledge regards as the ideal that philosophy must strive to attain, though it has so far striven in vain.

"True" and "false" belong among those determinate notions which are held to be inert and wholly separate essences, one here and one there, each standing fixed and isolated from the other, with which it has nothing in common. Against this view it must be maintained that truth is not a minted coin that can be given and pocketed ready-made. Nor *is* there such a thing as the false, any more than there *is* something evil. The evil and the false, to be sure, are not as bad as the devil, for in the devil they are even made into a particular *subjective agent;* as the false and the evil, they are mere *universals,* though each has its own essence as against the other.

The false (for here it is only of this that we speak) would be the other, the negative of the substance, which as the content of knowledge is the True. But the substance is itself essentially the negative, partly as a distinction and determination of the content, and partly as a *simple* distinguishing, i.e., as self and knowledge in general. One can, of course, know something falsely. To know something falsely means that there is a disparity between knowledge and its Substance. But this very disparity is the process of distinguishing in general, which is an essential moment [in knowing]. Out of this distinguishing, of course, comes their identity, and this resultant identity is the truth. But it is not truth as if the disparity had been thrown away, like dross from pure metal, not even like the tool which remains separate from the finished vessel; disparity, rather, as the negative, the self, is itself still directly present in the True as such. Yet we cannot therefore say that the false is a moment of the True, let alone a component part of it. To say that in every falsehood there is a grain of truth is to treat the two like oil and water, which cannot be mixed and are only externally combined. It is precisely on account of the importance of designating the moment of *complete otherness* that the terms "true" and "false" must no longer be used where such otherness has been annulled. Just as to talk of the *unity* of subject and object, of finite and infinite, of being and thought, etc., is inept, since object and subject, etc., signify what they are *outside* of their unity, and since in their unity they are not meant to be what their expression says they are, just so the false is no longer qua false, a moment of truth.

Dogmatism as a way of thinking, whether in ordinary knowing or in the study of philosophy, is nothing else but the opinion that the True consists in a proposition which is a fixed result, or which is immediately known. To such questions as, When was Caesar born?, or How many feet were there in a stadium?, etc., a clear-cut answer ought to be given, just as it is definitely true that the square on the hypotenuse is equal to the sum of the squares on the other two sides of a right-angled triangle. But the nature of a so-called truth of that kind is different from the nature of philosophical truths.

As regards *historical* truths—to mention these briefly—it will be readily granted that so far as their purely historical aspect is considered, they are concerned with a particular existence, with the contingent and arbitrary aspects of a given content, which have no necessity. But even such plain truths as those just illustrated are not without the movement of self-consciousness. To cognize one of them, a good deal of comparison is called for, books must be consulted, in some way or other inquiry has to be made. Even an immediate intuition is held to have genuine value only when it is cognized as a fact along with its reasons, although it is probably only the bare result that we are supposed to be concerned about.

As for *mathematical* truths, we should be even less inclined to regard anyone as a geometer who knew Euclid's theorems *outwardly* by rote, without knowing their proofs, without, as we might say, to point the contrast, knowing them *inwardly*. Similarly, if someone became aware, through measuring a number of right-angled triangles, that their sides do, in fact, have the well-known relation to one another, we should consider his [mere] awareness of the fact unsatisfactory. Yet, even in mathematical cognition, the *essentiality* of the proof does not have the significance and nature of being a moment of the result itself; when the latter is reached, the demonstration is over and has disappeared. It is, of course, as a *result* that the theorem is *something seen to be true;* but this added circumstance has no bearing on its content, but only on its relation to the knowing Subject. The movement of mathematical proof does not belong to the object, but rather is an activity external to the matter in hand. Thus the nature of the right-angled triangle does not divide itself into parts in just the way set forth in the construction necessary for the proof of the proposition that expresses its ratio. The way and the means by which the result is brought forth belong entirely to the cognitive process. In philosophical cognition, too, the way in which the [*outer*] *existence* qua existence of a thing comes about, is distinct from the way in which its *essence* or inner nature comes to be. But, to begin with, philosophical cognition includes both [existence and essence], whereas mathematical cognition sets forth only the genesis of the *existence,* i.e., the *being* of the nature of the thing in *cognition* as such. What is more, philosophical cognition also unites these two distinct processes. The inner coming-to-be or genesis of substance is an unbroken transition into outer existence, into being-for-another, and conversely, the genesis of existence is how existence is by itself taken back into essence. The movement is the twofold process and the genesis of the whole, in such wise that each side simultaneously posits the other, and each therefore has both perspectives within itself; together they thus constitute the whole by dissolving themselves, and by making themselves into its moments.

In mathematical cognition, insight is an activity external to the thing; it follows that the true thing is altered by it. The means employed, construction and proof, no doubt contain true propositions, but it must nonetheless be said that the content is false. In the above example the triangle is dismembered, and its parts consigned to other figures, whose origin is allowed by the construction upon the triangle. Only at the end is the triangle we are actually dealing with reinstated. During the procedure it was lost to view, appearing only in fragments belonging to other figures.—Here, then, we see the negativity of the content coming in as well; this could just as much have been called a "falsity" of the content as is the disappearance of supposedly fixed conceptions in the movement of the Notion.

But what is really defective in this kind of cognition concerns the cognitive process itself, as well as its material. As regards the former, we do not, in the first place, see any necessity in the construction. Such necessity does not arise from the notion of the theorem; it is rather imposed, and the instruction to draw precisely these lines when infinitely many others could be drawn must be blindly obeyed without our knowing anything beyond except that we believe that this will be to the purpose in carrying out the proof. In retrospect, this expediency also becomes evident, but it is only an external expediency, because it becomes evident only after the proof. This proof, in addition, follows a path that begins somewhere or other without indicating as yet what relation such a beginning will have to the result that will emerge. In its progress it takes up *these* particular determinations and relations, and lets others alone, without its being immediately clear what the controlling necessity is; an external purpose governs this procedure.

The *evident* character of this defective cognition of which mathematics is proud, and on which it plumes itself before philosophy, rests solely on the poverty of its purpose and the defectiveness of its stuff, and is therefore of a kind that philosophy must spurn. Its *purpose* or Notion is *magnitude*. It is just this relationship that is unessential, lacking the Notion. Accordingly, this process of knowing proceeds on the surface, does not touch the thing itself, its essence or Notion, and therefore fails to comprehend it [i.e., in terms of its Notion].—The *material*, regarding which mathematics provides such a gratifying treasury of truths, is *space* and the *numerical unit*. Space is the existence in which the Notion inscribes its differences as in an empty lifeless element, in which they are just as inert and lifeless. The *actual* is not something spatial, as it is regarded in mathematics; with nonactual things like the objects of mathematics, neither concrete sense-intuition nor philosophy has the least concern. In a nonactual element like this there is only a truth of the same sort, i.e., rigid, dead propositions. We can stop at any one of them; the next one starts afresh on its own account, without the first having moved itself on to the next, and without any necessary connection arising through the nature of the thing itself. —Further, because of this principle and element—and herein consists the formalism of mathematical evidence—[this kind of] knowing moves forward along the line of *equality*. For what is lifeless, since it does not move of itself, does not get as far as the distinctions of essence, as far as essential opposition or inequality, and therefore does not make the transition of one opposite into its opposite, does not attain to qualitative, immanent motion or *self*-movement. For it is only magnitude, the unessential distinction, that mathematics deals with. It abstracts from the fact that it is the Notion which divides space into its dimensions and determines the connections between and within them. It does not, for example, consider the relationship of line to surface; and, when it compares the diameter of a circle with its circumference, it runs up against their incommensurability, i.e., a relationship of the Notion, something infinite that eludes mathematical determination.

Nor does the immanent, so-called pure mathematics set time qua time over against space, as the second material for its consideration. Applied mathematics does indeed deal with time, as well as with motion and other concrete things; but the synthetic propositions, i.e., propositions regarding relationships determined by their Notion, it takes from experience and applies its formulae only on these presuppositions. The fact that the so-called proofs of propositions, such as those regarding the equilibrium of the lever, or the relation of space and time in the motion of falling, etc., are often given and accepted as proofs itself only proves how great is the need of proof for cognition, seeing that, where nothing better is to be had, cognition values even the hollow semblance of it, and obtains from it some measure of satisfaction. A critique of these proofs would be as noteworthy as it would be instructive, partly in order to strip mathematics of these fine feathers, partly in order to point out its limitations, and thus show the necessity for a different kind of knowledge.

As for *time,* which it is to be presumed would constitute, as the counterpart of space, the material of the other part of pure mathematics, it is the existent Notion itself. The principle of *magnitude,* of difference not determined by the Notion, and the principle of *equality,* of abstract lifeless unity, cannot cope with that sheer unrest of life and its absolute distinction. It is therefore only in a paralyzed form, viz., as the *numerical unit,* that this negativity becomes the second material of mathematical cognition, which, as an external activity, reduces what is self-moving to mere material, so as to possess in it an indifferent, external, lifeless content.

Philosophy, on the other hand, has to do, not with *unessential* determinations, but with a determination in so far as it is essential; its element and content are not the abstract or nonactual, but the *actual,* that which posits itself and is alive within itself—existence within its own Notion. It is the process which begets and traverses its own moments, and this whole movement constitutes what is positive [in it] and its truth. This truth therefore includes the negative also, what would be called the false, if it could be regarded as something from which one might abstract. The evanescent itself must, on the contrary, be regarded as essential, not as something fixed, cut off from the True, and left lying who knows where outside it, any more than the True is to be regarded as something on the other side, positive and dead. Appearance is the arising and passing away that does not itself arise and pass away, but is "in itself" [i.e., subsists intrinsically], and constitutes the actuality and the movement of the life of truth. The True is thus the Bacchanalian revel in which no member is not drunk; yet because each member collapses as soon as he drops out, the revel is just as much transparent and simple repose. Judged in the court of this movement, the single shapes of Spirit do not persist any more than determinate thoughts do, but they are as much positive and necessary moments, as they are negative and evanescent. In the *whole* of the movement, seen as a state of repose, what distinguishes itself therein, and gives itself particular existence, is preserved as something that *recollects* itself, whose existence is self-knowledge, and whose self-knowledge is just as immediately existence.

It might seem necessary at the outset to say more about the *method* of this movement, i.e., of Science. But its Notion is already to be found in what has been said, and its proper exposition belongs to Logic, or rather it is Logic. For the method is nothing but the structure set forth in its pure essentiality. We should realize, however, that the system of ideas concerning philosophical method is yet another set of current beliefs that belongs to a bygone culture. If this comment sounds boastful or revolutionary—and I am far from adopting such a tone—it should be noted that current opinion itself has already come to view the scientific regime bequeathed by mathematics as quite *old-fashioned*—with its explanations, divisions, axioms, sets of theorems, its proofs, principles, deductions, and conclusions from them. Even if its unfitness is not clearly understood, little or no use is any longer made of it; and though not actually condemned outright, no one likes it very much. And we should be sufficiently prejudiced in favor of what is excellent, to suppose that it will be put to use, and will find acceptance. But it is not difficult to see that the way of asserting a proposition, adducing reasons for it, and in the same way refuting its opposite by reasons, is not the form in which truth can appear. Truth is its own self-movement, whereas the method just described is the mode of cognition that remains external to its material. Hence it is peculiar to mathematics, and must be left to that science, which, as we have noted, has for its principle the relationship of magnitude, a relationship alien to the Notion, and for its material dead space and the equally lifeless numerical unit. This method, too, in a looser form, i.e., more blended with the arbitrary and the accidental, may retain its place, as in conversation, or in a piece of historical instruction designed rather to satisfy curiosity than to produce knowledge, which is about what a preface amounts to. In ordinary life, consciousness has for its content items of information, experiences, concrete objects of sense, thoughts, basic principles,—anything will do as a content, as long as it is ready to hand, or is accepted as a fixed and stable being or essence. Sometimes consciousness follows where this leads, sometimes it breaks the chain, and deals arbitrarily with its content, behaving as if it were determining and manipulating it from outside. It refers the content back to some certainty or other, even if only to the sensation of the moment; and conviction is satisfied when a familiar resting-place is reached.

But we have already pointed out that, once the necessity of the Notion has banished the slipshod style of conversational discussion, and along with it the pedantry and pomposity of science, they are not to be replaced by the nonmethod of presentiment and inspiration, or by the arbitrariness of prophetic utterance, both of which despise not only scientific pomposity, but scientific procedure of all kinds.

Of course, the *triadic form* must not be regarded as scientific when it is reduced to a lifeless schema, a mere shadow, and when scientific organization is degraded into a table of terms. Kant rediscovered this triadic form by instinct, but in his work it was still lifeless and uncomprehended; since then it has, however, been raised to its absolute significance, and with it the true form in its true content has been presented, so that the Notion of Science has emerged. This formalism, of which we have already spoken generally and whose style we wish here to describe in more detail, imagines that it has comprehended and expressed the nature and life of a form when it has endowed it with some determination of the schema as a predicate. The predicate may be subjectivity or objectivity, or, say, magnetism, electricity, etc., contraction or expansion, east or west, and the like. Such predicates can be multiplied to infinity, since in this way each determination or form can again be used as a form or moment in the case of an other, and each can gratefully perform the same service for an other. In this sort of circle of reciprocity one never learns what the thing itself is, nor what the one or the other is. In such a procedure, sometimes determinations of sense are picked up from everyday intuition, and they are supposed, of course, to *mean* something different from what they say; sometimes what is in itself meaningful, e.g., pure determinations of thought like subject, Object, Substance, Cause, Universal, etc.— these are used just as thoughtlessly and uncritically as we use them in everyday life, or as we use ideas like strength and weakness, expansion and contraction; the metaphysics is in the former case as unscientific as are our sensuous representations in the latter.

Instead of the inner life and self-movement of its existence, this kind of simple determinateness of intuition—which means here sense-knowledge—is predicated in accordance with a superficial analogy, and this external, empty application of the formula is called a "construction." This formalism is just like any other. What a dullard a man must be who could not be taught in a quarter of an hour the theory that there are asthenic, sthenic, and indirectly asthenic diseases, and as many modes of treatment;* and, since till quite recently such instruction sufficed, who could not hope to be transformed in this short space of time from an empirical into a theoretical physician? The formalism of such a "Philosophy of Nature" teaches, say, that the Understanding is Electricity, or the Animal is Nitrogen, or that they are the *equivalent* of the South or North Pole, etc., or represent it—whether all this is expressed as baldly as here or even concocted with more terminology—and confronted with such a power which brings together things that appear to lie far apart, and with the violence suffered by the passive things of sense through such association, and which imparts to them the Notion's semblance but saves itself the trouble of doing the main thing, viz., expressing the Notion itself or the meaning of the sensuous representation—confronted with all this, the untutored mind may be filled with admiration and astonishment, and may venerate in it the profound work of genius. It may be delighted, too, with the clarity of such characterizations, since these replace the abstract Notion with something that can be intuitively apprehended, and so made more pleasing; and it may congratulate itself on feeling a kinship of soul with such a splendid performance. The knack of this kind of wisdom is as quickly learned as it is easy to practice; once familiar, the repetition of it becomes as insufferable as the repetition of a conjuring trick already seen through. The instru-

---

*So-called Brownianism: John Brown, *Elementa medicinae*, 1780.

ment of this monotonous formalism is no more difficult to handle than a painter's palette having only two colors, say red and green, the one for coloring the surface when a historical scene is wanted, the other for landscapes. It would be hard to decide which is greater in all this, the casual ease with which everything in heaven and on earth and under the earth is coated with this broth of color, or the conceit regarding the excellence of this universal recipe: each supports the other. What results from this method of labeling all that is in heaven and earth with the few determinations of the general schema, and pigeonholing everything in this way, is nothing less than a "report clear as noonday"* on the universe as an organism, viz., a synoptic table like a skeleton with scraps of paper stuck all over it, or like the rows of closed and labeled boxes in a grocer's stall. It is as easy to read off as either of these; and just as all the flesh and blood have been stripped from this skeleton, and the no longer living "essence" [Sache] has been packed away in the boxes, so in the report the living essence of the matter [Wesen der Sache] has been stripped away or boxed up dead. We have already remarked that this way of thinking at the same time culminates in a style of painting that is absolutely monochromatic; for it is ashamed of its schematic distinctions, these products of reflection, and submerges them all in the void of the Absolute, from which pure identity, formless whiteness, is produced. This monochromatic character of the schema and its lifeless determinations, this absolute identity, and the transition from one to the other, are all equally products of the lifeless Understanding and external cognition.

The excellent, however, not only cannot escape the fate of being thus deprived of life and Spirit, of being flayed and then seeing its skin wrapped around a lifeless knowledge and its conceit. Rather we cognize even in this fate the power that the excellent exercises over the hearts, if not over the minds, of men; also the constructive unfolding into universality and determinateness of form in which its perfection consists, and which alone makes it possible for this universality to be used in a superficial way.

Science dare only organize itself by the life of the Notion itself. The determinateness, which is taken from the schema and externally

---

*An allusion to Fichte's *A Crystal Clear Report to the General Public Concerning the Actual Essence of the Newest Philosophy: An Attempt to Force the Reader to Understand (1801)*. The German Library, vol. 23, pp. 39–115.

attached to an existent thing, is, in Science, the self-moving soul of the realized content. The movement of a being that immediately is, consists partly in becoming an other than itself, and thus becoming its own immanent content; partly in taking back into itself this unfolding [of its content] or this existence of it, i.e., in making *itself* into a moment, and simplifying itself into something determinate. In the former movement, *negativity* is the differentiating and positing of *existence;* in this return into self, it is the becoming of the *determinate simplicity.* It is in this way that the content shows that its determinateness is not received from something else, nor externally attached to it, but that it determines itself, and ranges itself as a moment having its own place in the whole. The Understanding, in its pigeonholing process, keeps the necessity and Notion of the content to itself—all that constitutes the concreteness, the actuality, the living movement of the reality which it arranges. Or rather, it does not keep this to itself, since it does not recognize it; for, if it had this insight, it would surely give some sign of it. It does not even recognize the need for it, else it would drop its schematizing, or at least realize that it can never hope to learn more in this fashion than one can learn from a table of contents. A table of contents is all that it offers, the content itself it does not offer at all.

Even when the specific determinateness—say one like Magnetism, for example,—is in itself concrete or real, the Understanding degrades it into something lifeless, merely predicating it of another existent thing, rather than cognizing it as the immanent life of the thing, or cognizing its native and unique way of generating and expressing itself in that thing. The formal Understanding leaves it to others to add this principal feature. Instead of entering into the immanent content of the thing, it is forever surveying the whole and standing above the particular existence of which it is speaking, i.e., it does not see it at all. Scientific cognition, on the contrary, demands surrender to the life of the object, or, what amounts to the same thing, confronting and expressing its inner necessity. Thus, absorbed in its object, scientific cognition forgets about that general survey, which is merely the reflection of the cognitive process away from the content and back into itself. Yet, immersed in the material, and advancing with its movement, scientific cognition does come back to itself, but not before its filling or content is taken back into itself, is simplified into a determinateness, and has reduced itself to *one* aspect of its own existence and passed over into its higher truth. Through this process the simple, self-surveying whole itself emerges from the wealth in which its reflection seemed to be lost.

In general, because, as we put it above, substance is in itself or implicitly Subject, all content is its own reflection into itself. The subsistence or substance of anything that exists is its self-identity; for a failure of self-identity would be its dissolution. Self-identity, however, is pure abstraction; but this is *thinking*. When I say "quality," I am saying simple determinateness; it is by quality that one existence is distinguished from another, or is an existence; it is for itself, or it subsists through this simple oneness with itself. But it is thereby essentially a *thought*. Comprehended in this is the fact that Being is Thought; and this is the source of that insight which usually eludes the usual superficial [*begrifflos*] talk about the identity of Thought and Being.—Now, since the subsistence of an existent thing is a self-identity or pure abstraction, it is the abstraction of itself from itself, or it is itself its lack of self-identity and its dissolution—its own inwardness and withdrawal into itself—its own becoming. Because this is the nature of what is, and in so far as what is has this nature for [our] knowing, this knowing is not an activity that deals with the content as something alien, is not a reflection into itself away from the content. Science is not that idealism which replaced the dogmatism of assertion with a dogmatism of assurance, or a dogmatism of self-certainty. On the contrary, since [our] knowing sees the content return into its own inwardness, its activity is totally absorbed in the content, for it is the immanent self of the content; yet it has at the same time returned into itself, for it is pure self-identity in otherness. Thus it is the cunning which, while seeming to abstain from activity, looks on and watches how determinateness, with its concrete life, just where it fancies it is pursuing its own self-preservation and particular interest, is in fact doing the very opposite, is an activity that results in its own dissolution, and makes itself a moment of the whole.

Above we indicated the significance of the *Understanding* in reference to the self-consciousness of substance; we can now see clearly from what has been said its significance in reference to the determination of substance as being. Existence is Quality, self-identical determinateness, or determinate simplicity, determinate thought; this is the Understanding of existence [i.e., the nature of existence from the standpoint of the Understanding]. Hence, it is *Noûs,* as Anaxagoras first recognized the essence of things to be. Those who came after him grasped the nature of existence more definitely as *Eidos* or *Idea,* determinate Universality, Species, or Kind. It might seem as if the term *Species* or *Kind* is too commonplace, too inadequate, for Ideas such as the Beautiful, the Holy, and the Eternal that are currently in fashion. But as a matter of fact Idea expresses neither more nor less than Species or Kind. But nowadays an expression which exactly designates a Notion is often spurned in favor of one which, if only because it is of foreign extraction, shrouds the Notion in a fog, and hence sounds more edifying.

Precisely because existence is defined as Species, it is a simple thought; *nous,* simplicity, is substance. On account of its simplicity or self-identity it appears fixed and enduring. But this self-identity is no less negativity; therefore its fixed existence passes over into its dissolution. The determinateness seems at first to be due entirely to the fact that it is related to an *other,* and its movement seems imposed on it by an alien power; but having its otherness within itself, and being self-moving, is just what is involved in the *simplicity* of thinking itself; for this simple thinking is the self-moving and self-differentiating thought, it is its own inwardness, it is the pure Notion. Thus common understanding, too, is a becoming, and, as this becoming, it is *reason*ableness.

It is in this nature of what is to be in its being its own Notion, that *logical necessity* in general consists. This alone is the rational element and the rhythm of the organic whole; it is as much *knowledge* of the content, as the content is the Notion and essence—in other words, it alone is *speculative philosophy.* The self-moving concrete shape makes itself into a simple determinateness; in so doing it raises itself to logical form, and exists in its essentiality; its concrete existence is just this movement, and is directly a logical existence. It is for this reason unnecessary to clothe the content in an external [logical] formalism; the content is in its very nature the transition into such formalism, but a formalism which ceases to be external, since the form is the innate development of the concrete content itself.

This nature of scientific method, which consists partly in not being separate from the content, and partly in spontaneously determining the rhythm of its movement, has, as already remarked, its proper exposition in speculative philosophy. Of course, what has been said here does express the Notion, but cannot count for more than an anticipatory assurance. Its truth does not lie in this partly narrative exposition, and is therefore just as little refuted by asserting the contrary, by calling to mind and recounting conventional ideas, as if they were established and familiar truths, or by dishing up something new with the assurance that it comes from the shrine of inner divine intuition. A reception of this kind is usually the first reaction on the part of knowing to something unfamiliar; it resists it in order to save its own freedom and its own insight, its own authority, from the alien authority (for this is the guise in which what is newly encountered first appears), and to get rid of the appearance that something has been learned and of the sort of shame this is supposed to involve. Similarly, when the unfamiliar is greeted with applause, the reaction is of the same kind, and consists in what in another sphere would take the form of ultrarevolutionary speech and action.

What, therefore, is important in the *study* of *Science*, is that one should take on oneself the strenuous effort of the Notion.* This requires attention to the Notion as such, to the simple determinations, e.g., of Being-in-itself, Being-for-itself, Self-identity, etc.; for these are pure self-movements such as could be called souls if their Notion did not designate something higher than soul. The habit of picture-thinking, when it is interrupted by the Notion, finds it just as irksome as does formalistic thinking that argues back and forth in thoughts that have no actuality. That habit should be called material thinking, a contingent consciousness that is absorbed only in material stuff, and therefore finds it hard work to lift the [thinking] self clear of such matter, and to be with itself alone. At the opposite extreme, argumentation is freedom from all content, and a sense of vanity towards it. What is looked for here is the effort to give up this freedom, and, instead of being the arbitrarily moving principle of the content, to sink this freedom in the content, letting it move spontaneously of its own nature, by the self as its own self, and then to contemplate this movement. This refusal to intrude into the immanent rhythm of the Notion, either arbitrarily or with wisdom

*I.e., the strenuous effort required to think in terms of the Notion.

obtained from elsewhere, constitutes a restraint which is itself an essential moment of the Notion.

There are two aspects of the procedure of argumentation to which speculative [*begreifende*] thinking is opposed and which call for further notice. First, such reasoning adopts a negative attitude towards the content it apprehends; it knows how to refute it and destroy it. That something is *not* the case, is a merely negative insight, a dead end which does not lead to a new content beyond itself. In order to have a content once again, something new must be taken over from elsewhere. Argumentation is reflection into the empty "I," the vanity of its own knowing.—This vanity, however, expresses not only the vanity of this content, but also the futility of this insight itself; for this insight is the negative that fails to see the positive within itself. Because this reflection does not get its very negativity as its content, it is never at the heart of the matter, but always beyond it. For this reason it imagines that by establishing the void it is always ahead of any insight rich in content. On the other hand, in speculative [*begreifenden*] thinking, as we have already shown, the negative belongs to the content itself, and is the *positive*, both as the *immanent* movement and determination of the content, and as the whole of this process. Looked at as a result, what emerges from this process is the *determinate* negative which is consequently a positive content as well.

But in view of the fact that such thinking has a content, whether of picture-thoughts or abstract thoughts or a mixture of both, argumentation has another side which makes comprehension difficult for it. The remarkable nature of this other side is closely linked with the above-mentioned essence of the Idea, or rather it expresses the Idea in the way that it appears as the movement which is thinking apprehension. For whereas, in its negative behavior, which we have just discussed, ratiocinative thinking is itself the self into which the content returns, in its positive cognition, on the other hand, the self is a *Subject* to which the content is related as Accident and Predicate. This Subject constitutes the basis to which the content is attached, and upon which the movement runs back and forth. Speculative [*begreifendes*] thinking behaves in a different way. Since the Notion is the object's own self, which presents itself as the *coming-to-be of the object*, it is not a passive Subject inertly supporting the Accidents; it is, on the contrary, the self-moving Notion which takes its determinations back into itself. In this movement the passive Subject itself perishes; it enters into the differences and the content, and constitutes the determinateness, i.e., the differentiated content and its movement, instead of remaining inertly over against it. The solid ground which argumentation has in the passive Subject is therefore shaken, and only this movement itself becomes the object. The Subject that fills its content ceases to go beyond it, and cannot have any further Predicates or accidental properties. Conversely, the dispersion of the content is thereby bound together under the self; it is not the universal which, free from the Subject, could belong to several others. Thus the content is, in fact, no longer a Predicate of the Subject, but is the Substance, the essence and the Notion of what is under discussion. Picture-thinking, whose nature it is to run through the Accidents or Predicates and which, because they are nothing more than Predicates and Accidents, rightly goes beyond them, is checked in its progress, since that which has the form of a Predicate in a proposition is the Substance itself. It suffers, as we might put it, a counterthrust. Starting from the Subject as though this were a permanent ground, it finds that, since the Predicate is really the Substance, the Subject has passed over into the Predicate, and, by this very fact, has been sublated; and, since in this way what seems to be the Predicate has become the whole and the independent mass, thinking cannot roam at will, but is impeded by this weight.

Usually, the Subject is first made the basis, as the *objective,* fixed self; thence the necessary movement to the multiplicity of determinations or Predicates proceeds. Here, that Subject is replaced by the knowing "I" itself, which links the Predicates with the Subject holding them. But, since that first Subject enters into the determinations themselves and is their soul, the second Subject, viz., the knowing "I," still finds in the Predicate what it thought it had finished with and got away from, and from which it hoped to return into itself; and, instead of being able to function as the determining agent in the movement of predication, arguing back and forth whether to attach this or that Predicate, it is really still occupied with the self of the content, having to remain associated with it, instead of being for itself.

Formally, what has been said can be expressed thus: the general nature of the judgment or proposition, which involves the distinction of Subject and Predicate, is destroyed by the speculative proposition, and the proposition of identity which the former becomes contains the counterthrust against that subject-predicate relationship.—This conflict between the general form of a proposition and the unity of the Notion which destroys it is similar to the conflict that occurs in rhythm between meter and accent. Rhythm results from the floating center and the unification of the two. So, too, in the philosophical proposition the identification of Subject and Predicate is not meant to destroy the difference between them, which the form of the proposition expresses; their unity, rather, is meant to emerge as a harmony. The form of the proposition is the appearance of the determinate sense, or the accent that distinguishes its fulfilment; but that the predicate expresses the Substance, and that the Subject itself falls into the universal, this is the *unity* in which the accent dies away.

To illustrate what has been said: in the proposition "God is being," the Predicate is "being"; it has the significance of something substantial in which the Subject is dissolved. "Being" is here meant to be not a Predicate, but rather the essence; it seems, consequently, that God ceases to be what he is from his position in the proposition, viz., a fixed Subject. Here thinking, instead of making progress in the transition from Subject to Predicate, in reality feels itself checked by the loss of the Subject, and, missing it, is thrown back on to the thought of the Subject. Or, since the Predicate itself has been expressed as a Subject, as *the* being or *essence* which exhausts the nature of the Subject, thinking finds the Subject immediately in the Predicate; and now, having returned into itself in the Predicate, instead of being in a position where it has freedom for argument, it is still absorbed in the content, or at least is faced with the demand that it should be. Similarly, too, when one says: "the *actual* is the *universal,*" the actual as subject disappears in its predicate. The universal is not meant to have merely the significance of a predicate, as if the proposition asserted only that the actual is universal; on the contrary, the universal is meant to express the essence of the actual.—Thinking therefore loses the firm objective basis it had in the subject when, in the predicate, it is thrown back on to the subject, and when, in the predicate, it does not return into itself, but into the subject of the content.

This abnormal inhibition of thought is in large measure the source of the complaints regarding the unintelligibility of philosophical writings from individuals who otherwise possess the educational requirements for understanding them. Here we see the reason behind one particular complaint so often made against them: that so much has to be read over and over before it can be understood—a complaint whose burden is presumed to be quite outrageous, and, if justified, to admit of no defense. It is clear from the above what this amounts to. The philosophical proposition, since it *is* a proposition, leads one to believe that the usual subject–predicate relation obtains, as well as the usual attitude towards knowing. But the philosophical content destroys this attitude and this opinion. We learn by experience that we meant something other than we meant to mean; and this correction of our meaning compels our knowing to go back to the proposition, and understand it in some other way.

One difficulty which should be avoided comes from mixing up the speculative with the ratiocinative methods, so that what is said of the Subject at one time signifies its Notion, at another time merely its Predicate or accidental property. The one method interferes with the other, and only a philosophical exposition that rigidly excludes the usual way of relating the parts of a proposition could achieve the goal of plasticity.

As a matter of fact, nonspeculative thinking also has its valid rights which are disregarded in the speculative way of stating a proposition. The sublation of the form of the proposition must not happen only in an *immediate* manner, through the mere content of the proposition. On the contrary, this opposite movement must find explicit expression; it must not just be the inward inhibition mentioned above. This return of the Notion into itself must be *set forth*. This movement which constitutes what formerly the proof was supposed to accomplish, is the dialectical movement of the proposition itself. This alone is the speculative *in act,* and only the expression of this movement is a speculative exposition. As a proposition, the speculative is only the *internal* inhibition and the non*existential* return of the essence into itself. Hence we often find philosophical expositions referring us to this *inner* intuition; and in this way they evade the systematic exposition of the dialectical movement of the proposition which we have demanded.—The *proposition* should express *what* the True is; but essentially the True is Subject. As such it is merely the dialectical movement, this course that generates itself, going forth from, and returning to, itself. In nonspeculative cognition proof constitutes this side of expressed inwardness. But once the dialectic has been separated from proof, the notion of philosophical demonstration has been lost.

Here we should bear in mind that the dialectical movement likewise has propositions for its parts or elements; the difficulty just indicated seems, therefore, to recur perpetually, and to be inherent in the very nature of philosophical exposition. This is like what happens in ordinary proof, where the reasons given are themselves in need of further reasons, and so on ad infinitum. This pattern of giving reasons and stating conditions belongs to that method of proof which differs from the dialectical movement, and belongs therefore to external cognition. As regards the dialectical movement itself, its element is the one Notion; it thus has a content which is, in its own self, Subject through and through. Thus no content occurs which functions as an underlying subject, nor receives its meaning as a predicate; the proposition as it stands is merely an empty form.

Apart from the self that is sensuously intuited or represented, it is above all the name as name that designates the pure Subject, the empty unit without thought-content. For this reason it may be expedient, e.g., to avoid the name "God," since this word is not immediately also a Notion, but rather the proper name, the fixed point of rest of the underlying Subject; whereas, on the other hand, e.g., "Being" or "the One," "Singularity," "the Subject," etc., themselves at once suggest concepts. Even if speculative truths are affirmed of this subject, their content lacks the immanent Notion, because it is present merely in the form of a passive subject, with the result that such truths readily assume the form of mere edification. From this side, too, the habit of expressing the speculative predicate in the form of a proposition, and not as Notion and essence, creates a difficulty that can be increased or diminished through the very way in which philosophy is expounded. In keeping with our insight into the nature of speculation, the exposition should preserve the dialectical form, and should admit nothing except in so far as it is comprehended [in terms of the Notion], and is the Notion.

The study of philosophy is as much hindered by the conceit that will not argue, as it is by the argumentative approach. This conceit relies on truths which are taken for granted and which it sees no need to reexamine; it just lays them down, and believes it is entitled to assert them, as well as to judge and pass sentence by appealing to them. In view of this, it is especially necessary that philosophizing should again be made a serious business. In the case of all other sciences, arts, skills, and crafts, everyone is convinced that a complex and laborious program of learning and practice is necessary for competence. Yet when it comes to philosophy, there seems to be a currently prevailing prejudice to the effect that, although not everyone who has eyes and fingers, and is given leather and last, is at once in a position to make shoes, everyone nevertheless immediately understands how to philosophize, and how to evaluate philosophy, since he possesses the criterion for doing so in his natural reason—as if he did not likewise possess the measure for a shoe in his own foot. It seems that philosophical competence consists precisely in an absence of information and study, as though philosophy left off where they began. Philosophy is frequently taken to be a purely formal kind of knowledge, void of content, and the insight is sadly lacking that, whatever truth there may be in the content of any discipline or science, it can only deserve the name if such truth has been engendered by philosophy. Let the other sciences try to argue as much as they like without philosophy—without it they can have in them neither life, Spirit, nor truth.

In place of the long process of culture towards genuine philosophy, a movement as rich as it is profound, through which Spirit achieves knowledge, we are offered as quite equivalent either direct revelations from heaven, or the sound common sense that has never labored over, or informed itself regarding, other knowledge or genuine philosophy; and we are assured that these are quite as good substitutes as some claim chicory is for coffee. It is not a pleasant experience to see ignorance, and a crudity without form or taste, which cannot focus its thought on a single abstract proposition, still less on a connected chain of them, claiming at one moment to be freedom of thought and toleration, and at the next to be even genius. Genius, we all know, was once all the rage in poetry, as it now is in philosophy; but when its productions made sense at all, such genius begat only trite prose instead of poetry, or, getting beyond that, only crazy rhetoric. So, nowadays, philosophizing by the light of nature, which regards itself as too good for the Notion, and as being an intuitive and poetic thinking in virtue of this deficiency, brings to market the arbitrary combinations of an imagination that has only been disorganized by its thoughts, an imagery that is neither fish nor flesh, neither poetry nor philosophy.

On the other hand, when philosophizing by the light of nature flows along the more even course of sound common sense, it offers at its very best only a rhetoric of trivial truths. And, if reproached with the insignificance of these truths, it assures us in reply that their meaning and fulfillment reside in its heart, and must surely be present in the hearts of others too, since it reckons to have said the last word once the innocence of the heart, the purity of conscience, and such like have been mentioned. These are ultimate truths to which no exception can be taken, and beyond which nothing more can be demanded. It is just the point, however, that the best should not remain in the recesses of what is inner, but should be brought out of these depths into the light of day. But it would be better by far to spare oneself the effort of bringing forth ultimate truths of that kind; for they have long since been available in catechisms or in popular sayings, etc.—It is not difficult to grasp such vague and misleading truths, or even to show that the mind in believing them is also aware of their very opposite. When it labors to extricate itself from the bewilderment this sets up, it falls into fresh contradictions, and may very well burst out with the assertion that the question is settled, that so and so is the truth, and that the other views are sophistries. For "sophistry" is a slogan used by ordinary common sense against educated reason, just as the expression "visionary dreaming" sums up, once and for all, what philosophy means to those who are ignorant of it.—Since the man of common sense makes his appeal to feeling, to an oracle within his breast, he is finished and done with anyone who does not agree; he only has to explain that he has nothing more to say to anyone who does not find and feel the same in himself. In other words, he tramples underfoot the roots of humanity. For it is the nature of humanity to press onward to agreement with others; human nature only really exists in an achieved community of minds. The antihuman, the merely animal, consists in staying within the sphere of feeling, and being able to communicate only at that level.

Should anyone ask for a royal road to Science, there is no more easygoing way than to rely on sound common sense; and for the rest, in order to keep up with the times, and with advances in philosophy, to read reviews of philosophical works, perhaps even to read their prefaces and first paragraphs. For these preliminary pages give the general principles on which everything turns, and the reviews, as well as providing historical accounts, also provide the critical appraisal which, being a judgment, stands high above the work judged. This common road can be taken in casual dress; but the high sense for the Eternal, the Holy, the Infinite strides along in the robes of a high priest, on a road that is from the first no road, but has immediate being as its center, the genius of profound original ideas and lofty flashes of inspiration. But just as profundity of this kind still does not reveal the source of essential being, so, too, these skyrockets of inspiration are not yet the empyrean. True thoughts and scientific insight are only to be won through the labor of the Notion. Only the Notion can produce the universality of knowledge which is neither common vagueness nor the inadequacy of ordinary common sense, but a fully developed, perfected cognition; not the uncommon universality of a reason whose talents have been ruined by indolence and the conceit of genius, but a truth ripened to its properly matured form so as to be capable of being the property of all self-conscious Reason.

Since I hold that Science exists solely in the self-movement of the Notion, and since my view differs from, and is in fact wholly opposed to, current ideas regarding the nature and form of truth, both those referred to above and other peripheral aspects of them, it seems that any attempt to expound the system of Science from this point of view is unlikely to be favorably received. In the meantime, I can bear in mind that if at times the excellence of Plato's philosophy has been held to lie in his scientifically valueless myths, there have also been times, even called times of ecstatic dreaming,* when Aristotle's philosophy was esteemed for its speculative depth, and Plato's *Parmenides* (surely the greatest artistic achievement of the ancient dialectic) was regarded as the true disclosure and positive expression of the divine life, and times when, despite the obscurity generated by ecstasy, this misunderstood ecstasy was in fact supposed to be nothing else than the pure Notion. Furthermore, what really is excellent in the philosophy of our time takes its value to lie in its scientific quality, and even though others take a different view, it is in fact only in virtue of its scientific character that it exerts any influence. Hence, I may hope, too, that this attempt to vindicate Science for the Notion, and to expound it in this its proper element,

---

*This was what the English Enlightenment called "enthusiasm," but the word has no religious overtones now.

will succeed in winning acceptance through the inner truth of the subject matter. We must hold to the conviction that it is the nature of truth to prevail when its time has come, and that it appears only when this time has come, and therefore never appears prematurely, nor finds a public not ripe to receive it; also we must accept that the individual needs that this should be so in order to verify what is as yet a matter for himself alone, and to experience the conviction, which in the first place belongs only to a particular individual, as something universally held. But in this connection the public must often be distinguished from those who pose as its representatives and spokesmen. In many respects the attitude of the public is quite different from, even contrary to, that of these spokesmen. Whereas the public is inclined good-naturedly to blame itself when a philosophical work makes no appeal to it, these others, certain of their own competence, put all the blame on the author. The effect of such a work on the public is more noiseless than the action of these dead men when they bury their dead. The general level of insight now is altogether more educated, its curiosity more awake, and its judgment more swiftly reached, so that the feet of those who will carry you out are already at the door. But from this we must often distinguish the more gradual effect which corrects the attention extorted by imposing assurances and corrects, too, contemptuous censure, and gives some writers an audience only after a time, while others after a time have no audience left.

For the rest, at a time when the universality of Spirit has gathered such strength, and the singular detail, as is fitting, has become correspondingly less important, when, too, that universal aspect claims and holds on to the whole range of the wealth it has developed, the share in the total work of Spirit which falls to the individual can only be very small. Because of this, the individual must all the more forget himself, as the nature of Science implies and requires. Of course, he must make of himself and achieve what he can; but less must be demanded of him, just as he in turn can expect less of himself, and may demand less for himself.

Translated by A. V. Miller

ENCYCLOPEDIA
OF THE
PHILOSOPHICAL
SCIENCES
IN OUTLINE

For Use in His Lectures

by
Dr. Georg Wilhelm Friedrich Hegel
Professor of Philosophy at the University
of Heidelberg

Heidelberg,
August Oswald's University Bookstore
1817

Preface

The most immediate reason why I let this overview of the entire scope of philosophy appear earlier than expected is in order to give my listeners a guide to my philosophical lectures.

But the nature of an outline not only precludes a more exhaustive treatment of the content of the ideas. It also limits the discussion of the systematic derivation of the evidence which such an encyclopedia must contain, and which is indispensable for a scientific philosophy. The title should suggest partly the scope of the whole, and partly the intent to leave the details for oral delivery.

Further, the arrangement and organization of an outline would be of merely superficial utility if the contents, which must be presented in deliberate brevity, were already known. Such is not the case with the present account. It offers a new treatment of philosophy using a method which will, I hope, be recognized as the only one truly identical to its contents. Thus it would have been better for the public, I believe, if circumstances had allowed me to begin with a more thorough work on the other parts of philosophy, as I have done with the first part, the *Logic*. In addition I believe that, although the contents of the representation and the empirical connections had to be limited, because the transitions in the argument can only be mediated through the concept, my methodology differs considerably not only from the superficial order in which the other sciences arrange their materials. The method also differs from a manner which has become common in philosophy, namely, to presuppose a schema and thus to arrange the materials in a way even more superficial and arbitrary than the former approach. Here, a strange misunderstanding attempts to meet the necessity of the concept with contingencies and arbitrary associations.

We have seen this arbitrariness temporarily seize control of the contents of philosophy and embark on an intellectual adventure that has dominated honest and truehearted effort, although it is occasionally considered a grotesque style often exaggerated to madness. Instead of being seen as imposing or mad, however, the contents were recognized more frequently and properly as familiar trivialities, and the form as the mere trick of a deliberate, easily acquired, and methodical wit, driven by baroque associations and a strained eccentricity, with an earnest face thinly masking both self-deception and deception of the public. On the other hand, we have seen shallowness and a lack of thought assume the character of a self-congratulatory skepticism and a thinly reasoned criticism, and the obscurity and vanity of this position have increased in exact proportion to the emptiness of its ideas.—For some time, these two intellectual tendencies have toyed with German seriousness, exhausting its deeper need for philosophy, and resulting in an indifference, even a contempt for the science of philosophy. Now, a self-conscious modesty dares to join the conversation concerning the deepest philosophical problems, and presumes to dismiss rational cognition in the form once understood as proof.

The first of these attitudes can be seen in part as the youthful joy of a new era that has emerged in both the scientific and the political realms. Although this joy greeted the dawn of the rejuvenated spirit with rapture, and without deeper work immediately began to enjoy the idea and briefly reveled in the hopes and prospects that it offered, one can more readily forgive its excesses. There was an underlying kernel of truth, and the superficial haze surrounding it was bound to disappear on its own accord. But the other attitude is more repulsive because it betrays exhaustion and impotence, and strives to conceal them with an obscurantist conceit that acts as the master of the philosophical thoughts of all centuries, yet mistakes them, and most of all, mistakes itself.

It is thus all the more gratifying to perceive and to remark how, contrary to both tendencies, the interest in philosophy and the earnest love of higher knowledge have been maintained without conceit and vanity. If occasionally these interests have embraced the form of immediate knowledge and feeling, they nevertheless exemplify the progressive, inward-moving drive of rational insight, which alone gives dignity to humanity. Such interests reveal above all that a true standpoint will only be the result of philosophical knowledge, for although this knowledge may seem dismissible at first it is at least acknowledged as a prior condition.

To this interest in knowing the truth I dedicate the following, as an attempt to provide an introduction or contribution towards its achievement. May such a purpose receive a favorable reception.

Heidelberg, May 1817.

Introduction

#1.*

All sciences other than philosophy deal with issues that are assumed to be immediate to representation. Such issues are thus presupposed from the beginning of the science and, in the course of its further development, determinations considered necessary are also derived from representation.

Such a science does not have to justify the necessity of the issues it treats. Mathematics, jurisprudence, medicine, zoology, botany, and so on, can presuppose the existence of magnitude, space, number, law, diseases, animals, plants, and so on. These are assumed to be ready at hand for representation. It does not occur to us to doubt the being of such issues, nor do we expect to be shown conceptually that magnitude, space, disease, animals, or plants must exist in and for themselves.—In the first place such an issue is given its familiar name. This name is fixed, yet for the moment gives only the representation of the object. Still further determinations of the object also have to be made. They can, of course, be derived from the immediate representation. At this point the difficulty may easily arise, however, that certain determinations are apprehended which, it will readily be admitted, are already at hand in the object and are essential to the object. For the formal aspect of this problem, logic or the doctrine of definitions and classifications can be used; but for content one usually proceeds in an empirical manner, in order to discover for oneself and for others whether attributes like those in fact occur in the representation of the general issue. The assessment of this fact can then give rise to sharp controversy.

#2.

By contrast, the beginning of philosophy involves the awkward problem that its object immediately and necessarily provokes doubt and controversy. 1) There is a problem regarding content: in order to be seen as not merely a representation, but as the very object of philosophy, the content must not be found in the representation.

*The numbers in the translation follow the original.

Indeed, the cognitive procedure in philosophy is actually opposed to representation, and the faculty of representation should be brought beyond itself through philosophy.

#3.

(2) The beginning of philosophy faces the same embarassment regarding form, for the beginning as beginning is immediate, but presents itself as mediated. The concept must on the one hand be recognized as necessary and at the same time the cognitive method cannot be presupposed, since its derivation occurs within philosophy itself.

If nothing could be done but to show that representation in itself is the entirely indeterminate topic of philosophy, then one could take refuge in the customary belief that human beings begin with sensory perception and desire, soon feel themselves driven beyond that point to the feeling and intimation of a higher being, an infinite being and infinite will, and then become aware of general concerns: What is the soul, what is the world, what is God? What can I know? On what basis should I act? What should I hope, and so on? Religion and its topics could then be addressed more directly. Yet despite the fact that such questions and issues can themselves be met with doubt and negation, immediate consciousness and even religion in its own way already contain in part the dissolution of such questions and doctrines concerning these topics. But the specific quality that turns these concerns into the contents of philosophy is not expressed in this way.—

Hence one can indeed refer to the topic of philosophy, but neither to its authority nor to a general agreement over what is understood as philosophy. Even the requirement stated earlier, that the knowledge of necessity only occurs through the concept, is not accepted, for there are many who believe that they have grasped philosophy more from immediate feeling and intuition than from the knowledge of necessity, and in fact such immediacy of perception is even called reason. In this sense Newton and the English confuse experimental physics with philosophy, so that electrical machines, magnetic appliances, pumps and the like are called philosophical instruments. But surely it is only thought which should be called the instrument of philosophy, and not a mere assemblage of wood, iron, or other materials.*

#4.

Because the topic of philosophy is not immediate, the concept of the topic and the concept of philosophy itself can only be comprehended within philosophy. What is said here of the topic as well as of philosophy is something said prior to philosophy, and is therefore somewhat anticipatory, still ungrounded for itself. It is also, therefore, incontrovertible and intended to provide only an indeterminate, tentative, and historical introduction.

#5.

Philosophy is here represented as the science of reason, particularly insofar as reason becomes conscious of itself as of all being. All knowledge other than philosophy is knowledge of finite things or a finite knowledge, for by this knowledge reason is presupposed as subjective, given, and thus does not recognize itself in this knowledge. Even when topics are found in self-consciousness, such as laws, duties, and values, these are still particulars seen in contrast to both the self-consciousness that is aware of them and the remaining variety of the universe. To be sure, the topic of religion is the infinite topic for itself, which is supposed to contain everything within itself. But the representations of religion do not stay true to themselves. For here again the world remains independent, apart from the infinite, and what religion offers as the highest truth remains at the same time unfathomable, a secret, unknowable, given, and available to differentiating consciousness only in the form of a given and external entity. In religion the true is presented as feeling, intuition, presentiment, as representation or as worship in general, as well as interwoven with thoughts, but truth is not presented in the form of truth. Above all, religion constitutes its own world, separate from the rest of consciousness, even though its attitude is all-embracing.

---

*There is also a journal, published by Thomson, entitled *Annals of Philosophy or Magazine of Chemistry, Minerology, Mechanics, Natural History, Agriculture, and the Arts.* It is hard to imagine how the materials named in the title could be seen as philosophical.—*Hegel's note*

Philosophy can also be seen as the science of freedom, because in philosophy the heterogeneity of topics and with it the finitude of consciousness disappear. Thus only in philosophy do contingency, the necessity of nature, and the relation to exteriority in general fall away, as well as dependence, longing, and fear. Only in philosophy is reason altogether by itself.—On the same basis, reason in this science does not concern itself with the one-sidedness of subjective rationality, neither as the property of an unusual talent nor as the gift of a particularly divine favor or disfavor, like the possession of artistic skill. Since it is nothing but reason conscious of itself, it is capable by its very nature of being a general science. Nor is it an idealism in which the content of knowledge is determined merely by the self, or has subjective validation enclosed within self-consciousness. Since reason is conscious of itself as being, the subjectivity of the self, which sees itself as something particular in contrast to objects and can distinguish its own determinations in itself as different from others outside of itself and over against itself, is suspended and transformed into rational generality.

#6.

Philosophy is the encyclopedia of the philosophical sciences, insofar as its entire scope is presented through the specific differentiation of its parts, and it is a philosophical encyclopedia insofar as the differentiation and the connection of its parts are presented according to the necessity of the concept.

Since philosophy is rational knowledge throughout, each of its parts is a philosophical whole, a circle of totality containing itself within itself, but the philosophical idea is also within each particular determinacy or element. The individual circle thus ruptures itself because it is in itself a totality, it breaks through the limit of its own elements and establishes another sphere. The whole presents itself then as a circle of circles in which each circle is a necessary moment, so that the system of its characteristic elements constitutes the whole idea, which also appears in each individual part.

#7.

Philosophy is also essentially encyclopedic, since the true can only exist as totality, and only through the differentiation and determination of its differences can it be the necessity of totality and the freedom of the whole. It is, therefore, necessarily systematic.

Philosophizing without a system can not be scientific. Moreover, if it expresses for itself primarily a subjective perspective its contents are contingent. For the contents are only justified as a moment of the whole, and outside of the whole rest on ungrounded presuppositions or have only subjective certainty.

#8.

It is a mistake to confuse a system of philosophy with a philosophy that is derived from a single principle. On the contrary, the principle of true philosophy contains all particular principles in itself. Philosophy demonstrates this both in itself and in its history: on the one hand, the philosophies that appear different in history are only one philosophy at different stages of development; and on the other hand, the particular principles that underlie particular systems are only branches of one and the same whole.

Here the general and the particular must be distinguished according to their own determinations. Formal logic places the general next to the particular, but in itself it becomes another particular. Concerning the objects of everyday life such an arrangement would strike one as inadequate and awkward, as if for example someone who has asked for fruit would refuse cherries, pears, or grapes, and so on, because they are cherries, pears, and grapes, but not fruit.—

Concerning philosophy, however, one allows this procedure, partly to justify contempt for philosophy with the argument that there are so many different philosophies, and each one is only *a* philosophy but not *the* philosophy. The procedure is also allowed in order to place a philosophy whose principle is general next to one whose principle is particular, even to place one of these next to doctrines that insist there is no philosophy. These names are also used for a movement of thought that presupposes that truth is given and immediate, and on this basis constructs its further reflections.

#9.

As an encyclopedia, however, science is not to be presented in the specific development of its particularity, but is to be limited to the beginnings and basic concepts of the particular sciences.

How many of its particular components are needed to constitute a particular science is to a certain extent entirely indeterminate, since, in order to be true, the component must be not only an isolated moment but also a totality. In truth, therefore, the whole of philosophy constitutes one science; but it may also be viewed as a whole composed of several particular sciences.

#10.

What is true in any one science is so through and by virtue of philosophy, whose encyclopedia thus comprises all true sciences.

The philosophical encyclopedia can be distinguished from other, ordinary encyclopedias by the fact that the ordinary one is an assemblage of sciences, taken up in a contingent and empirical manner, and it sometimes includes topics that merely bear the names of sciences but are otherwise only collections of bits of information. The unity that brings the sciences together in such an assemblage is, because they are gathered extrinsically, at the same time only external, an ordering. For the same reason this arrangement must, especially since the materials are also of a contingent nature, remain an experiment, and will always exhibit incongruent aspects.

The encyclopedia of philosophy thus excludes (1) mere assemblages of information, such as philology; and (2) pseudosciences that have mere arbitrariness as their basis, such as for example heraldry. Sciences of this type are thoroughly positive. (3) Other sciences are also called positive, however, that have a rational basis and beginning. This part belongs to philosophy; whereas the positive side remains peculiar to the sciences themselves.

Such sciences are those, for example, that exist for themselves outside of philosophy in general. (1) Their beginning, though very true, ultimately gives way to contingency, when they have to bring their universal truth into contact with empirical facts and the phenomena of experience. In this field of contingency and instability it is not the concept but only the ground that can be validated. The study of law, for example, or the system of direct or indirect taxation, ultimately require exact decisions that lie outside the determinacy in and for itself of the concept. Thus a certain latitude of determination is left open, so that for one reason something can be said in one way but for another reason it can be said in another, and neither is capable of definite certainty. Similarly, when it is separated into details the idea of nature dissolves into contingencies, and natural history, geography, and medicine stumble over descriptions of reality in terms of kinds and differences, which are not determined by reason but rather by chance and by games. Even history belongs under this category, insofar as the idea is its essence, whose manifestation, however, lies in contingency and the field of arbitrary decisions. (2) These sciences are also positive in that they do not recognize their concepts as finite, nor do they see how these concepts and their entire realm undergo a transition into a higher sphere, but they see them as valid in any case. Together with this finitude of form, as with the finitude of content, goes the (3) ground of cognition, partly since the sciences are based on rationalizations, but partly, however, since the feeling, faith, and authority of others, or inner and outer intuition in general, are taken as the ground of cognition. This group includes religion, but also the type of philosophy that attempts to base itself on anthropology, facts of consciousness, inner intuition or outer experience,—as well as natural history, and so on. (4) It may happen, however, that "empirical" or "nonconceptual" are epithets pertinent only to the form of scientific exposition, while sensory intuition arranges mere phenomena according to the inner sequence of the concept. In such a case it may also happen that through the contrasts between the assembled phenomena and their variety, the external, contingent circumstances of their conditions suspend themselves, and generality can then emerge into view.—A sensory form of experimental physics, history, and so on, would present in this way the rational science of nature, and of human events and deeds, in an external picture mirroring the concept.

#11.

The whole of science is the presentation of the idea; its division, therefore, can only be conceptualized on this basis. Now since the idea is reason identical to itself, which, in order to be for itself stands in opposition to itself and is itself an other, but in this other is identical to itself, science falls into three parts: (1) logic, the science of the idea in and for itself; (2) the philosophy of nature, as the science of the idea in its otherness; (3) the philosophy of spirit, the science of the idea as it returns to itself from its otherness.

(1) The division of a science that is projected in advance of itself is at first only an external reflection of its topic, for the differentiation of its concept can be achieved only through knowledge of the concept, which, however, that very science is. Thus the division of philosophy is an anticipation of what is produced by the necessity of the idea itself. (2) As observed in #6, the differences among the various philosophical sciences are only determinations of the idea itself, and it is thus only the idea that manifests itself in these different elements. In nature it is not an other that needs to be recognized as the idea; the idea is in the form of alienation; in the spirit, the same idea has asserted itself as being for itself and becoming in and for itself. Every such determination in which the idea appears is, however, a fleeting moment, and therefore the individual science must not only recognize its contents as an existing topic, but must also recognize in the same act, at once and directly, the transition of its contents into its higher circle. The representation of the relation between the contents as a division is therefore inconsistent in that it places the particular components or sciences next to each other as if they were merely at rest and their differences were substantial, like the differences between kinds.

A.

The Science of Logic

Preliminary Concepts

#12.

Logic is the science of the pure idea, that is, of the idea in the abstract element of thought.

The same point applies to the determinations contained in this section as to prefatory concepts in general prior to philosophy, namely, that they are also anticipations or, what is the same, they are determinations from and according to a survey of the whole.

Logic might be described as the science of thought, its determinations and laws. But thought is in the first place the pure identity of knowledge with itself, and therefore constitutes only general determinacy or the element in which the idea exists as distinctly logical. The idea may well be thought, though not in formal terms but as the totality of the particular determinations which it develops for itself.

Logic is to a certain extent the most difficult science because it does not deal with intuitions, nor, like geometry, with abstract representations of the senses, but with pure abstractions, and a certain force is required for withdrawing into pure thought, keeping firm hold on it, and moving within it. On the other hand logic can be seen as the easiest science, because its contents are nothing but our own thought and its familiar determinations, and these are, at the same time, the simplest ones. The uses of logic are concerned with the relation to the subject, in the sense that it yields a certain development for other purposes. Development through logic is achieved by being an exercise in thought, since this science is the thought of thought. Insofar, however, as logic is the absolute form of truth and, furthermore, also pure truth itself, it is altogether different from something merely useful.

#13.

In formal terms logic has three aspects: (a) the abstract or understandable side; (b) the dialectical or negatively rational side; and (c) the speculative or positively rational side.

These three sides do not constitute the three sides of logic, but are rather moments of each logically real entity, that is, of each concept or of each truth in general. They can again be posited under the first or understandable moment, and thereby held in separation apart from each other, but under this rubric they are not seen in their truth.

#14.

(a) Thought as understanding remains at the point of fixed determinacy and its differentiation in contrast to other moments. Such a limited abstraction is taken to be existent and lasting for itself.

#15.

(b) The dialectical moment is the self-suspension of such determinations and their transition into an opposing form.

(1) Skepticism is constituted by the assumption that the dialectical moment of understanding is separated for itself, particularly as it appears in scientific concepts; it contains mere negation as the result of the dialectic. (2) Dialectics are usually seen as an external art which, through arbitrary design, produces confusion in specific concepts and the mere appearance of contradictions in them. Hence it is not the determinations but rather this appearance which is seen as nothing, and the understanding, by contrast, becomes true. The dialectic, however, should be seen as the proper, true nature of the categories of the understanding, of things and of finitude in general. Reflection is initially the transition past isolated determinacy, into a relation which is posited as relationship and retains its isolated validity. The dialectic, by contrast, is this immanent movement past isolation, in which the one-sidedness and limitation of the categories

of the understanding show themselves as what they are, namely, as the negation of the dialectic. The dialectic, therefore, constitutes the moving soul of further development, and is the principle whereby an immanent connection and necessity enter the contents of science; thus only within the dialectic lies the true, not external, elevation beyond the finite.

#16.

(c) The speculative or positively rational moment apprehends the unity of the determinations in their opposition, the positive moment which is contained in their dissolution and devolution.

(1) The dialectic has a positive result because it has determinate content, and because the result is not really empty, abstract nothingness but the negation of certain determinations. (2) Thus this rational moment, although it is a thought and abstract entity, is at the same time concrete, not because it is a simple, formal unity, but because it is the unity of different determinations. Philosophy in general, then, has nothing at all to do with mere abstractions or formal thoughts, but only with concrete thoughts. (3) The mere logic of the understanding is contained in speculative logic and can, therefore, be constructed from it; it requires nothing more than to leave out the dialectic and rational elements. In this way it becomes what logic usually is, a history of many kinds of assembled categories of thought, which in their finitude are considered to be infinite.

#17.

In terms of content, the determinations of thought are seen in and for themselves in logic.—They are in this way the concrete, pure thoughts of the concept, with the value of determinations based in the fundamental ground. Logic is therefore essentially speculative philosophy.

In speculation, form and content in general are not as distinct as they have been treated in the previous entry. The forms of the idea are their determinations, and it would not be possible to say where another, truer content should derive from than from these determinations themselves. The forms of the simple logic of the understanding, by contrast, are not only untrue in themselves, but are even unable to be forms of the true. Moreover, since they are linked as merely formal with an essential antithesis to content, they are nothing more than forms of the finite, of the untrue.—

Since, however, logic as purely speculative philosophy still includes the idea in thought, or the absolute in its eternity, it is on the one hand subjective and hence the first science; it nevertheless lacks the side of the complete objectivity of the idea. Not only, however, does it remain the absolute ground of the real, but since logic presents itself as this ground, it also proves itself to be a real, general, and objective science. In the assumed generality of its concepts it appears for itself as subjective, particular speculation, next to which the entire richness of the sensory as well as the concrete, intellectual world maintains its essence. Since this, however, is also recognized in the real part of philosophy, and it has shown itself going back into the pure idea and there having its last ground and truth, logical generality thus no longer presents itself as merely another particularity but as a concrete generality. It thus achieves the significance of speculative theology.

#18.

Logic, in the essential meaning of speculative philosophy, emerges in place of what is often dismissed as a separate science and is otherwise called metaphysics. The nature of logic and the standpoint on which scientific cognition posits itself were clarified more precisely: first, by the nature of metaphysics and then by critical philosophy, through which metaphysics reached its final stage. At this point the concept of these sciences and the relation of logic to itself should be elaborated more fully.—Metaphysics, after all, is only outmoded in relation to the history of philosophy. For itself, it is in general as it has become, particularly in recent times: the view from the understanding of the objects of reason.

#14.*

This science thus viewed the determinations of thought as the ground for the determinations of things. It stood, on the basis of this presupposition, at a higher level than recent critical philosophizing, since that which is, by being thought, is recognized in itself. How-

*The manuscript shows the number "14" following "18."

ever, (1) it took those determinations in their abstraction as valid for themselves and able to be predicates of the true. It presupposed in general that knowledge of the absolute could occur in this way, that predicates could simply be designated as true, although it did not investigate the determinations of the understanding either in their actual contents or in their forms. It nevertheless tried to determine the absolute through the attribution of predicates.

Such predicates are, for example, existence, as in the thesis: God has existence; finitude or infinitude, as in the question whether the world is finite or infinite; and simple or complex, as in the proposition: the soul is simple. Other predicates include the question of whether the thing is one, whole, and so on.

#20.

(2) To be sure, its objects were totalities which belong in and for themselves to reason—the soul, the world, God—but metaphysics took these from the sphere of representation, established them basically as complete, given subjects by applying the categories of the understanding, and then had for representation only the criterion of whether the predicates were appropriate and satisfactory or not.

#21.

(3) It thus became dogmatism, because it had to assume, in accordance with the nature of finite determinations, that of two opposed assertions, both propositions, one had to be true but the other had to be false.

#22.

The first part of this metaphysics, after it acquired an ordered shape, was constituted by ontology, the doctrine of abstract determinations of essence. This doctrine is lacking a principle for the multiplicity of the determinations and their finite validity. They must be assumed empirically and contingently, and their more precise contents can only be based on representation, presuming that one thinks this literally, namely, as etymology. The issue becomes, then, mere analytical accuracy and empirical completeness in accordance with linguistic convention, and has nothing to do with the truth and necessity of such determinations.

The question of whether being, existence, finitude, simplicity, composite structure, and so on are true concepts in and for themselves becomes significant if one believes that it could be merely a question of the truth of a thesis, and at that point we need only to ask whether a concept can be attributed (as it is called) to a subject with truth or not. Untruth would depend on the contradiction to be found between the subject and the concept to be attached to the subject as predicate. In such a representation the concept is taken as simple determinacy. But the concept is in general a concrete entity, and this determinacy itself is essentially a unity of different determinations. If truth, then, were nothing more than the lack of contradiction, it would first have to be observed with each concept whether or not it contained such an inner contradiction.

#23.

The second part of this metaphysics was rational psychology, or pneumatology, which concerns the metaphysical nature of the soul, or the nature of the spirit as a thing.

Immortality was sought in a sphere dominated by composite structure, time, qualitative change, and quantitative increase or decrease.

#24.

The third part, cosmology, dealt with the world, its contingency, necessity, eternity, and limited being in time and space; the changes in formal laws, human freedom, and the origin of evil.

The following were taken by cosmology as absolute opposites: contingency and necessity; external and internal necessity; effective and final causes, or causality in general, and the goal of a process; essence or substance and appearance; form and matter; freedom and necessity; happiness and pain; good and evil.

#25.

The fourth part, natural or rational theology, considers the concept of God or its possibility, the proofs of God's existence, and God's qualities.

(a) In this view of God from the understanding the issue is whether a predicate accords or does not accord with what we conceive of as God. The antithesis of reality and negation, or of positive and negative, occurs here as absolute. For the concept, as the understanding takes it, remains in the end only the empty abstraction of the indeterminate essence, of pure reality or positivity.

(b) The proof of finite cognition contains: either the backward position that the objective ground of God should be stated, and that this being thereby presents itself as a mediated entity; or, insofar as the ground must be subjective for our knowledge, this proof, which proceeds from the identity of the categories of the understanding, can not make the transition from the finite to the infinite, and thus God can not be freed from the positive finitude of the existing world. Hence, God must determine Himself as the immediate substance of the world;—He remains, as an object, opposite from the subject, and thereby a finite entity.

(c) The qualities actually disappear in the abstract concept if it is introduced this way. Insofar, however, as the finite world remains a true being and God remains in opposition to it in the representation, even the representation of different relations of God emerge as determinate qualities, on the one hand as relations to finite conditions of a finite type (for example: just, good-natured, powerful, wise, and so on), but, on the other hand, these should also be infinite. This contradiction provokes, in regards to the standpoint of natural or rational theology, a meager and nebulous dissolution through quantitative intensification, namely, by driving it into an indeterminate condition, the *sensum eminentiorem*. In the process, however, its attribute is in fact negated for representation and left as a mere name.

#26.

This metaphysics is subject to two attacks, which come from antithetical sides: (I) The one is philosophizing based on empiricism, which takes not only the entire content of the representation but also all the content and determination of thought, as it is found in sensory perception, with feeling and intuition as an external or internal fact of consciousness. It takes, in the process, the sensory world and its analysis for the source of truth, but either denies the supernatural altogether, or at any rate all knowledge of the supernatural, and makes only the form of abstraction, or of identical positing, available for thought.

#27.

(II) Kantian philosophy contains the opposite view. It has investigated the value of the concepts of the understanding used in metaphysics, and found that they do not derive from sensory perception, but belong rather to the spontaneity of thought. They also contain relations which have generality and necessity, that is, objectivity: synthetic propositions a priori.

#28.

This philosophy offers, as the determinate ground of the concepts of the understanding, the original identity of the "I" in thought—the transcendental unity of self-consciousness. In terms of content, the representations given by feeling and intuition are manifold; they are equally made manifold through their form, through the self-externality of sensory perception in its two forms of space and time. This manifold quality, in which the "I" relates to itself and is united in itself as in one consciousness ("pure apperception"), is thereby brought into identity, into an originary connection. The determinate aspects of this relation are now the pure concepts of the understanding, the categories.

#29.

On the one hand, mere perception arises through objectivity, but on the other hand these concepts, simply as unities of subjective consciousness, are conditioned by the given material, empty for themselves, and have their only application and use in experience.

#30.

Due to this finitude they are unable to be determinations of the absolute, which is not given in perception; thus the understanding, or knowledge through categories, is unable to recognize things in themselves.

#31.

Now it is reason, as the faculty of the unconditioned, which conditions this knowledge of experience and has the insight that it is only appearances. If reason, however, in accordance with its nature, makes the infinite or the thing in itself the object of knowledge, and wants, since it would have nothing else, to apply the categories, it begins to rise up, to become transcendent, yields paralogisms, and falls into antinomies. Reason thus delivers nothing but formal unity to the simplification and systematization of experiences. It is a canon, not an agent, of truth, and can not deliver a doctrine of the infinite, but only a critique of knowledge.

#32.

This philosophy now correctly recognizes the categories of the understanding as finite, hence as unable to grasp the true. But it is also one-sided, since it does not view the categories in and for themselves, but considers them merely as belonging to self-consciousness, and preserves them in this antithesis.

A particular weakness in the Kantian derivation of the above theses becomes evident here. For the categories, apart from the fact that they are incomplete if taken directly from the description, are derived empirically from ordinary logic, without showing how the "transcendental unity of self-consciousness" determines itself in the first place. Similarly, it is not shown how this unity achieves the multiplicity of the determinations of the categories. Nor is it shown how the categories are to be deduced in terms of their determinacy.—In the discussion of the "paralogisms" and "antinomies" of reason, the table of categories is again presupposed. Moreover, instead of deducing the object it is simply put into a model already at hand, an approach which has since become fashionable. I have pointed out further difficulties in the treatment of the antinomies in my *Science of Logic* (Nürnberg bei Schrag, 1812–15).—

In and for itself, however, the thought that the contradiction which is posited in reason by the categories of the understanding is essential and necessary should be regarded as one of the deepest, most important, and progressive achievements of modern philosophy. Of course, this is represented in the *Critique of Pure Reason* as if the contradiction were not in the concepts themselves, but emerges only in their application to the unconditional. Nevertheless, the great service of Kantian philosophy should be recognized. For it elevated the "I" as "pure apperception," moved the search for knowledge away from the question of whether the "soul-thing" exists or not, and focused on the true essence of the self, namely, the pure identity of self-consciousness with itself, or freedom. The grasping of this freedom as the essence and substance of the "soul" established the absolute ground for philosophical knowledge.

#33.

Kantian criticism is thus only a philosophy of subjectivity, a subjective idealism. It diverges from empiricism merely in consideration of what constitutes experience, but agrees with empiricism entirely in its view that reason does not recognize anything supernatural, rational, and divine. It remains fixed in finitude and untruth, namely, in a knowledge that has only subjectivity, exteriority, and a "thing in itself," a formless abstraction, an empty beyond, as its condition.

#34.

At the same time it goes beyond the two sides of the antithesis which it assumes as final, precisely in the sense that it recognizes the knowledge of the understanding as merely an appearance, and the product of reason as only a one-sided, formal unity. The "thing in itself," however, is taken as an indeterminate emptiness which in itself should be true, and at the same time should contain the concept.

It is the greatest inconsistency to admit, on the one hand, that the understanding knows only appearances, and to claim on the other hand that this knowledge is absolute, by such statements as: "Cognition can go no further"; "Here is the natural and absolute limit of human knowledge." For any limit or lack is only recognized through comparison with the idea of the whole and the complete. It is thoughtless, therefore, not to see that precisely the designation of something as finite or limited contains the proof of the actuality and presence of the infinite and unlimited.—One need only think of religious and moral perspectives as having a knowledge of the absolute. These are undeveloped, to be sure, but nevertheless take a position which does not relate directly in contrast to the "in itself," as if it were in contrast to an unknown and indeterminate beyond. They have also given up the belief in a fixed antithesis between subjective cognition and the absolute as a negative entity.—

Of course in relation to morality, but also to some extent in relation to religiosity, one is accustomed to seeing theory and practice as two particular faculties or powers, and at the same time as two kinds of realms. Such a view accords with the representation of the soul in general as a thing which in itself is just as originary and multiple as atomic matter. Moreover, this separation belongs to the presuppositions and assumptions which, once they have become fixed in the imagination, are taken as true without further critique. It is easy to see, however, that it contradicts the presupposed unity of self-consciousness, and that it would not be possible to say what practical faculty could exist without a theoretical one, without knowledge.

#35.

In order now to return to the standpoint of the objective sciences, it is necessary to summarize the difficulties contained in the subjective and finite methods of philosophical cognition: (1) the fixed validity attributed to contrary and limited categories of the understanding; (2) the presupposition of a given, preestablished substratum as a criterion, whether one of the categories of thought accords with it or not; (3) the presupposition that cognition functions as a mere relation between fixed, completed predicates and any given substratum; and (4) the presupposition of an eternal antithesis between the cognitive subject and its object, such that each side should remain equally fixed and true for itself.

#36.

To move beyond these presuppositions it is not yet sufficient to say that they are false, for the science which introduced them in the first place must be the one to show this. They may be rejected, however, for the reason that they belong to the imagination and to immediate thought, thought which is caught up in the given, an opinion; or, in general, because they are given and presuppositions, and science presupposes nothing but that it is pure thought.

Earlier, in the *Phenomenology of Spirit,* I have treated the scientific history of consciousness as the first part of philosophy, since it was meant to precede pure science and to generate its concept. At the same time, however, consciousness and its history, like every other philosophical science, are not an absolute beginning, but an element in the circle of philosophy. Skepticism, if it is made a negative science and systematically applied to all forms of knowledge, might seem a suitable introduction, as it would point out the emptiness of such assumptions. Yet a skeptical introduction would not only be a dissatisfying but also a superfluous path to take, because the dialectic, as stated above, is itself an essential moment of positive science. Moreover, skepticism would only be able to grasp finite forms empirically and unscientifically, and to assume them as given. The demand for such an accomplished skepticism is the same as to insist that science be preceded by universal doubt or, perhaps even more, by universal desperation, that is, the total lack of all presuppositions. Actually, this demand is met by the decision to want to think purely, in freedom, which abstracts from everything and grasps its pure abstraction, the simplicity of thought.—

The demand made fashionable by Kantian philosophy, that prior to actual cognition the faculty of cognition should be investigated critically, offers itself on first glance as a plausible alternative. But this investigation is itself cognitive, and to claim that it could be initiated without cognition is meaningless. Furthermore, even the assumption of a faculty of cognition before actual cognition is a presupposition, both of the unjustified category or determination of a faculty or power, and of a subjective cognition;—a presupposition which belongs to the former one. Logic, by the way, is also part of that required investigation, and more truly than the critical method, which would have to proceed in a limited way on the basis of its own presuppositions and according to the nature of its own ability.

#37.

Pure science or logic divides into three parts: into the logic of being, the logic of essence, and the logic of the concept or the idea.—That is, it divides into the logic of the immediacy of thought, of the reflection of thought, and of the thought which returns from reflection into itself and abides by itself in its reality.

I
The Doctrine of Being

A.
Quality

#39.*

(a.) Being

Pure being constitutes the beginning, because it is both pure thought and simple immediacy; the first beginning, however, can neither be mediated nor further determined.

The true first definition of the absolute is therefore: it is pure being.

This definition is the same as the known assumption that God is the sum total of all realities. Since a determination should be abstracted which contains every reality, or states that God is the only reality in all reality, the most real; and since reality contains a reflection in itself, thus the following can be uttered directly: God is the being in all existence.—All doubts and admonitions, which might be brought as an argument against beginning science with abstract, empty being, will disappear through the simple consciousness of what a beginning naturally implies. Being can be determined as "I = I," as absolute indifference or identity, and so on. These forms can on hindsight be seen as if they must be first, due either to the necessity of an awareness of certainty or to a sense of the absolute truth. But each of these forms contains a mediation, and thus they are not really first: for mediation implies a precedence deriving from something different. If "I = I," and intellectual intui-

*This numbering is in the original.

68

tion is taken truly as first, this is in its pure immediacy nothing but being; just as, conversely, pure being is pure thought or intuition, especially if it is no longer abstract but includes mediation within itself. Moreover the form of the definitions, "the absolute is being," or "absolute indifference," emerges only through a substratum of representation, here in the name of the absolute, which interferes in advance—a substratum whose thought, which is the central point, is contained entirely in the predicate; the subject, then, as well as the form of the thesis, is completely superfluous.

#40.

This pure being, in so far as it is pure abstraction, is also the absolute negative, which, if taken similarly in an immediate sense, is nothingness.

(1) Thus was derived the second definition of the absolute, that is, as nothingness. In fact, this definition is implied by saying that the thing in itself is indeterminate, utterly without form and so without content;—or in saying that God is only the supreme being, for this is also to describe him as negativity. This negativity can be taken as the indeterminacy of a positive, but this positive is itself a determinacy which at the same time should be suspended;—further, the indeterminacy itself is suspended, since in itself the thing in itself and God could not be this emptiness, but would contain form and content, and therefore neither determinacy nor indeterminacy could be their attributes.

(2) If the antithesis is stated this directly as being and nothingness, it appears so striking that being could be nothingness that we might try to fix being and to secure it against this transition. Such reflection would try to discover a fixed determination for being, in order to distinguish it from nothingness; for example, being is indentified with what persists amid all change, with infinitely determinable matter, or even, unreflectively, with any single being. But all such additional and more concrete characterizations cause being to lose that purity which it has immediately in the beginning. On the basis of pure indeterminacy it is nothingness;—something unsayable; the distinction from nothingness is merely an opinion.—

Precisely this awareness of beginnings should be kept in mind:

they are nothing but empty abstractions, and one is as empty as the other. The drive to find a fixed significance in being or in both is the very necessity which leads further and gives them true significance. This procedure is the logical deduction and the movement of thought that manifests itself in the following. The reflection that finds deeper determinations for being and nothingness is logical thought, through which such determinations evolve, though not in an accidental but in a necessary way.—Every following significance, therefore, is only to be seen as a more precise specification and truer definition of the absolute; such a definition is then no longer an empty abstraction like being and nothingness, but rather a concrete entity in which both being and nothingness are moments. When the difference emerges in such a concrete entity, then it is further determined in itself.—The highest form of nothingness for itself is freedom, but freedom is negativity when it sinks into itself to its greatest intensity, and is itself also affirmation.

#41.

Conversely, if it is immediate and the same as itself, nothingness is also the same as being. The truth of being and nothingness is accordingly the unity of both; this unity is becoming.

(1) The thesis that being and nothingness are the same seems so paradoxical to the imagination that it may not be taken seriously. And indeed it is one of the hardest tasks thought poses for itself, for being and nothingness present an antithesis in all its immediacy, that one term is not invested with any attribute which would involve its connection with the other.—This determination, however, as the above paragraph points out, is implicit in them—the determination which is the same in both. So far the deduction of their unity is entirely analytical; indeed, the whole process of philosophizing, if it is to be methodical, that is to say necessary, is nothing but the making explicit of what is already implicit in a concept.—It is just as correct, however, to posit the unity of being and nothingness as to say that being and nothingness are altogether different, that the one is not what the other is. But since the distinction here has not yet assumed definite shape, for being and nothingness are still immediate, it is something unsayable, a mere opinion.—

(2) It requires no great expenditure of wit to ridicule the thesis

that being and nothingness are the same, or to adduce absurdities through the erroneous assertion that these are the consequences and illustrations of that thesis. The objection could be made, for example, that according to the thesis it amounts to the same thing if my house, my property, the air for breathing, this city, the sun, the law, the spirit, and God exist or do not exist. In some of these cases the particular purpose or utility that something has for me is introduced, and the question is asked whether it is indifferent to me that the useful thing exists or not. Indeed, the teaching of philosophy is precisely what frees people from an infinite crowd of finite aims and intentions, by making them so indifferent that it would be all the same to them if such things exist or not.—Moreover, in regards to the air, the sun, the law, or God, philosophy is the disregard of their essential purposes, and the observation of their absolute existence and ideas simply under the rubric of being. Such concrete objects are more than mere beings or nonbeings. Barren abstractions, like being and nothingness—and they are the most barren, precisely because they are characterizations of the beginning—are inadequate to express the nature of these objects. If, therefore, such a concrete entity is introduced, something quite typical of thoughtlessness occurs, namely, it takes up an issue that was entirely out of the question, for here the discussion concerns only abstract being and nothingness.—

(3) It can easily be said that it is difficult to form a concept of the unity of being and nothingness. The concept of unity, however, is developed in the previous sections, and it is nothing more than this: to understand what it means to have comprehended this unity. What is understood by "forming a concept," though, is actually more, namely, a more differentiated and richer state of mind, so that such a concept will appear as a concrete case and one more familiar to the ordinary practices of thought. Insofar, however, as this incomprehensibility expresses the unfamiliarity of holding onto abstract thoughts without any sensible elements, there is nothing left to say but that philosophical knowledge is different from the knowledge one is accustomed to every day, as well as from the knowledge that dominates the other sciences.—Incomprehensibility here seems only to mean that one is unable to represent the unity of being and nothingness. In fact, however, this is not the case; indeed, everyone tends to have infinitely many representations of this unity, and a lack

of representation can only mean that we do not recognize the concept in one of our representations and are not aware that they exemplify it. The nearest example of it is "becoming." Everyone has a mental image of becoming, and will even admit that it is one image. Further, if it is analyzed closely, it exhibits the attributes of being, but also what is the very opposite of being, namely, nothingness. Moreover, these two lie undivided in one representation, so that becoming forms the unity of being and nothingness.—

Another equally plain example is "beginning." The thing does not yet exist in its beginning, but it is more than merely nothing, for its being is already in its beginning. "Beginning" is used with an awareness of further advance; "becoming" is in fact however also only a beginning, for it must proceed further. It becomes, because it contains this contradiction in itself, that which has become, determinate being.

(b.) Determinate Being

#42.

The being in becoming, which is one with nothingness so that nothingness is one with being, exists only in disappearance.

Becoming collapses through its inherent contradiction into the unity in which both elements are absorbed. The result of this is determinate being.

Only by holding fast to results in their truth can an advance and a development in knowledge be secured. Whenever a contradiction is shown in any object or concept—(and there is nothing whatever in which a contradiction or contrary attributes can not be shown; the abstraction made by understanding is the violent insistence on a single aspect, a rigorous effort to obscure and to remove the consciousness of the other aspect involved)—whenever such contradiction, then, is recognized, the usual conclusion is: hence, this object is nothing. Thus Zeno, who first demonstrated that motion contradicts itself, concluded that there is no motion, and the ancients, who recognized origination and passing away, the two kinds of becoming, as untrue categories, used the expression that the one, that is the absolute, neither originates nor passes away. This dialectic considers only the negative side of the result, and abstracts a definite result from that which is actually at hand, here a pure nothingness, but a nothingness which includes being, and equally, a being which includes nothingness. Hence (1) determinate being is the unity of being and nothingness, in which the immediacy of these determinations, and thus the contradiction in their relation, disappears—a unity in which they are only moments—, and (2) since the result is the suspended contradiction, it comes in the form of a simple unity with itself as a being, but a being with negation or determinacy.

#43.

Determinate being is being with determinacy, which is an immediate or subsisting mode or quality. Since, however, nothingness constitutes its ground, nonbeing is posited as an equally immediate aspect of determinate being,—an otherness. The quality exists in itself, therefore, as a relation to another, because it is its own moment. In this being-for-another, which subsists at the same time as a relation to itself, quality is reality.

#44.

Reality as pure relation to itself, and immediately and indifferently contrasted to otherness, is something with qualities or realities that are different from the breadth of its determinate being, namely, relations to others.

#45.

In something, however, determinacy is one with its being; otherness, therefore, is not an indifferent moment outside of something but its own moment. By its quality, then, something is in the first place finite and in the second place changeable, so that changeability belongs to its being.

#46.

Something becomes an other, but the other is itself a something, thus it also becomes an other, and so on to infinity.

#47.

This infinity is the bad or negative infinity, in that it is nothing but the suspension of the finite which, however, also arises again, and is therefore never entirely suspended. In other words, this infinity expresses only the potential suspension of the finite. The progression to infinity never goes further than the statement of the contradiction contained in the finite, that it is both something and its other. It sets up a perennially ongoing alternation between these two terms, each of which brings on the other.

#48.

In fact what occurs is that something becomes an other and the other in general becomes an other. Something is in relation to an other, itself already an other against the same; so that what it passes into is entirely the same as what it passes over. Both have no other than one and the same characteristic, namely, to be an other.— Therefore it follows that something in transition only joins with itself, and this relation to itself in transition and in the other is the true infinity. Or seen negatively: what is changed is the other, it becomes the other of the other. Thus being is restored, but as the negation of the negation, and is being for itself.

(c.) Being for Itself

#49.

Being for itself as relation to itself is immediacy, and this, as the relation of the negative to itself, is self-sufficiency, or unity.

#50.

The relation of the negative to itself is a negative relation, the absolute repulsion of unity, that is, the positing of many unities. In terms of the immediacy of being for itself these are many beings, and the repulsion of unity is to that extent their repulsion of each other as existing beings, or reciprocal exclusion.

#51.

The many are, however, the one that the other is; they are therefore one and the same. Or considering the repulsion in itself, it is, as the negative relation of many unities against each other, just as essentially their relation to each other. Since those to which unity is related in its repulsion are one, it relates in them to itself. The repulsion is therefore just as essentially an attraction, and exclusive unity or being for itself suspends itself. The qualitative determinacy which in unity has reached its determinateness in and for itself has thereby passed over into suspended determinacy, that is, into being as quantity.

Atomistic philosophy takes this standpoint, for which the absolute determines itself as being for itself, as unity and as many unities. Further, its basic force is assumed to be the repulsion showing itself in the concept of unity. Instead of attraction, however, it is supposedly chance or mere thoughtlessness which brings them together. As long as unity is fixed as unity, its convergence with others is seen as something quite external.—The void, which is assumed as the principle complementary to the atom, is represented as repulsion itself, as the nothingness that exists between atoms.—More recent atomism—and physics retains this principle—has partially given up atoms and focuses instead on small particles or molecules. In doing so physics has moved itself closer to sensory representation, but has given up thoughtful observation. Since, moreover, an attractive force is set alongside the repulsive force, the antithesis is of course completed, and the discovery of this "natural force" has been very productive. But the mutual relation of the two, which constitutes what is concrete and real in them, has until now remained only an obscure confusion.

B.
Quantity

(a.) Pure Quantity

#52.

Quantity is pure being, for which determinacy is no longer posited as one with being itself, but either as suspended or indifferent.

(1) The expression "magnitude" is inappropriate for quantity, particularly since it signifies determinate quantity. (2) Mathematics usually defines magnitude as that which can be increased or reduced. As defective as this definition is, since it already contains the thing defined, nevertheless it also posits that the category of magnitude is changeable and indifferent, so that, despite a change in it—an increased extension or intension—the thing, for example a house or the color red, does not cease to be a house or red. (3) The absolute is pure quantity. This view is to some extent the same as to say that the absolute has the character of matter in which, although form of course is present, it is an indifferent characteristic. For determinacy is not lacking quantity, it is rather one of the moments from which quantity results. Quantity also constitutes the basic character of the absolute in the concept, when the absolute is regarded as absolutely indifferent, and for which all difference should only be quantitative. Otherwise, pure space, light, and so on, could be taken as examples of quantity, if by space we take the real as the indifferent fullness of space, or by light we take figuration as well as darkness as an external difference.

#53.

Moments in quantity are suspended, and hence they are characteristics of quantity only in their unity. In the determination of attraction posited as an identity to itself, quantity is continuous magnitude, whereas in the determination of unity it is discrete magnitude. The continuous, however, is also to some extent discrete, for it is only a continuity of many; and the discrete is equally continuous, for its continuity is one as the same of many ones, or unity. (1) Continuous and discrete magnitude, therefore, must not be seen as two types of magnitude, as if the determination of the one did not bear on the other, but rather as if they are only distinguished in terms of the same whole quantity put directly under one, or at another time under another of its determination. (2) The antinomies of space, time, or matter, in regards to their infinite divisibility or their constitution as indivisible units, is nothing else than the assertion of quantity at one moment as continuous, and at another moment as discrete. If space, time, and so on are posited only as characteristic of a continuous quantity, then they are infinitely divisible, whereas if they are posited as characteristic of discrete magnitude, they are divided in themselves and consist of indivisible units.

(b.) Quantum

#54.

In the immediate simplicity of quantity the negative of the unit is the limit, and the quantity is essentially quantum.

#55.

The quantum reaches its completed determinacy in the number, because the element of the number constitutes the unit. In terms of the moment of discreteness, number is the sum, whereas in the moment of continuity it is unity. This qualitative difference is suspended in the unit, that is, the entire number, sum and unity, the essence of the quantum that is identical with its limit.

(c.) Degree

#56.

This limit, as a multiple determination in itself, is extensive, but as a simple determination in itself it is the intensive magnitude or degree.

The difference between continuous and discrete magnitude, on the one hand, and extensive and intensive on the other, is that the former applies to quantity in general, whereas the latter applies to the limit or determination of it as such. Extensive and intensive magnitude are also not two kinds, of which the one contains a determination not possessed by the other.

#57.

The concept of quantum is posited in degree. It is magnitude as simple and for itself, but in such a way that its determination essentially lies outside it in other magnitudes. In this indifference of the quantum as determinacy, where being for itself is absolute exteriority, infinite quantitative progress is posited.

Of course number is a thought, as the identity of determinacy for itself with itself, but thought as fully self-externalized being. Because it is a thought, it does not belong to intuition; but it is a thought containing the exteriority of intuition in itself.—

Not only, therefore, can the quantum be increased or decreased to infinity, but the very concept of quantum is this sending out beyond itself. Again, the infinite quantitative progress is nothing more than the thoughtless repetition of one and the same contradiction, which posits the quantum in general and in its determinacy as degree. Concerning the superfluity of pronouncing this contradiction in the form of an infinite progress, Zeno, as recorded by Aristotle, rightly says: It is the same to say something once, and to say it forever.

#58.

This determination of the quantum in its being for itself as being external to itself constitutes its quality. In this externality it is itself and related to itself. Or, it is united precisely in externality, that is, the quantitative realm, and being for itself, that is, the qualitative realm. Thus posited the quantitative is in the first place nothing immediate but rather a quantitative relationship.

#59.

The sides of the quantitative relationship are themselves, however, still only immediate quanta, and their relation is therefore itself indifferent, a quantum (the exponent), or the qualitative and quantitive determinations are themselves still external. But in their truth, where the quantitative itself is in relation to itself in its externality, or being for itself and the indifference of determinacy are united, it is measure.

C.
Measure

#60.

Measure is the qualitative quantum, in the first place as immediate, a quantum to which a determinate being or a quality is attached.

The modality or kind and manner of being could appear as the third element with quality and quantity, insofar as the qualitative has become an external, indifferent being through its unity with the quantitative. But the mode expresses this indifference or accidental quality only in general. This external manner is, however, also at the same time an expression of qualitative being, as one says in relation to a thing that everything depends on the kind and manner. The mode is at the same time, however, in accordance with this qualitative side, only the indeterminate kind and manner; in its true determination it is measure.

#61.

Since in the measure quality and quantity exist only in immediate unity, their difference presents itself in a similarly immediate manner. Either the specific quantum is merely quantum, and capable of an expansion or diminution without the suspension of measure, which to that extent is a rule, or the change of the quantum is also a change of the quality.

#62.

Initially it seems that measurelessness is this excess of measure, passing through its quantitative nature beyond its qualitative specificity. Since, however, the other quantitative relationship, the measurelessness of the first, is just as qualitative, measurelessness is equally a measure. These two transitions, from quality to quantum and from the latter back to the former, can be represented as infinite progress.

#63.

What indeed is posited here is that the transition in general suspends itself. Since quality and quantity themselves are qualitatively different, but the quality suspends itself in the indifferent determinacy of the quantum, and in this exteriorization only meets itself, hence negativity is also posited, to suspend itself in its otherness and as this otherness. Being which relates to itself in this way is the essence.

II
The Doctrine of Essence

#64.

Essence, as being which comes into mediation with itself through the negativity of itself, contains the negative, as immediately suspended determination, as appearance, and is reflection,—related to itself only in that it is related to another, and is immediate only as something posited and mediated.

The absolute is the essence.—This definition is to some extent the same as the one that says it is being, to the extent that being is equally simple self-relatedness. But it is at the same time higher, because the essence is being that has gone into itself, that is, its simple self-relatedness is this relation through the negation of the negative, or pure negativity. Since the absolute is determined as essence, however, negativity is often taken only in the sense of an abstraction of all specific predicates. Such negative activity falls outside of the essence, and the essence is itself only apart from its premises, the *caput mortuum* of abstraction. But since this negativity is its own dialectic, and not external to being, the truth of essence is that being which goes into itself, or the being in itself of being. The reflection constitutes the difference between essence and immediate being, and is the unique determination of essence itself.

#65.

In the sphere of essence, the dominant characteristic consists in relativity. In the sphere of being, identity is immediate self-relatedness, and the negative is merely otherness. In the present sphere, by contrast, everything is posited only as being which at the same time has gone beyond this point. It is a being of reflection, relationship.

A.
The Pure Categories of Reflection

(a.) Identity

#66.

The essence shines in itself or is pure reflection, and thus it is identity with itself—self-relatedness, however, not as immediate, but as reflected.

(1) This identity is formal or for the understanding if it is held fast and abstracted from difference. Or, rather, abstraction is the positing of this formal identity, the transformation of something inherently concrete into the form of simplicity,—unless a part of the multiplicity found in the concrete entity is excluded, and only one of the same is taken, or the different multiplicities are concentrated into one determinacy, so that here, in regards to the content, nothing is changed. Considered from the position of the truth, both are the same; for each being or general determination is concrete in itself as a concept. It is, therefore, the same contingency or arbitrariness to leave the entity which appears to representation or to thought as simple and self-identical in that form, or to pull together what appears as concrete into the form of simple determinacy.

(2) If identity is linked with the absolute as the subject of a sentence, it implies that the absolute is identical with itself. As true as this thesis is, it is still doubtful whether it is meant in truth; at least in its expression, therefore, it remains incomplete. For it is undecided whether the abstract identity of the understanding—that is, in contrast to the other characteristics of essence—is meant, or if it is the identity which is concrete in itself. In the latter case, as will be shown, it is the ground, but in higher truth, it is the concept. Even the word *absolute* itself often has no other significance than "abstract," and thus the phrases "absolute space" or "absolute time" signify nothing more than "abstract space" or "abstract time."

(3) The categories of essence can also be taken as essential determinations, and in this case they become predicates of a presupposed subject. Since, as categories of essence, they are themselves, they are essentially in themselves the generally essential categories. To them,

therefore, the subject "everything" is given, and the theses that then arise have been treated as the general laws of thought. Accordingly, the principle of identity reads: everything is identical with itself, A = A, and negatively: A can not be at the same time A and not-A. This thesis, instead of being a true principle, is nothing but the law of the abstract understanding. The form of the sentence contradicts itself, since a proposition promises a difference between subject and predicate, but this one does not achieve what its form requires. It is, however, suspended by the following "laws of thought," which are placed beside the first law with the same validity.

(b.) Difference

#67.

The essence is pure identity and appearance in itself only as it is the negativity of being or negativity itself in relation to itself. It essentially contains, therefore, the characteristic of difference.

Otherness is here no longer qualitative, determinacy, negation, or limit. It is now the same as in essence, itself relating to itself, and therefore the negation is a relation, difference, posited being, mediated being.

#68.

Difference is first of all immediate difference, or, since immediacy and being in essence are suspended and only posited, it is only a posited difference. In diversity the different entities are each for themselves what they are, and indifferent to their relations to others. This relation is therefore external to them.

It can also be said that diversity is posited being as posited being, that is, only as appearance, as the difference is only appearance in essence. Now because the posited being as posited being is the negative as negative, the diverse is being for itself, and thus rather the opposite of appearance. Being for itself, in that it denies relativity, and does not want to exist merely in the difference, which, however, constitutes its essence, is in that case precisely not posited as it truly is, and only initially is it the showing of difference.

#69.

In consequence of the indifference of the diverse entities towards the difference between them, it falls outside them into a third entity, an agent of comparison. This external difference, as an identity of the objects related, is equality; as a nonidentity, it is inequality.

(1) Equality and inequality are means, as identity and difference are for the understanding. Both lie in the concept of difference, for it is a relation that constitutes the sides of the equality, as difference itself as such constitutes the sides of the inequality. Because, however, equality and inequality are nothing more than difference external to itself, they are thus posited in difference, and indifferent, by contrast, whether equal or unequal. These determinations themselves fall apart, and the equal is only equal, the unequal only unequal. If the comparison has one and the same substratum for equality and inequality, these are the sides and points of view, according to which it is equal, but different from them, according to which it is unequal.

(2) Diversity has, like identity, been transformed into a principle, namely, that "Everything is different," or that "There are no two things completely like each other." Here, "everything" is put into a pedicate that is the reverse of the identity posited in the first proposition. However, as diversity is understood only in relation to external comparison, something taken for itself is understood only as identical with itself, so that the second proposition does not contradict the first. In addition, however, diversity does not belong to something or to everything; it constitutes no intrinsic characteristic of this subject. This second proposition, then, can not actually be said. In as far as diversity is a wholly indeterminate difference, mere multiplicity, then the proposition that everything is many, or something in its complete multiplicity, is in any case tautological. If, however, this something is itself diverse, it must be so in virtue of its own proper character. In this case it is the specific difference, and not diversity as such, that is meant.

#70.

Equality is an identity only of those entities that are not the same, not identical with each other, and inequality is a relation of unequal entities. The two do not fall, therefore, on different sides or perspectives without any mutual affinity, but one throws light onto the other. Diversity is therefore a difference of reflection, or difference in itself.

#71.

Difference, in the second place, is essential difference in itself, positive and negative, such that the positive is the identical self-relation that is not the negative, and the negative is the difference for itself that is not the positive. Since each is for itself in such a way that it is not the other, each appears in the other, and is only insofar as the other is. Essential difference is therefore an opposition, according to which the different is not confronted by *any* other, but by *its* other. That is, either the positive or the negative has its own determination only in relation to the other, and is only reflected into itself as it is reflected into the other.

Difference in itself yields the following proposition: everything is essentially distinct, or, as it has also been expressed, of two opposite predicates the one can only be assigned to something, and there is no third possibility.—This principle of antithesis contradicts the principle of identity: the one says that something exists only in relation to itself, the other says, however, that it should be only in relation to its other.—It is the distinctive thoughtlessness of abstraction which places two such contradictory propositions next to each other without even comparing them.—The principle of the excluded middle is the principle of the determinate understanding, which wants to avoid contradiction and, in so doing, commits the same. For the predicate, precisely in that it is set in opposition, is the third unit, in which it contains itself, but also its opposite. A should be either $+A$ or $=A$, it says. With these words a third A is declared which is neither $+$ nor $=$, and which at the same time is posited as $+A$ and as A.

#72.

The positive is, then, that diversity which should be independent and at the same time should not be indifferent to its relation to its other. The negative should be equally as independent, thus the negative relation to itself, being for itself, but as negative should have its relation to itself, its positive, only in the other. Both positive and negative are therefore a posited contradiction, both are in themselves the same, but both are also for themselves, since each is the suspension of the other and of itself. In this way they fall to the ground. Or directly, the essential difference, as difference in and for itself, is only the difference from itself, and thus contains the identical. As self-relating difference it is likewise articulated as self-identical, and the opposite is in general that which includes the one and its other, itself and its opposite.

(c.) Ground

#73.

The ground is the unity of identity and difference, the truth of what difference and identity have turned out to be—the reflection into itself which is equally a reflection into another and vice versa. It is the essence posited as totality.

The principle of the ground states: everything has its sufficient ground, that is, the true essentiality of any thing is neither the determination of something as identical with itself, nor as diverse, neither as merely positive nor merely negative, but as having its being in another, which as identical with itself is the essence. And to this extent the essence is not abstract reflection into itself, but into another. The ground is the essence in its own being, but it is essentially ground only insofar as it is the ground of something, of another.

#74.

The essence is in the first place shining and mediation in itself, the category of reflection is the specific character of mediation and therefore essentially mediated. Once this mediation suspends itself into itself, this is the restoration of immediacy or being, but being insofar as it is mediated by suspending mediation;—existence.

The ground still has neither content nor purpose, therefore it is still neither active nor productive. An existence only arises from the ground. The determinate ground is therefore a formal matter, because the content of existence and its ground are not one with its form, and the ground is not something determined in and for itself.

A ground can therefore be found and adduced for everything, and a good ground (for example, a good motive for action), can effect something or not, can have a consequence or not. A motivation may effect something through, for example, its reception into a will, where it first becomes active and is made into a cause.—The ground as such does not, therefore, remain back from and for itself inwardly against the existence which derives from it, but passes entirely into the existence. The ground is reflection into self as immediate reflection into another, and existence is the immediate unity of both, in which the mediation of the ground has suspended itself.

B.
Appearance

(a.) Existence

#75.

Existence is the immediate unity of reflection into self and reflection into another, and thus it is not only as unity or reflection into self but different in these two determinations. As the latter it is the thing, and fixed in its abstraction it is the thing in itself.

The thing in itself, which has become so famous in the philosophy of Kant, shows itself here in its genesis, namely, as the abstract reflection into self which is clung to at the exclusion of different determinations as the empty basis for them. Ground is therefore posited as thing in itself, as it is for itself in its truth as the indeterminate and inactive entity, since it is only suspended mediation without content and purpose.

#76.

The thing as reflection into another has the differences in itself, by virtue of which it is a specific thing. These determinations are different from each other; they have their reflection into self as part of the thing, and not on their own part. These are properties of the thing, and their relation to the thing is expressed as "having."

"To have" as a term of relation takes the place of "to be." Of course something also "has" qualities, but this transference of having onto being is imprecise, because determinacy as quality is immediately one with something, and something ceases to be when it loses its quality. The thing, however, is reflection into itself, for it is an identity distinct from its differences. In many languages *having* is used to denote the past. With reason: for the past is suspended being, and the spirit is its reflection into itself in which it alone continues to subsist. Spirit, however, also distinguishes this suspended being in itself from itself.

#77.

Reflection into another is, in the ground and in truth, also reflection into self. Hence the properties of the thing are not merely different from each other, they are also self-identical, independent, and relieved from their attachment to the thing. Still, as they are the determinations of the thing distinguished from one another as reflected into self, they are not themselves things, as those with the reflection into another are in the relation of having, but only things as abstract determinacies, materials.

Nor are materials, for example magnetic or electric, named "things." They are actual qualities, one with their being, determinacy which has reached immediacy, but an immediacy which is existence.

#78.

Matter is abstract or indeterminate reflection into another, or reflection into itself at the same time as determinate, it is consequently existent thingness, the subsistence of the thing. In contrast to it, however, is the determinate difference which to that extent is form.

#79.

Form and matter, the thing in itself and the material entities of which the thing consists, are one and the same antithesis of inessential and essential existence, with the difference that the form for itself is the abstraction of reflection into another, whereas the thing in itself is by contrast the abstraction of the reflection into itself. Matter is, however, in contrast to form, the essential existence, in which reflection into self is contained, but also at the same time the determination in itself. The many material entities which constitute the thing are equally the thing's essential existence, since they are at the same time reflection into another as well as reflection into self.

#80.

The thing has its essential existence as well as matter in addition to many independent material entities, which, moreover, are absorbed into the form, insofar as matter is essential existence, but since the material entities are equally essential existence, which is suspended into abstract, empty thingness, the thing is thus appearance.

(b.) Appearance

#81.

The essence must appear. Its shining forth in itself is the suspension of its immediate existence, which, however, is not the immediacy of being, but has reflection as its ground. It is therefore such an essence which is immediately suspended and has its ground in a nonexisting identity with itself. Its interiority, however, is immediately just as much reflection into another as existence, but another existence than the first. In the sense that something exists rather as an entity existing in another than in itself, and is a mediated entity, the essence is in the appearance. Essence accordingly is not behind or beyond appearance, but rather, precisely because it is the essence which exists, the existence is appearance.

#82.

That which exists in truth, therefore, is an entity for itself, which immediately exists as another. It exists immediately as mediacy. It is therefore one and the same, which is the distinction and relation between these doubled forms of existence. These forms have, moreover, determinacy as the difference of the reflection against each other, so that the one is reflection into itself, whereas the other is reflection into another.

#83.

That which exists or appearance in its determinacy is therefore the relation, which is one and the same the opposition of independent existences, and only in this identical relation are differences what they are.

(c.) Relation

#84.

(1) The immediate relation is that of the whole and the parts. The whole consists of parts, of the opposite of its own. The parts are diverse and independent of each other. They are, however, only parts in their identical relation to each other, or insofar as they, taken together, constitute the whole. But this togetherness is the opposite of the part.

#85.

(2) The unity and sameness of this relation are immediately, then, its negative relation to itself. The relation is, in short, the mediating process whereby one and the same are first indifferent towards difference, and secondly are the negative self-relation, which repels itself as reflection into self to difference, and invests itself as reflection into something else with existence, while it conversely leads this reflection back into another, to self-relation and indifference;—force and its manifestation.

The relation of the whole and its parts is the immediate and therefore thoughtless relation, the overturning of identity with itself into diversity. It passes thus from the whole to the parts, and from the parts to the whole, and in one its antithesis to the other is forgotten, while each on its own for itself is taken as an independent existence. In other words, when the parts are declared to subsist in the whole, and the whole to consist of the parts, then it is at one moment the one and at another moment the other to be subsistent, and equally each time the other of the same is inessential. In its superficial form the mechanical relation consists in the parts being independent of each other and the whole.

This relation may be adapted for progression ad infinitum in the case of the divisibility of matter, and then it becomes a thoughtless alternation between the two sides. A thing is at one time taken as a whole, then we go on to specify the parts; this determination is then forgotten, and what was a part is viewed as a whole; the determination of the part comes up again, and so on forever. But if this infinity is taken as the negativity that it is, it is the negative self-relating element in the relation—force, the self-identical whole, or immanency—which yet suspends this immanency and gives itself expression, and conversely, the expression which vanishes and returns into force.

Force, notwithstanding this infinitude, is also finite. It requires solicitation from without for its expression, is blind in its effect, and has only a determinate, finite content. It has a content, like the relation of the whole and the parts, because one and the same posit themselves in the diverse determinations of form, and indeed, as unity of these formal determinations is at the same time indifferent towards this distinction. But this one and the same are only at first in themselves this identity, because both sides of the relation are still neither themselves for themselves the concrete identity of the same nor totality. They are, therefore, various for each other, and the entire relation is finite. Force requires, then, solicitation from outside, and the determinacy of the content is a contingent one. It does not yet have the infinitude of concept and purpose, which is in and for itself a specific one.—

It is often said, moreover, that the nature of force is unknown and that only its manifestation is apprehended. But, on the one hand, the entire specific content of force is exactly the same as that of its expression; the explanation of a phenomenon by force is to that extent a mere tautology. What is supposed to remain unknown, therefore, is really nothing but the empty form of reflection into itself, the force is only different from the manifestation,—and that form, too, is something quite familiar. On the other hand, however, the nature of force is of course unknown, because its relatedness is to be sure probably infinite, although only at first abstractly negative, whereas its determinacy is actually finite. This requires, therefore, a necessity of connection and of origin which are entirely lacking. It is thus the contradiction between the shine of independence that the force has and its presence in finitude that must have conditions. For these conditions lie outside of force, and are therefore not recognized in it.

#86.

Force, as the whole which in itself is the negative relation to itself, is as such a whole which it continually pushes itself off from and which manifests itself. But since this reflection into another, corresponding to the difference between the parts and the whole, is equally a reflection into itself, this manifestation is the mediation by which the force returns to itself as force. Its manifestation consists therefore in positing the identity in itself of reflection into itself and reflection into another. The truth of force is hence the relation in which the two sides are distinguished only as inward and outward.

#87.

(3) The interior is the ground, as it is in truth a side of the appearance and the relation, the empty form of reflection into self. As a counterpart to it stands the exterior, existence, also as a side of the relation, with the empty determination of reflection into another. The identity of interior and exterior is brought to fullness in the content, that unity of reflection into self and reflection into other which was posited in the movement of force.

#88.

Primarily, then, the exterior has the same content as the interior. What is inward is also found outwardly, and vice versa. The appearance shows nothing that is not in the essence, and in the essence there is nothing that does not manifest itself.

#89.

In the second place, *inward* and *outward* as formal terms are also reciprocal and thoroughly opposed, as the abstractions of identity with itself and of mere reality. They are essentially identical, however, so that whatever is at first put only in the one abstraction is also immediately and only in the other. Therefore what is only internal is also only external, and what is only external is also only external.

It is the customary mistake of reflection to take the essence as the purely interior. If it is merely so taken, even this observation is purely external, and that sort of essence is the empty external abstraction. "Into the interior of nature," says the poet:

> No created spirit penetrates,
> Too happy if it only
> Knows the outer shell.

He ought rather to have said that only if the essence of nature is determined as interior, does one know the outer shell. In being as a whole, the concept is at first only inward, and for that very reason external, a merely subjective thinking and devoid of truth. In nature itself, as well as in spirit, to the extent that the concept, purpose, or law are at first inner capacity or pure possibilities, they are only at first an external, inorganic nature, the knowledge of a third, foreign violence, and the like.

#90.

The empty abstractions, through which the identical content should still be in the relation, suspend each other into an immediate transformation of the one into the other. They are the shining forth of the essence as appearance, or what has become entirely inessential essentiality. By the manifestation of force the interior is posited as existence, but this positing is an empty mediation by empty abstractions. In its own self the mediating process disappears into immediacy, since the interior and the exterior are in and for themselves identical. This identity is reality.

C.
Reality

#91.

Reality is the immediate unity of essence with existence, or of interior with exterior. The manifestation of the real is the real itself, so that in this manifestation it remains just as essential, and only is essential, insofar as it is in immediate external existence.

Earlier, being and existence were mentioned as forms of immediacy. Being is, in general, unreflected immediacy and the transition into something other. Existence is the immediate unity of being and reflection, thus appearance; it comes from the ground and falls to the ground. In reality this unity is stated explicitly, and the two sides of the relation become identical. Hence the real is exempted from transition, and its externality is its energy. In that energy it is reflected into itself, for its existence is only the manifestation of itself, and not of an other.

#92.

Viewed as an identity in general, reality is (1) the difference between its immediacy and its mediation with itself, its possibility;—the reflection into self which, in contrast to the concrete unity of the real, is taken and posited as an abstract and inessential essentiality.

It was probably the determination of the possibility which enabled Kant to regard it along with necessity and reality as modalities: "since these categories do not in the least increase the concept as object, but only express its relation to the faculty of knowledge." Indeed, possibility is at first the empty abstraction of the reflection into self, such that it belongs only to subjective thought. It is the same as what was formerly called the interior, only that in reality the interior is now suspended, it is now taken to mean the external interior, suspended out of reality with the being of a mere supposition, and thus, to be sure, posited only as a bare modality, an empty abstraction. It is different with actuality and necessity, for they are anything but a mere kind and mode of something else, in fact they are the very reverse of that.

Since possibility is, moreover, in contrast to the concretely real the empty form of identity with itself, everything is possible. For this form can be given through abstraction to every content. But everything is equally impossible, for in every content, which is and must be concrete, the determinacy of its nature may be viewed as a specific antithesis and thus as contradiction. Nothing, therefore, could be more meaningless than to speak of such a possibility and impossibility. In philosophy in particular there should never be a statement made which says that "It is possible," or that "There is still another possibility," nor even, in another phrase, that there is "any kind of plausibility."

#93.

(2) But the real in its difference from possibility as reflection into self is itself only outward immediacy. Or, the real is primarily and immediately itself only in the abstraction of the reflection into self. It is in this way, as reality, determined only as a possibility. When thus valued as a mere possibility or inessential reality, it is a contingency.

#94.

This shining forth posited as appearance, however, mere possibility and contingency, has no real reflection into itself of reality. Therefore only content is posited here, from which arises the essential ground of determination. The finitude of the contingent and the possible thus lies in the distinction between the formal determination, identity with itself, and the content, so that it depends on the content alone whether anything is contingent and possible.

#95.

Reflection into self is, however, no longer the abstract determination of the real, as in the simple essence, but the self-suspending positing or mediation. Contingency, as immediate reality, is essentially identical with itself as a supposition whose positing is just as much suspended. Contingency is therefore something presupposed, the immediate existence of which is a possibility, and at the same time has the determination of being suspended,—the possibility of an other, the condition.

#96.

(3) If possibility is full of content, so that the condition belongs to it, it is the real possibility. But if it is distinct from content and immediate reality it is form for itself, and not the abstract identity in the sphere of the real but the concrete totality of form for itself, the immediate self-translation of the interior into the exterior and

the exterior into the interior. This movement of the form, activity, is the ground as reflected into self, and to be sure, the real ground, which suspends itself to actuality and carries into effect the contingent reality, the condition, their reflection into self and their suspension to another reality. This identity of possibility and reality is necessity.

#97.

Necessity is therefore unity with itself, identical, but full of content, essence which shines in itself so that its differences have the form of independent realities, and thus is identical at the same time as absolute form, the activity of suspending immediacy into mediation and mediation into immediacy. Necessity exists through an other that has collapsed into the mediating ground, into immediate reality, and into a contingent entity which is at the same time condition. Necessity that is through an other is not in and for itself, but merely posited. This mediation, however, is just as immediately the suspension of itself. The ground posits itself as ground, and is suspended as contingent condition into immediacy, through which the former positing is, rather, suspended into reality and converges with itself. This identity makes the real into the necessary. In its truth, then, it is the relation of necessity.

#98.

That which is necessary is (a) the relation of substance and accident. The absolute identity of this relation is substance as such, which as necessity gives negativity to this form of interiority, and thus posits itself as reality, but that is also the negative of this exterior entity. In this negativity the actual, as immediate, is only accidental and through this mere possibility passes over into another reality. This transition is the identity of substance regarded as the activity of form (#97).

#99.

Substance is accordingly the totality of accidents in which it reveals itself as absolute power and, at the same time, as the richness of all content. This content, however, is nothing but these manifestations itself, since the determinacy reflected into itself is not indifferent to form, but passes into the power of substance. Or, the substance is much more itself the absolute activity of form and the power of necessity.

#100.

That which is necessary is, (b) at the stage where substance is absolute power—power in relation to itself as to an inner possibility—effective, and it is causal. Substance is therefore essential causality.

#101.

This, however, is also a relationship of causality, to the extent that substance reflects into itself as against its passage into accident and thus stands as the primary fact. It again, however, no less suspends this reflection into self or its mere possibility, but posits itself as the negative of itself, and thus produces an effect, a reality which at the same time is only posited and not yet necessary.

Cause and effect are in opposition to each other, as substance or primary fact and as mere posited being. Cause in necessity, whose identity constitutes its primary quality, passes into effect. There is no content in the effect which is not in the cause; the former identity is content, but it is equally the determination of form. The primary quality of the cause is suspended in the effect, in which it makes itself into a posited being. This posited being is, however, equally and immediately suspended, it is moreover in the reflection of the cause into itself, its primordiality. In the effect it is actually the cause.—The concept of necessity is one of the most difficult in philosophy, because it is precisely the concept itself but not, however, in its manifestation.—Substance is the necessity still taken immediately; it is, however, at least essentially relation. The substance for itself and the accident are empty abstractions. In its reality, however, the infinite relation of substance is the relation of causality: it is not the substance of an exterior abstraction, itself in relation to itself, but it is this itself, and therefore cause. In this form, however, it is itself infinitude and its effectiveness, but infinite effectiveness which returns to itself in the effect and is only then original and actual. The cause is finite only in the moment of the antithesis which suspends itself immediately. If this antithesis is maintained and the concept of the cause in that case is relinquished, it produces the finite cause and the general representation of the causal relationship. Its finitude also passes into the antithesis of form and content, and is taken as if the cause is finite, because according to its content it is a determined actuality. The cause appears, for the sake of this finitude, as a posited entity or as an effect. This has, then, another cause in turn, and thus there occurs an infinite process of effects to causes.

#102.

Since the cause in its effect is not only positing, but this mediation is also suspended into reflection into itself and immediacy, it is at the same time a presupposition. There is, in this case, another substance at hand on which it has an effect.

#103.

As immediate, the presupposed substance is determined not as a self-relating negativity and active, but as passive. Yet as a substance it is also active; it therefore suspends the immediacy it was originally put forward with and the effect which was put into it, and reacts, that is, suspends the activity of the first substance. But this first substance also in the same way suspends its own immediacy, or the effect which is put into it; it thus suspends the activity of the other substance and reacts. In this manner, (c) causality is transformed into the relation of reciprocity.

In reciprocity the progress of causes and effects into infinity is truly suspended; the rectilinear movement outward from causes to effects and from effects to causes is bent around and back into itself. The cause, which has an effect, is itself an effect, but not of a cause that lies behind and beyond its own effect, rather of a cause that arises in the first place within its own effect. Or the cause is not effect in a sense different from the effect it has, but the effect that has been brought forth is the positing of the cause,—which, however, is just as immediately reflection into self, actuality, and presupposed substance, the other cause—; but the cause as immediate should be real and, indeed, original. Precisely this immediacy is only a posited being or effect.

#104.

Reciprocity is the truth of causality, that is to say, causality only exists as reciprocity. Since cause is determined only by effect, whereas passivity is noneffecting immediacy, the cause assumed to be first is, on account of its immediacy, passive, a dependent being, and an effect. Accordingly, the distinction of the causes spoken of as two has vanished, and there is in itself only a cause which suspends itself as substance in its effect and thereby establishes itself as independent.

#105.

But this unity is also for itself, since the entire reciprocation is the cause in the act of constituting itself and only in such constitution lies its being. The effect or passivity, which the cause received in the reciprocation, is moreover its original moment, and the immediacy revealed by the mediation of its suspended mediation. Its activity is this constitution of itself as effect or as a constituted being, and, conversely, to introduce this constitution into its effect is its primordiality and independent being.

#106.

This pure self-reciprocation is, therefore, unveiled or posited necessity. The link of necessity with necessity is identity in a still inward form, because it is the identity of what should be realities, though their very self-subsistence is bound to be necessity. The circulation of substance through causality and reciprocity is therefore only the proposal that self-subsistence is the negative self-relation—negative, because the acts of distinction and mediation become a primordiality of realities independent against each other—and self-relation, because their independence lies only in their identity.

#107.

This truth of necessity is, therefore, freedom, and the truth of substance is the concept—an independence which, though self-repulsive into distinct independent entities, is as this repulsion identical with itself, and in this movement of reciprocity is with itself and remains by itself.

#108.

The concept is thus the truth of being and of essence, since the shine of self-reflection is itself at the same time independent immediacy, and this being of a different reality is immediately in itself only a shining forth.

(1) The concept has manifested itself as the truth of being and of essence, and both have returned to the concept as into their ground. Conversely, the concept has been developed out of being as out of its ground. The former side of the advance can be viewed as a deepening into being, thereby disclosing its interior, and the latter side as an emerging of the more complete from the incomplete. The more specific meaning which the superficial thoughts of complete and incomplete have here is to indicate the difference of being as an immediate unity with itself from the concept as free mediation with itself. Since being has shown itself as a mere moment of the concept, the concept has precisely in this way exhibited itself as the truth of being. As its reflection into itself and suspension of the mediation, the concept is the presupposition of the immediate—a presupposition which is identical with the return to itself, and in this identity lie freedom and the concept. If, therefore, the moment is called incomplete, then the concept, or the complete, is certainly a development from the incomplete, for it is essentially this suspension of its presupposition. But it is the concept alone which, in the act of positing itself, constitutes the presupposition. The dead concept is, to be sure, without freedom and movement in itself, and therefore also without moments which could be called incomplete.—Since the moment is viewed as independent, and the presupposition as a primordial and lasting principle, this determination is like the concept that would be bound to such a moment, not a concept but an empty abstraction, like the opposition of complete and incomplete, as though the latter would be something in and for itself.

(2) In regards, then, to the relation of being and essence to the concept, the concept is the essence which has returned to being as simple immediacy—the shining forth of the essence thereby has reality, and its reality is at the same time a free appearance in itself.

The concept has being as its simple self-relation or as the immediacy of its immanent unity. Being is so poor a category that it is the least which can be shown in the concept.

(3) The transition from necessity to freedom, or from reality to the concept, is the very hardest, because it proposes that independent reality should be thought as having its only substance in the transition and the identity with the other independent reality. The concept, too, is extremely hard, because it is itself precisely this identity. But the actual substance as such, the cause, which in its being for itself resists all invasion, is already subjected to necessity or to destiny, and this subjection is the hardest. The thinking of necessity, however, is the dissolution of that hardness, for the thinking of necessity is one's meeting oneself in the other. It means a liberation which is not the flight of abstraction, but consists in that which is real having itself not as something else, but as its own being and positing in the other reality with which it is bound up by the power of necessity. The great intuition of substance in Spinoza is in itself the liberation from finite being for itself; but the concept itself is for itself the power of necessity and substantial freedom.

III
The Doctrine of the Concept

#109.

The concept is free as the pure negativity of the reflection of essence in itself or the power of substance, and as the totality of this negativity determined in and for itself.

#110.

The further movement of the concept is development, for the

different entities are immediately posited as identical, and the specific character of each is a free being of the concept.

#111.

The doctrine of the concept divides itself into the doctrine of: (1) the subjective or formal concept; (2) the concept as immediate, or objectivity; (3) the idea, the subject-object, the unity of the concept and objectivity, absolute truth.

Conventional logic includes only those issues which appear here as a part of the third part of the whole, together with the "laws of thought" named above and, in applied logic, some aspects of cognition. It is unnecessary to show the insufficiency of this coverage, since it only offers itself as a contingent selection of material and no other legitimation, for example that it could be more or less than this, can be conceived. On the other hand, the coverage given in this presentation of logic is accompanied and legitimized by its own development. In relation to the preceding logical categories, those of being and essence, it can be said that they are not only categories of thought; they prove to be concepts in their transition, their dialectical moment, and in their return into themselves and totality. But they are only determined concepts, concepts in themselves, or what is the same thing, concepts for us. The other term, into which each category passes or in which it appears, is not characterized as particular. Neither is the third term characterized as an individual or subject, nor is the identity of the category characterized in its antithesis, nor is its freedom posited, because the category is not generality. (2) In its conventional treatment the logic of the concept is understood as a merely formal science, and understood to deal with the form of the concept, judgment, and syllogism as such, without in the least considering whether anything is true. Presumably, this consideration depends entirely on the content. If the logical forms of the concept were really dead, ineffective and indifferent containers for representations or thoughts, then the knowledge of them would be a highly superfluous and dispensable history. In fact, however, they are the opposite: as forms of the concept they are the living spirit of the real, and only that is true of the real which is true by the force of these forms, through them and in them. But as yet the validity and truth of these forms have never been considered and examined on their own account, any more than their necessary interconnection.

A.
The Subjective Concept

(a.) The Concept as Such

#112.

The concept as such contains the moments of generality, as free equality with itself in its determinacy; particularity, that determinacy in which the general remains serenely equal to itself; and individuality, that reflection of determinacy into itself whose negative self-unity is at the same time determined in and for itself and identical with itself or general.

Individual is the same as real, though only the former emerged from the concept and is, as a generality, posited therefore as a negative identity with itself. The real, because at first it is only in itself or immediately the unity of essence and existence, can have effect; the individuality of the concept, however, is absolute effectiveness, and indeed, no longer as the cause is, with the appearance of effecting another, but self-effectiveness.

#113.

The concept is the absolutely concrete, because the negative unity with itself constitutes individuality, its relation to itself, generality. The moments of the concept can to this extent not be separated. The categories of reflection are supposed to be accepted and apprehended apart from their opposites. But in the concept, where their identity is posited, each of its moments can be immediately apprehended only from and with the others.

Ordinarily, one hears nothing more often than that the concept is something abstract. This is entirely true, to the extent that the concept is not the idea. To this extent the subjective concept is still formal, though not at all as if it should have or receive another content than itself. As the absolute form itself it is all determinacy, but determinacy in its truth. Although it is therefore equally abstract, it is concrete, and indeed absolute concreteness, the subject as such. To the extent that the concept exists as concept different from its objectivity, it is spirit. Everything else concrete is not as concrete, least of all that which is generally understood as concrete, a multiplicity held together externally. What are ordinarily called concepts, and indeed specific concepts, such as person, house, animal, and so on, are nothing less than concepts, but simple characterizations and abstract representations, abstractions, which take only the moment of generality from the concept and leave aside the particularity and individuality. Precisely in doing so they abstract from the concept.

#114.

The moment of individuality first differentiates the moments of the concept. Individuality is the negative reflection of the concept into itself, therefore the first free differentiation of the concept as the first negation by which the determinacy of the concept is posited, but as particularity. That is, the differentiations have in the first place only the determinacy of moments in the concept against each other, and equally, their identity is posited, the one being said to be the other. This stated particularity of the concept is the judgment.

It is an issue for abstraction, or for the understanding which holds itself to the reflective category of identity, to retain the general, particular, and individual as separate concepts. Further, if the classes of the concept as concept would be given, specific concepts insofar as a content from elsewhere is not introduced to constitute their determinacy, then these moments alone would be the true kinds.

The ordinary classification of concepts as clear, distinct, and adequate does not belong to the concept; it belongs to psychology. In this case, clear and distinct concepts are synonymous with mere representations: a clear concept is taken as an abstract, simply determined representation, whereas a distinct concept is one where, in addition to the simplicity there is a mark, namely, a sign for subjective knowledge. The adequate concept alludes more to the concept, or even to the idea, but after all expresses only the formal correspondence between a concept or a representation with its object, an external thing. The division into subordinate and coordinate concepts implies a mechanical distinction of the general from the particular, and grounds their correlation in external reflection. Again, an enumeration of such kinds as contrary and contradictory, affirmative, or negative concepts, and so on, is merely a chance selection of determinations of thought which only exist by virtue of concepts that have treated them as such, but otherwise are contents or determinations which have nothing to do with the specific determinacy of concepts as such.—The true distinctions of the concept, the general, the particular, and the individual, also constitute kinds of the concept, but only when they are kept apart from each other by external reflection. The concept is, moreover, only the general which determines itself and is therefore particular, suspends its particularity as determinacy in an equally immediate way, in this turns back into itself, and hence becomes individual and general in one identity.—The immanent differentiation and reflection of the concept itself are posited in the judgment.

(b.) Judgment

#115.

The judgment is the concept in its particularity, as the differentiating relation of its moments, which are at the same time posited as being for themselves and identical with themselves such that they emerge reciprocally as individual and universal.

(1) Ordinarily one thinks of the judgment first as the independence of two extremes, the subject and the predicate. The former is taken as a thing or a determination for itself, and the predicate as a general determination outside of the subject, something in my head.—They are then brought together by me and in this way judged. Since, however, the copula *is* articulates the predicate of the subject, that external, subjective subsumption is again suspended, and the judgment is taken as a determination of the object itself.—The etymological meaning of judgment in our language is deeper. The word (*Urtheil*) expresses the unity of the concept as primary

and its differentiation as the original division. That is what judgment is in truth.

(2) In its abstract sense a judgment expresses in the first place the thesis: The individual is the general, for these are the essential determinations of the subject and predicate reciprocally.—This thesis is a contradiction, and precisely this leads to the necessity that the judgment determines itself further as the identity of its subject and predicate. It also immediately reveals that such abstract judgments contain no truth; in other words, they can be correct by virtue of their content, they can contain for example a truth in the sphere of perception, the sphere of finite thought in general, but they can not achieve truth in and for itself. For the subject and the predicate, the abstract individual and the general (whether it is taken as the concept or as reality is indifferent), do not correspond. One should be, instead, what the other is not. Thus it is not dependent on the content whether, for example, the judgment that "this rose is red" has truth or not. Truth is not to be found in such sensory content, and the form of such a judgment can not, as form, comprehend truth.—

It is precisely for this reason that philosophical truth can not be expressed in a single judgment: spirit, life, the concept in general, are only movement in itself, which is especially deadened by judgment. It is, therefore, principally by virtue of the form of the judgment that such content does not have truth.—

(3) The copula, *is,* comes to be identical with itself in its alienation from the nature of the concept. The individual and the general are, as moments of the concept, specific determinacies that cannot be isolated.—The earlier categories of reflection in their correlations also refer to one another, but their interconnection is only "having" and not "being," neither identity posited as such nor generality. The judgment is for this very reason the true particularity of the concept, for this is the determinacy or differentiation of the latter which, however, at the same time remains a generality.

#116.

The judgment is usually taken in a subjective sense as an operation and a form occurring only in self-aware thought. Since, however, this distinction does not exist in logic it appears, therefore, quite general, and all things are a judgment. That is, they are individuals which are a generality or have an inner nature in themselves, a generality that is individualized. The generality and individuality are differentiated, but at the same time identical.

Subjective judgments are different from propositions. The latter contain statements about the subject that do not stand to it in any general relationship but express some single action, or some state, or the like. It is entirely empty to say, for example, that such statements as "I slept well last night," or "Present arms!" may be turned into the form of a judgment. The sentence "A carriage is passing by" would be a judgment only if it were doubtful, whether the passing object was a carriage, or whether it and not the standpoint from which we observed it was in motion. Here, within the subject, the object which constitutes the subject of the sentence and the determination which should be attached to it are separated from each other. Each of these is at first viewed in my head as an independent entity, the object as an external thing and the determination as a general representation still separated from the object. The combination of the two then becomes a judgment.

#117.

The judgment is an expression of finitude. Things from this standpoint are said to be finite, because their definite being and their general nature (their body and their soul), though united indeed—otherwise they would be nothing—, are also in any case separable and have independence from each other.

#118.

In the abstract terms of the judgment, "The individual is the general," the subject as individual is immediately concrete, while the predicate is what is abstract, general, and in short, abstraction itself. But the two elements are connected together by an *is,* and thus the determination of the concept has the entire concept within it, so that the predicate in its generality must also contain the determinacy of the subject and must, therefore, have particularity. Because, further, the identity of subject and predicate is posited, hence unaffected by the difference in form, it is the content.

#119.

Since individuality and generality constitute the reciprocal, general, formal determinations of the subject and predicate, the further determinacy of the judgment, by which it is a particular entity in contrast to others, falls in the content, the particularity. Insofar, however, as this formal determination has at the same time a relation to individuality and generality, it is determined further with them.

Since the content of the judgment as immediate falls in the particularity of the predicate, the formalism of the judgment emerges from the side of the content. The subject first has its determinacy and content in the predicate; for itself, therefore, it is a mere representation or an empty name. In the judgments "God is the most real of all things," or "The absolute is identical with itself," *God* and *the absolute* are mere names. What they are is only said in the predicate. What the subject may be in other respects, as concrete entity, is no concern of this judgment. Should, however, the predicate express only an individual quality, precisely for the reason that the subject is concrete, the predicate would not correspond to its subject. According to the conceptual determination, one side of the judgment, the subject, is the concrete totality, as well as the other side, the predicate, namely as the unity of particularity and generality. The judgment, therefore, is identical with itself in its subject and predicate. The formalism of the immediate judgment (and it is usually taken in this sense, so that the positive judgment or form of the judgment in general is understood as the enduring type) consists, then, in the fact that the content of the predicate is immediate, and the particularity is a determination indifferent to generality. Consider for example the generality of the predicate: red is a color, although the color could just as well be blue, yellow, and so on.

#120.

(1) The immediate judgment is the judgment of determinate being. The subject is invested with generality as its predicate, which is an immediate quality and therefore does not correspond to the concrete nature of the subject, neither as immediate particularity nor as the generality of the predicate, nor as the unity of the concepts in its determinations.

It is one of the fundamental prejudices of logic that qualitative judgments, such as "The rose is red" or "is not red," can contain truth.

#121.

This untrue judgment splits into a doubled relationship. Since neither the particularity nor the generality of the predicate, both different determinations in this immediate judgment, correspond to the concrete subject, it must (1) be abstracted from them, and only the empty, identical relation that the individual "A" is the individual "A" can be posited, which produces an identical judgment. (2) The other relation is the total incongruity of subject and predicate, which produces an "infinite" judgment.

Examples of the latter are: "The spirit is not an elephant," "A lion is not a table," and so on; propositions which are correct but absurd, exactly like the identical propositions: "A lion is a lion," or "The spirit is spirit." Propositions like these are undoubtedly true for the immediate or, as it is called, qualitative judgment. But they are not judgments at all, and can only occur in subjective thought where even an untrue abstraction may hold its ground. Viewed objectively, they express the nature of beings or of sensory things, since they collapse into both an empty identity and into a fully charged relation, except that this relation is the qualitative otherness of the things related, their total incongruity. The different forms of the judgment in general are the spheres of being and essence which circulate through the concept.

#122.

(2) The suspended judgment of immediacy is the judgment of reflection, the subject with the kind of predicate which is not immediate, but shows itself as essential and comprising a relation.

#123.

The subject, initially immediate or singular, is raised in this relation above its individuality. This enlargement is external, due to subjective reflection, and is at first indefinite particularity. Modified by the individuality of the subject, however, in which it exists, particularity becomes allness.

#124.

Since the subject is equally determined as general, the identity of the subject and of the predicate is posited in such a way that the determination of the judgment is itself indifferent. The unity of the content as the posited simple concept makes the relation of the judgment, in the variety of its formal determinations, a necessary one.

#125.

(3) The judgment of necessity contains in the predicate partly the substance or nature of the subject, concrete generality, the genus (categorical judgment); partly the form of the independent reality of both sides, whose identity is inward only; the reality of the one is not its own, but that of the other (hypothetical judgment). From the alienation of the concept, the judgment, this alienation and its identity, the real concept itself now arises;—the general, which is identical to itself in its exclusive individuality. This judgment, which has generality for both its terms, at one moment as such, at another moment as the totality of its self-excluding particularization—or that individuality which has become general—is the distinctive judgment.

#126.

(4) The judgment of the concept has for its content the concept, which has appeared through the judgment of the necessity, the general with its determinacy. And since as judgment it is also its antithesis, as subject it is individual, in the sense that it is immediately general and exterior, determinate being, and as predicate it is the reflection of the specific determinate being on the general,—the correspondence or noncorrespondence of these two determinations, such as good, true, correct, and so on.

#127.

This judgment is consequently the judgment of the truth (the apodictic). All things are a genus and a purpose in an individual reality of a particular constitution. Their true being is this subjectivity in general, which both contain in themselves, although the particular in them may or may not conform to the general.

#128.

Subject and predicate are in this way each the whole judgment. At the same time the particularity of the subject, its immediate constitution, is the mediating ground between the individuality of the real and its generality, namely, the ground of the judgment. In this way the empty *is* of the copula is filled, and a relation of the subject and predicate is posited that is no longer immediate but now mediated. The mediating element, however, is not the ground as such, but in the determination of the concept, into whose unity the different forms of the judgment have returned. This is the syllogism.

(c.) Syllogism

#129.

The syllogism is the unity of the concept and the judgment;—it is the concept as the simple identity of its determinations, and the judgment as it is also posited in its reality, namely, in the difference of its determinations. The syllogism is thus rational and everything rational.

Of course the syllogism is ordinarily taken as the form of rationality, but only a subjective form, and no connection is shown between it and any other rational content, such as a rational principle, a rational action, idea, and so on. Indeed, it is also the formal syllogism which is taken as rational in such an unreasonable way that it has nothing to do with any rational content. But as such content can only be rational through the determinacy which posits thought as reason, then it can be so in form only, which is the syllogism.—This is nothing else than the posited, initially formal, real concept. Accordingly, the syllogism is the essential ground of all that is true, and the definition of the absolute is that it is the syllogism, or, stating the principle in a proposition: everything is a syllogism. Everything is a concept, and the existence of the concept is the differentiation of its moments, so that the general nature of the concept gives itself external reality by means of particularity, and with this is made individual.—Or, conversely: the real entity is an individual, which by means of particularity rises to generality. The real is one, but it is also the dissociation of the moments in the concept, and the syllogism is the circle of mediation of its elements by which it posits itself as unity.

#130.

In the immediate syllogism the form of the determinations of the concept confronts the others abstractly. There are the two extremes, individuality and generality, and then the concept as the mean which locks the two extremes together, but the concept is also only abstract, simple particularity, the general posited at the same time in determinacy. Here the extremes are posited just as much in contrast to each other as in contrast to their mean. This syllogism contains reason but without concept,—and is therefore the formal syllogism of the understanding.—Objectively considered, such a syllogism expresses the nature of external and determinate beings. In the case of determinate beings subjectivity as thinghood is separable from their properties or their particularity, but also separable from their generality, when this generality is both the genus of the thing and its external connections with other things.

#131.

(1) The first syllogism is a syllogism of definite being, a qualitative syllogism, as stated in the previous paragraph. Its form is I-P-G (Individual-Particular-General), that is, a subject as an individual is coupled with a general character by means of a particular quality.

#132.

This syllogism is entirely contingent in the matter of its terms. The middle term, as an abstract particularity, is only a quality of the subject, but the subject has many others, and thus can be coupled together with exactly as many other generalities. Similarly a single particularity may have various determinations in itself, so that the same *medius terminus* would serve to connect the subject with several different generalities.

With such syllogisms, therefore, the most diverse conclusions can,—as people say, be proven. All that is required is to take a *medius terminus,* from which the transition to the desired proposition can be made. Something different can be proven with another *medius terminus.*—The more concrete an object is, the more sides it has which belong to it, and can serve as *medii termini.* To determine which of these sides is more essential than another again requires a syllogism of this kind, which fixes on the single quality and can with equal ease discover in it a side or consideration by which it can realize its claims to be considered important and necessary.

#132.*

This syllogism is just as contingent in the form of relation which is found in it. According to the concept of the syllogism, truth lies in the relation of different things through a middle term which is their unity. But relations of the extremes with the middle term (the "premises," "major" and "minor") are themselves immediate relations.

This contradiction in the syllogism expresses itself again in an infinite progression, the requirement that each premise will be proven by a syllogism. As the new syllogism itself also has immediate premises, the demand for proof repeats and doubles itself at every step without end.

#133.

This contradiction is in the syllogism itself, as its own dialectic. The problem, however, disappears in the further determination of the syllogism, and particularly in terms of the concept. For in the concept, as in the judgment, the opposite determination is not merely present potentially, but is posited explicitly. The syllogism and its determinacy are therefore not merely related to one another like the determinations of reflection, but they are posited as identical, because they are moments of the concept. The individual is the

---

*This numbering is in the original.

particular, and the particular is the general. Since in the immediate syllogism I-P-G the individual is mediated with the general, it is posited in this conclusion as general. The individual as subject, which includes generality in itself, is therefore itself the unity of the two extremes and the mediating agent.

#134.

The second figure of the syllogism, G-I-P, is expressed in the truth of the first. It shows, namely, that mediation occurs in the individual, and is therefore something contingent. This figure brings together the general (as subject, for in the conclusion of the first figure it received its determinacy through individuality) with the particular. By this conclusion the general is posited as particular, and therefore as the mediation between the extremes, whose places are occupied by the others. This is the third figure of the syllogism: P-G-I.

The "figures" of the syllogism (Aristotle justly recognizes only three; the fourth is a highly superfluous, even absurd addition by the moderns) are in the usual manner of treatment put side by side, without the slightest thought of showing their necessity, and still less their significance and value. Their necessity derives from the fact that each moment is a determination of the concept, and therefore is the whole itself and mediating ground. But to specify which determinations of the theses, for example whether they are generalities or negatives, are needed to enable a correct conclusion in the different figures, is a merely mechanical inquiry which its nonconceptual mechanism and inner meaninglessness have predictably consigned to oblivion. And Aristotle would have been the last person to support those who try to attach importance to such inquiries or to the syllogism of understanding in general. To be sure he described these, as well as numerous other forms of spirit and nature, and examined and elaborated their determinacies. But the syllogisms of the understanding appear in Aristotle as nothing else than the subsumption of the individual or the particular under the general. Not only does he distinguish explicitly between absolute thought and thought which can be true or false, or which can be supported or rejected—these propositions belong for him in the latter sphere—but in his metaphysical theories as well as his theories of nature and mind, he was very far from taking the form of the syllogism as a basis and criterion. Indeed it might be maintained that neither one of these theories would have emerged or have been allowed to exist, if he had been compelled to submit to the syllogisms of the understanding. Aristotle was evidently much too speculative for such a form. Despite all the many descriptions and analyses which he has, the dominant issue is, after all, the concept. How could he have gone further with the syllogism of the understanding?

#135.

Since each moment has to go through the middle and the extremes, their specific difference from each other is suspended. In this form, where there is no distinction between its moments, the syllogism has for its relation in the first place the external identity of the understanding,—equality;—the quantitative or mathematical syllogism.

#136.

(2) As a consequence of this determinacy, the mediating unity of the concept can no longer be seen as the essence of the syllogism in its abstraction, but as a developed particularity which constitutes the determination of the individual as the universal. This is the syllogism of reflection, in which, as the syllogism of allness, induction, and analogy, the middle term also runs through the three determinations of the concept.

#137.

In the syllogism of reflection the concept that shines forth is the middle term, but both extremes, the determinations of the concept in general, are themselves nothing but the shine of the concept. Since this middle term also runs through all determinations of the concept, or conversely, the extremes also assume the determination of the middle which joins them, the shining forth of the shine suspends itself, and produces the substantial unity of the concept, or true generality.

#138.

(3) The syllogism of necessity situates the particular explicitly in the meaning of the determinate species (in the categorical syllogism),

and the individual explicitly in the meaning of immediate being (in the hypothetical syllogism), as mediating determinations. At this point the mediating generality is posited as the totality of its particulars and as an individual particular, or exclusive individuality (in the disjunctive syllogism).

#138.*

The syllogism of understanding has in the process suspended its determinacy and the self-externality in which the concept immediately exists. For, in the first place, each of the determinations enters into the functions of the two others, so that, in the second place, the immediate relations are also mediated, and in the third place, the unity, outside of which the determinations were initially extremes, posits at the same time their reflected relation, which it initially has in itself, and then posits itself as their substantial unity.

#139.

With this is realized: (1) that each mediated relation presupposes reciprocally the two immediate entities which it contains, so that every positing is also a presupposing; (2) that the concept in its individual differences is itself posited as totality and a whole syllogism; and (3) that the difference within the concept as unity with itself falls away as the concept in the extremes. In this process the concept is completely realized, and is, as this unity of its differences with itself, the object.

The relation of the concept to being, or the subject to the object, has been until most recently one of the most interesting, if not the most interesting, and therefore the most difficult, points of philosophy, and has not yet been clarified. Its most important significance has been in the effort to prove the existence of God on the basis of the concept of God. This actually means, however, that the concept, which as yet has nothing to do with remote abstractions of being, or even of objectivity, is taken for its determination as a concept alone, to see when and where it passes into a very different form. One then finds that the concept and the object are implicitly the same. But it is equally correct to say that they are different. In short, the two modes of expression are equally correct and incorrect.—

*Hegel uses this numbering in the original.

Anselm, in whom the highly memorable thought of this proof first occurs, says briefly: Certe id, quo majus cogitari nequit, non potest esse in intellectu solo. Si enim vel in solo intellectu est, potest cogitari esse *et in re:* quod majus est. Si ergo id, quo majus cogitari non potest, est in solo intellectu; id ipsum, quo majus cogitari non potest, est, quo majus cogitari potest. Sed certe hoc esse non potest. (Certainly that, beyond which nothing greater can be thought, cannot be in the intellect alone. For even if it is in the intellect alone, it can also be thought to exist in fact: and that is greater. If, then, that, beyond which nothing greater can be thought, is in the intellect alone, then the very thing which is greater than anything which can be thought can be exceeded in thought. But certainly this is impossible.)—

This argumentation is in the first place an external one; admitting this, however, it also contains a merely subjective concept, the highest being that is only thought, and, in as much as thought has its antithesis in being, it is only finite and not a true essence. Instead, this subjectivity should be suspended. The complete and fundamental thought of this argumentation, moreover, has acquired an entirely incorrect and shallow perspective through its forced employment in the form of the syllogism of the understanding. The concept of the most real essence should contain all realities, including, therefore, the reality of existence. This expresses, however, only the positive side, according to which being is a moment of the concept, but not the negative side, according to which the one-sidedness of the subjective concept is to be suspended. The identity of the concept and objectivity has appeared until now in philosophy in the two forms that they could have, either as a reflective relationship—namely, with the presupposition of a merely relative relation between the absolute differentiation and independence of the concept for itself and objectivity for itself—or, by contrast, as their absolute identity. The latter has then become the basis of each and every philosophy, either as it has been for Plato and Aristotle, for all their predecessors and ancient philosophy in general, or as a presupposed definition, axiom (as it is, for example, for Descartes and Spinoza), as immediate certainty, faith, or intellectual intuition.—

It has already been indicated above, however, that it is an outstanding feature of critical philosophy, in conjunction with all unphilosophical thought, to remain fixed on finite knowledge, and the subjective concept as such, as an absolute. Anselm had, even in his time, already experienced the contradiction that even nonexistent and false things could be thought. Indeed, there is nothing more false than the merely subjective thought of the being of God; it should therefore be dropped, and conceived rather as objective. If, however, the identity of subjectivity and objectivity are taken as the primary basis of philosophy, then (1) this basis, definition, immediate certainty, intellectual intuition, taken as immediate, since it is mediated according to its nature as well as its explicit form, and because it is essentially not an abstract-simple entity, but rather its identity is already differentiated, contains therefore in itself negativity and the dialectic. (2) The requirement that it be proven hence makes itself necessary;—that is, the requirement that its identity be shown as deriving from these differentiations because they exist as such. The need for this proof was raised by critical philosophy, but the result was only to show the inability of critical philosophy to achieve it.—

An external dialectic can, perhaps, represent the contradictions which emerge from the separation of the subjective and the objective, and the merely relational figure which appears. This dialectic, however, is in the first place only negative, and the transition it makes to the positive idea is again only a syllogism of the understanding. But the dialectic is in any case the activity of the concept, and in the present effort it is particularly the concept as such which is the object. The only true form of proof, which shows the subjective in its truth just as much as the objective, is to show the self-determination of the concept as objectivity. This movement, however, is the self-determination of the concept as judgment, then as syllogism, and then as the complete suspension of its development, which it undergoes in the same manner as in the form of the determinations of the understanding and their relation. Since the moments of the concept determine themselves as the whole concept, their differences are suspended in and for themselves, and equally through their negative relation, so that the presupposition of the same is both a positing and a mediation. The concept, thus realized by itself, has in the first place been translated into the object. This object is thus in and for itself concept, and determines itself by the reemergence of the concept from the object on the way to the idea, the idea differentiating itself into object and concept as the absolute unity of both.

B.
The Object

#140.

As being is to determinate being, essence to existence, in this way the concept is related to objectivity, to that immediacy in which mediation joins together with itself through judgment and the syllogism into simple unity. Immediacy is, therefore, only in itself and not for itself the totality of the concept or being in and for itself.

The definition of the absolute as the object is most certainly to be found in all those forms of representation and philosophizing in which God has a relationship external to the concept. The object in such a relation, however, has in such a relation only the abstract meaning of true being in contrast to the subject, and the subject's inner reason is not the concept, because it must be unknowable. The definition which states that the absolute is the object is strongly implied in the Leibnizian monad. The monads are each objects, but in themselves representative, and implicitly contain the total representation of the world. Nothing from outside comes into the monad: it is the whole concept in itself, distinguished only by its greater or lesser development.

#141.

The object, because it is in itself the totality of the concept, is indeterminate, but responsive to all determinations while at the same time remaining indifferent to all. It is, therefore, just as much a differentiated multiplicity in itself as an identity of differences, a dependent and an independent entity, and these nonconceptual determinations are external both to the object and to each other.

(a.) Mechanism

#142.

Because the object is the concept only in itself, the concept is initially outside it and all its determinacy is posited into it from the outside. As a unity of differences it is, therefore, a composite, an aggregate, and its capacity for acting on anything else is an external relation;—the formal mechanism.

#143.

Indeterminacy is precisely, then, because it stands in opposition to determinacy, determinacy. These are objects of determinate differentiation, which however retain an external characteristic as a reflective relation to each other. To the extent that they portray themselves as indifferent, in contrast to this external determination, they appear to be independent and able to offer resistance. To the extent, however, that they also suffer external determination in this independence, they suffer violence.

#144.

In violence the nonindependence of objects manifests itself, that is, negativity as the proper element of their nature. In this way, however, the reflective relation, according to which determinacy as the negative is only an external part of the object, suspends itself.

#145.

This inner negativity is the immanent independence of the object, which in this case is identical with its exteriority. Identity, as the concept pushing itself away from itself, forms the syllogism so that the immanent negativity, as the central individuality of an object, relates itself to nonindependent objects as the other extreme, by a middle term which unites the centrality and nonindependence of the objects in themselves;—absolute mechanism.

#146.

This syllogism is a triad of syllogisms. The false individuality of nonindependent objects, in which formal mechanism is at home, is, by reason of that nonindependence, no less general, though it is only external. Hence these objects also form the middle term between the absolute and the relative center (in the form of the syllogism as G-I-P): for it is by this nonindependence that the two are kept separate and made extremes, as well as related to one another. Similarly, absolute centrality, as substantial generality (illustrated by the gravity that remains identical), which as pure negativity equally includes individuality in itself, is the mediating element between the relative center and the nonindependent objects, with the form of syllogism being P-G-I. It does so no less essentially as a diremptive force, in its character of immanent individuality, than as a generality, acting as an identical bond of union and tranquil being in itself.

#147.

The negativity or selfhood of the object in the absolute mechanism is still general or internal; its multiplicity is therefore still indifferent, and qualitatively only that of abstract being for itself or not for itself, independence or nonindependence. As the concept, however, it determines itself, and the particularity of the concept yields an objective difference in the object.

(b.) Chemism

#148.

The different object is the chemical object. It has an immanent determinacy which constitutes its nature and in which it has existence. Because its essence is the concept, however, it involves the contradiction between its totality and the determinacy of its existence. Consequently it is striving to suspend this contradiction and to make its determinate being equal to the concept.

#149.

The product of the chemical process is thus the neutral object, itself inherent in the two extremes. The concept or general moment, by means of the difference of the objects, their particularity, converges with the individuality of the product. In this process, too, the other syllogisms are equally involved. The mediating role is played both by individuality as activity, and by generality, the essence of the strained extremes, which achieves determinate being in the product.

#150.

In the product the specific qualities, which the extremes had against one another, are merged. But since the extremes are only implicitly the concept, the neutral product is appropriate to the concept, though the inspiriting principle of differentiation does not exist in this and is external to it. The object is still indifferent towards the negative unity of the concept as concept, does not yet exist in it for itself, and the neutral body is therefore separable.

#151.

Therefore the judging principle, which breaks up the neutral body into different extremes, and gives to the undifferentiated object in general its difference, its spirited relation to an other, and the process as intensifying separation, falls outside of that first process and constitutes only a particular side of it.

#152.

The externality of these processes, however, which allows them to appear independent in relation to each other, shows their finitude by their transition into products in which they are suspended. The concept is liberated, then, by that determinacy through which it is the same in each, by that differentiation in which each suspends the other, and by its extinction in the product, and emerges for itself in opposition to the object,—as the purpose.

(c.) Teleology

#153.

The purpose is the concept existing for itself, and is constituted only implicitly by mechanism and chemism. Because it is determined in and for itself as concrete generality, which as absolute form has its determination in itself—for as it has passed through each of the previous phases in which the determinations of form have an external reality it has become free of them and general—it has gained determinacy as content in itself. As differentiated form it is subjective, but as the negativity of this it exists as formal determinacy in it;—the drive translates itself into objectivity.

The concept of the purpose is justly called the concept of reason, in contrast to abstract generality and particularly to the causal relationship of the understanding. The relation of abstract generality to the particular is understood as a subsumption, in the sense that the particular does not have particularity within itself. But in this way it is abstract. We can determine the absolute as pure being, first cause, or ground, and proceed to further knowledge in this mode of relation, but then it is not determined as reason, in the sense that its essence is not grasped as the goal. Of course on the whole it is superfluous to speak of the concept of reason, for the concept is nothing else but reason, and that which is called the concept of reason is not the concept at all, but rather the abstract determination of the generality, or that content which is preserved in the form of this simple abstraction. Nevertheless the expression "the concept of reason" can actually be a concept and grasped as such. Concepts of reason would include in this case those, as for example being, quality, identity, force, causality, and so on, which are not yet posited in terms of their contents as concepts. It can of course occur, however, that what is conceptual in content, such as the concept itself, or even purpose and reason, becomes nonconceptual in form, as for example the syllogism in the perspective of conventional logic, and this perspective is itself nonconceptual, unreasonable, and merely understandable. The perspective of the goal is similarly flawed if a content, or even the realization of the content, is sought elsewhere or externally. It becomes pure or reasonable only in view of its finitude, and not as a concept. It has already been remarked that the purpose: (1) has a content determined from itself as the absolute first. This constitutes a side of reality in which the concept exists as goal, as the self-reflective identity of the concept, and thereby as indifferent to the determination of form. Here the goal is generality existing for itself, and different from particularity and individuality: an extreme in the whole teleological syllogism, in contrast to the mediating realization, and in contrast to the goal posited as realized in individuality. This generality is, however, at the same time the identity which passes through all termini of the syllogism, retains itself in these, and forms their substance. The goal is: (2) the disjunctive syllogism. The general is the immediate individuality by which it is made disjunctive. On the one hand, here, it is set as the content against the form, a particular against other particulars, in contrast to merely different, but at the same time it is the particular subjective. On the other hand, however, the disjunctive individuality is, as a negative unity, just as much the mediating element between the two sides and the suspension of this antithesis: the activity of translating the subjective into the objective.—The concept passes through the various forms of the formal syllogism (cf. nos. 131–38), and produces thereby the first immediate realization, without which it would be posited still primarily as the moving or dialectical entity, though it is this only implicitly. Since, however, it is posited in itself as objectivity through the suspension of the object, and produces the negative self-relation, it becomes the self-sustaining concept,—that subjective element which is itself required by the realization, and the dialectic as immanent activity.

#154.

The teleological relation is initially of external purposiveness, for the concept is still immediately in opposition to the object: the concept has not yet generated the object out of itself. The goal is consequently finite, and that partly in its content, partly in the fact that it has an external condition in the object which has to be found existing and which is taken as material for its realization. Its self-determination is to that extent only formal, enclosed within the subjective purpose, and the realized goal is only an external form.

This finite goal belongs to an external, finite reason, and therefore actually to external understanding. The concept, too, in its immediate determinations, the judgment of the understanding, and the syllogism have existence as such only in subjective understanding. But the goal does not merely involve the form which it has in consciousness as a mode of merely mental representation. Through the concept of inner purposiveness Kant has resuscitated the idea in general and in particular the idea of life. He liberated practical reason from external purposiveness only insofar as he recognized the formalism of the will, self-determination in the form of generality, as absolute. The content, however, is indeterminate. Purposive action is conditioned by material and accomplishes only formal goodness, or, what amounts to the same thing, realizes only the means. Even Aristotle's concept of life contains inner purposiveness, and thus is far in advance of the concept in modern teleology.

#155.

The teleological relation is the syllogism in which the subjective purpose coalesces with objectivity through a middle term which is the unity of both. This unity is both purposive action and, as objectivity posited directly subservient to the goal, the means.

#156.

(1) The subjective purpose is the syllogism in which the general concept coalesces with individuality by means of particularity, in such a way that the individual as self-determination particularizes the general concept or makes it into a determinate content. At the same time the individual is the return to itself, for it holds up the particularity of the concept, presupposed in opposition to objectivity, as a lack (cf. #153), and thereby at the same time turns itself outwards.

#157.

(2) This outwardly directed activity is related to individuality, which in the subjective purpose is identical with particularity and under which, together with the content, it also comprised external objectivity. The action throws itself in the first place immediately upon the object, and appropriates the object to itself as a means. The concept is this immediate power over mechanism and chemism, because it is their truth and at the same time their self-identical negativity. The whole middle term is now this inner power of the concept as activity, with which the object is immediately united as means.

#158.

(3) Purposive action, with its means, is still outwardly directed, because the purpose is also not identical with the object, and must first, consequently, be mediated with it. The means stands as object in this second premise in direct relation to the other extreme of the syllogism, namely, the objectivity or material which is presupposed. This relation is the sphere of mechanism and chemism, which are now serving the goal. That this subjective purpose, the power of those processes in which objective entities suspend one another, stands itself outside of them and preserves itself in them, is the cunning of reason.

#159.

The realized goal is thus that generality which preserves itself in the objective process; the universal which, in the very course of the process, has achieved objectivity. But since this objectivity was already in the finite goal as a presupposed and preexisting material, the accomplished goal is also as broken within itself as the means were. It is, therefore, only a form posited extraneously on the material, the means which have arisen and which, like the accomplished goal, are because of the contents at the same time a contingent determination, and which therefore again become a material for other purposes.

#160.

What appears in the first place is that the posited subjectivity of the purpose and the independence of the object lie in opposition to each other. But what happens in the realization of the goal is that its own subjectivity and the mere appearance of objective independence are suspended. In grasping the means the concept posits itself as the self-sustaining essence of the object. In the mechanical and chemical processes the independence of the object has already implicitly been dissipated, and in the course of its movement under the domination of the goal the appearance of that independence, the negative which opposes the concept, is suspended. But this negative is the particularity and outward orientation which the concept manifested as its self-determination. Through this process it turns back into itself, as a negative relation to itself, or a self-sustaining entity, which has equally become the objective in itself as for itself.—This realized goal is the idea.

C.
The Idea

#161.

The idea is the true in and for itself, the absolute unity of the concept and objectivity. Its ideal content is nothing but the concept in its determinations; its real content is only the presentation made by the concept in the form of external existence.

The definition which declares the absolute to be the idea is itself the absolute. All previous definitions come back to this. Everything real, insofar as it is true, is the idea, and has its truth only by and in virtue of the idea. Individual being is one side of the idea, for which, therefore, further realities are needed, which then appear to be equally self-sustaining. It is only in them together and in their relationship that the concept is realized. The individual for itself does not correspond to its concept. This limitation of its existence constitutes the finitude and downfall of the individual.

The idea is, moreover, not to be taken as an idea of any one thing or other, any more than the concept is to be taken as merely a specific concept. Since the idea emerges in determinate being, it throws its own moments apart, but since it remains ground and essence it is in them, and in them it is a specific idea. But the absolute is this general and one idea, the idea itself, which is just as much the system of specific ideas and into which these return as into their truth.

Consciousness, which abides in the sphere of representation and whose only thoughts are interwoven with representations, normally begins with existing things, and if it rises to the thought of its ideas, takes the relation between idea and representation as if existent things were real, and as if the idea were only a subjective abstraction whose content derived from the existent. Further, the idea as such, which has no specific content and has no existent thing as either its starting point or underpinning, is taken as a merely formal-logical entity. Here, however, we can no longer speak of such relationships: the existing thing and all further determinations of it have exposed themselves as untrue and have turned back into the idea as their last ground. The idea is thereby revealed as in and for itself true and real, and all content which it has in addition can only be given through the idea itself.

It is just as false to represent the idea as if it were merely an abstraction. Of course it is abstract insofar as everything untrue is consumed within it; but in its own self it is essentially concrete, because it is the free concept determining itself and determining itself as reality. It would only be an abstract form if the concept, which is its principle, were taken as the abstract unity and not as it is, namely, the negative return into itself and individuality.

#162.

The idea may be described in many ways: as reason, as subject-object, as the unity of the ideal and the real, of the finite and the infinite, of the soul and the body, as the possibility which has its actuality in itself, the nature of which can be thought of as existing, and so on. For in general all these descriptions apply, because the idea contains all the relations of understanding but in their self-return and self-identity.

It is easy for the understanding to show that everything said of the idea is self-contradictory. But that can just as well be rejected, or rather the rejection is already implied in the idea. This work, which is the work of reason, is certainly not as easy as the work of the understanding. It is quite possible, therefore, for the understanding to show that the idea contradicts itself, because for example the subjective is only subjective, and is always confronted by the objective; because being is something quite different from the concept, and therefore can not be picked out of it; because the finite is finite only, and precisely the opposite of the infinite, therefore not identical with it; and so on with every term of the description. The doctrine of logic, however, is the reverse of this. For logic shows that the subjective which is only subjective, the finite which is only finite, the infinite which is only infinite, and so on, have no truth, contradict themselves, and pass over into their opposites. Hence this transition, and the unity into which the extremes are suspended as an appearance or moments, reveals itself as their truth.

The understanding, which creates itself in the idea, is a double misunderstanding. It first takes the extremes of the idea—be they expressed as they will, as long as they are in their unity—not in the sense as if they were in their concrete unity, but abstractions outside of it. It overlooks, for example, the copula in the judgment, which affirms that the individual, or subject, is after all not individual, but general. And secondly, the understanding holds its reflection—that the self-identical idea contains its own negative, or contradiction—to be an external reflection which does not lie in the idea itself. This belief, however, is really not the unique wisdom of the understanding, but because the idea is this negativity, it is itself the dialectic, which forever divides and distinguishes the self-identical from the differentiated, the subjective from the objective, the finite from the infinite, the soul from the body, and only on these terms is it an eternal creation, eternal vitality, and eternal spirit. While it is thus the transition into the abstract understanding, it is also forever reason. The idea is the dialectic which makes this rational diversity understand its nature and the false appearance of independence in its productions, and which brings diversity back to unity. Since this double movement is neither temporally nor in any other way separate and distinct—otherwise this would be merely the abstract understanding again—it is the eternal perception of itself in the other. It is the concept which in its objectivity has achieved itself, the object, which is inner purposiveness and essential subjectivity.

The different ways of apprehending the idea, as unity of ideal and real, of finite and infinite, of identity and difference, and so on, are more or less formal, since they designate some stage of the specific concept. Only the concept itself, however, is free, and truly general; in the idea, therefore, its determinacy is only the concept itself, an objectivity into which it carries itself further as general, and in which it has only its own, total determinacy. The idea is the infinite judgment, of which its sides are equally identical as the independent totality, and precisely in this way, as each has been completed, it has passed into the other. None of the otherwise determined concepts exhibits this totality completed on both its sides as does the concept itself and objectivity.

#163.

The idea is essentially a process, because its identity is the absolute and free identity of the concept only insofar as it is absolute negativity and hence dialectical. It is the path in which the concept, as generality which is individuality, gives itself the character of objectivity; this externality, which has the concept as its substance, leads itself back to subjectivity through its immanent dialectic.

(a.) Life

#164.

The immediate idea is life. The concept is realized as soul in a body, of whose exteriority the soul is the immediate, self-relating generality. The soul is also its particularity, so that the body expresses no other distinctions than follow from the determinations of its concept. Finally, individuality is on the one hand the dialectic of objectivity, which is led back into subjectivity from the appearance of its independent subsistence, so that all members are as reciprocally means as they are momentary purposes and determinations of the concept. On the other hand, life is constituted as something alive by the individuality of the concept.

#165.

The living being has individuality because its individuality is the subjectivity of the concept. Since this is inseparably unified, but the objective differences have an indifferent exteriority, the living being is essentially the process of itself in itself, and its parts are only transitional.

The relation between the whole and the parts is therefore the most inappropriate for the living being, or if it is viewed according to this relation it is taken as dead, because the parts manifest such differences as an independent subsistence should have for itself. Spirit is similarly a living being, though it is also seen as dead if the abilities and powers active within it are taken as those it should have. It is then the thing of many attributes, a collection of characteristics subsisting indifferently in opposition to each other. The finitude of the living thing consists in the fact that soul and body are separable; this consitutes the mortality of the living being. Only when the living being is dead, however, are these two sides of the idea different components.

#166.

(2) This process is enclosed in the concept or in the immediacy of the living being. In the judgment of the real concept, however, the objective element is equally an independent totality, and the negative relation of the living thing to itself implies the presupposition of an opposed, inorganic nature. As this negative of the animate is equally a moment in the concept of the animate itself, it exists consequently in the animate, which is at the same time general, as a lack. The dialectic by which the object, as implicitly null, suspends itself, is the action of the self-assured living thing, which in this process against an inorganic nature thus retains, develops, and objectifies itself.

#167.

(3) The living individual, which in its first process is as subject and concept, through its second has assimilated its external objectivity. It is now therefore implicitly a genus, with substantial generality. The judgment of this concept is the relation of the subject to another subject, the sexual difference.

#168.

The process of genus formation brings it to a being for itself. Since life remains the immediate idea, the product of this process falls apart into two sides. On the one hand, the living individual, which was initially presupposed as immediate, is seen now to be mediated and engendered. On the other hand, however, the living individuality, which, on account of its first immediacy relates negatively to generality, sinks into generality, and thereby the idea as a free genus enters into existence for itself: the death of individual vitality is the emergence of spirit.

(b.) Cognition

#169.

The idea exists freely for itself, insofar as it has generality as the element of its existence, or objectivity is itself as the concept. Individuality, which is suspended in the idea, is pure differentiation within the idea, and intuition holds itself in this identical generality. But as this individuality of totality it is the judgment which repels itself from itself, and presupposes itself as an external universe.

#170.

The relation of these two ideas, which implicitly or as life are identical, is thus at first relative. It is the relationship of reflection, in which the distinguishing of the idea is the first judgment, and the presupposition of the one is not yet the positing of the other. For the subjective idea therefore the objective is the immediate world found ready to hand, or the idea as life is in appearance the individual existence.

#171.

(A) The subjective idea, as the idea in the determination of generality, is itself for itself and its other. It therefore has to realize the drive itself as such a unity. Because, however, that other is itself initially in opposition to the drive, this prior drive is organized to suspend its lack into itself, and the certainty of the identity of the objective world with itself, and to raise this certainty by assimilation of the subsisting world in itself to truth. The realization of this drive is cognition as such.

#172.

This cognition is finite, because it has the presupposition of a preexisting world, and in that sense its identity with the world is not for itself. The truth it is able to achieve is therefore also merely finite, and not the infinite truth of the concept. Thus this knowledge is understanding beyond cognition. Infinite truth as a self-subsisting goal is without reason; the assimilation of the given object in the form of the concept that remains external to it.

#173.

Finite cognition, when it presupposes what is different as a being already preexisting and confronting it—facts of external nature or of consciousness—has (1) only formal identity or abstraction for itself. Its activity therefore consists in analyzing the given concrete object, isolating its differences, and giving them the form of abstract generality. Or it leaves the concrete object as a ground, and by the abstraction of the inessential-looking particulars brings into relief a concrete generality, the genus or power and the law. This is the analytical method.

#174.

(2) This generality is at the same time determinate, its truth is the concept. In this case, however, since it does not have infinity in finite cognition, it is merely the rational, determined concept. The absorption of the object in this form is the synthetic method.

#175.

(a) If the object of cognition is brought into the form of the specific concept, so that its genus and its general determinacy are posited, it is the definition.

#176.

(b) The statement of the second moment of the concept, the determinacy of a generality as particularization, is division.

#177.

(c) In concrete individuality, the object is a synthetic relation of different determinations. This is a theorem. The identity of this relation is mediated. To supply the materials which constitute the middle members is the construction, and the mediation itself, from which cognition derives the necessity of the relation, is the proof.

As the difference between the synthetic and analytical methods is commonly stated, it appears entirely optional which of the two we employ. If the concrete entity, which the synthetic yields as a result, is assumed, we can analyze from it as consequences the abstract theses which formed the presuppositions and material for the proof. Thus the algebraic definitions of curved lines are theorems in the operations of geometry. Similarly, even the Pythagorean theorem, if it is made the definition of a right triangle, might yield to analysis those theses which geometry had already demonstrated on its behalf. The arbitrariness of the choice between methods is due to the fact that both begin from an external presupposition. As far as the nature of the concept is concerned, analysis is prior, since it has to raise the given concrete material in the first place into the form of general abstractions, which may then be set before the synthetic method as definitions.

That these methods are useless for philosophical cognition is selfevident, for they contain an initial presupposition, and cognition is thereby debased to the understanding and the procedure of formal identity. In place of the abuse which the formalism of these methods , generated in philosophy and the sciences, there has arisen in recent times the abuse of "construction." Kant brought into use the idea that mathematics "construes" its concepts, which means nothing other than that mathematics has no concepts, but only depicts abstract determinations in sensory intuitions. The phrase "a construction of concepts" has since been given to a statement of sensory attributes derived from perception but in avoidance of the concept, to the additional formalism of classifying scientific and philosophical objects in a tabular form according to some presupposed model, and classified by the way according to fancy and discretion. Here, basically, is a dim representation of the idea, the unity of the concept and objectivity. But this game of "construing" is very far from presenting this unity adequately, a unity which only the concept as such can present.

Another point should be noticed. Geometry has to do with the sensory but also abstract intuitions of space, and in space it can easily fix simple determinations of the understanding. Geometry alone, therefore, has the synthetic method of finite cognition in its perfection. Ultimately, however, geometry also stumbles upon incommensurabilities and irrationalities, and at that point any attempt at further specification drives it beyond the principle of the understanding. (Here also, as often, occurs an instance of perverse terminology, whereby the term *rational* is applied to the activity of the understanding, while what is called *irrational* may indicate rather a beginning and a trace of rationality.) Other sciences, if they reach the limits of their understanding, help themselves easily: they interrupt the sequence of their procedure and take what they need, often the opposite of the preceding, from an external quarter, from a representation, an opinion, a perception, or any other source. The blindness of finite cognition as to the nature of its own procedure through definitions, divisions, and so on, is really led on by the necessity of the determinations of the concept. For the same reason it cannot see when it has reached its limit; nor, if it has transgressed that limit, does it perceive that it is in a field where the categories of the understanding are no longer valid, though it crudely continues to apply them.

#178.

The necessity brought forth by finite cognition in the proof is external, for the subjective insight as determinacy in the definition is a characteristic, and the basis for division is any external consideration,—because this knowledge in general adheres to the formal concept, antithetical to the concept of the thing. Necessity as such is implicitly the concept, and the truth of the formal and external mediation is the mediation of itself with itself, independent subjectivity. Thus the idea as cognition passes from the externally subsisting determinacy into an inner one which is immanent in the subject, into the idea of the will.

#179.

(B) The subjective idea is that which is determined in and for itself as the good. Its drive to realize itself has the reverse relation to the idea of the true, and no longer attempts to absorb the object and to determine itself accordingly, but instead tries to determine the world it finds at hand, according to its purpose.

#180.

This will has on the one hand the certainty of the nothingness of the presupposed object, since in necessity the validity of immediate being has suspended itself. On the other hand, however, it presupposes the independence of the object, because the suspension of being by cognition is its first and formal negation, and the purpose of the good is still a subjective idea.

#181.

The finitude of this will, therefore, lies in the contradiction that in the contradictory determinations of the objective world the purpose of the good is just as much achieved as not achieved, the purpose is posited as just as inessential as essential, just as real as at the same time merely possible. This contradiction disappears, however, when the action suspends the subjectivity of the purpose, which is not in itself and organized according to content, and along with it the objectivity, with the contrast which makes both finite. With this the presupposition of cognition reestablishes itself and the objective world as an immediately subsisting entity, in its antithesis to the final purpose of the good, disappears.

#182.

The truth of the good as purposive is therefore the unity of the theoretical and practical idea which achieves the good in and for itself,—the objective world is in and for itself the concept. This life, which has returned to itself from the difference and finitude of cognition, and which by the activity of the concept has become identical with it, is the speculative or absolute idea.

(c.) The Absolute Idea

#183.

The idea as unity of the subjective and objective idea is the concept, of which the concept as such is the object, or of which the object is the concept;—an object in which all determinations have converged. This unity is consequently the absolute and all truth, the idea thinking itself.

#184.

Because there is in it neither transition nor presupposition, and in general no specific character other than that which is fluid and transparent, the absolute idea is for itself the pure form contemplating its contents as itself. It is its own content, insofar as it distinguishes itself from itself, and one of the distinctions is the identity with itself, in which however the totality of the form as determination is contained. This content is logic. As form nothing remains for the idea but the method of this content.

#185.

The moments of the speculative method are (a) the beginning, which is being or immediacy, self-subsistent for the simple reason that it is the beginning. But viewed from the speculative idea, being is now its self-determination, which as the absolute negativity or movement of the concept judges and posits itself as the negative of itself. Being, which for the beginning as such appears as a position, is thus rather negation. But because it is the negation of the concept, which in its otherness is identical with itself and the certitude of itself, it is the concept not yet posited as concept, or the concept that is implicitly concept.—This being, therefore, as the still indeterminate concept, is equally general.

The beginning, merely in the abstract sense of immediate being, is a beginning taken from intuition and perception. It is the beginning of the analytical method of finite cognition. In the abstract sense of generality, it is the beginning of the synthetic method. Since, however, logic is immediately as much general as subsisting, and presupposed as much by the idea as it itself immediately is, its beginning is a synthetic as well as an analytical beginning.

#186.

(b) Progressive motion is the judgment of the idea. Immediate generality is in itself not simple, but differentiated, or rather its very immediacy and generality constitute its determinacy. It is therefore the negative of the beginning, or posits the beginning in its determinacy. It is, for one, the relation of differences, which however is not external but immanently dialectical. This advance is equally analytical, since the immanent reflection posits only what is contained in the immediate concept;—and synthetic, since in this concept the distinction is not yet posited.

#187.

This advance is, in being, an other and a transition into an other; in the essence it is the appearance in the antithetical; in the concept it is the differentiation of the individual from the general, which continues itself as, and is as an identity with, that which is differentiated from it. In the idea this middle term is already the second negation, the negation of the negation, the living soul of totality.

#188.

(3) The end is this: it posits the difference as that which is in the idea. The end is in itself the negative of the first, and as the identity with that it is the negativity of itself. It is consequently the unity in which both of these firsts, the ideal and the real, exist, or are suspended.—In the idea this end is still only the disappearance of appearance, as if the beginning were immediate, and the end were a result;—it is the knowledge that the idea is one totality.

#189.

The method is in this way not an extraneous form, but the soul and the concept of the content itself, and is only different from it insofar as the determinations of the concept are as content also in themselves the totality of the concept. This concept, however, shows itself to be inappropriate to the elements and contents as long as it is without form.

#190.

But since the content leads itself through the concept back to the idea, thus the idea presents itself as a systematic totality which is only one idea, of which particular moments are implicitly the idea in part, and partly produce the simple being for itself of the idea through the dialectic of the concept. The difference between form or method and content thus makes itself disappear.

#191.

The speculative idea, which is thus the idea for itself, is therefore infinite reality, and in this absolute freedom does not merely pass over into life, or as finite cognition allow life to appear in it. In its own absolute truth it resolves to let the moment of its particularity, or of the first determination and otherness, the immediate idea as its reflected image, release itself as nature freely out of itself.

B.

The Philosophy of Nature

Preliminary Concepts

#192.

Nature has presented itself as the idea in the form of otherness. Since in nature the idea is as the negative of itself, or is external to itself, nature is not merely external in relation to this idea, but the externality constitutes the determination in which nature as nature exists.

#193.

In this externality the determinations of the concept have the appearance of an indifferent subsistence and isolation in regards to each other. The concept therefore exists as an inward entity. Hence nature exhibits no freedom in its existence, but only necessity and contingency.

For this reason nature, in the determinate existence which makes it nature, is not to be deified, nor are the sun, moon, animals, plants, and so on, to be regarded and adduced as the works of God, more excellent than human actions and events. Nature in itself, in the idea, is divine, but in the specific mode by which it is nature it is suspended. As it is, the being of nature does not correspond to its concept; its existing actuality therefore has no truth; its abstract essence is the negative, as the ancients conceived of matter in general as the *non-ens*. But because, even in this element, nature is a representation of the idea, one may very well admire in it the wisdom of God. If, however, as Vanini said, a stalk of straw suffices to demonstrate God's being, then every representation of the spirit, the slightest fancy of the mind, the play of its most capricious whim, every word, offers a ground for the knowledge of God's being that is superior to any single object of nature. In nature, not only is the play of forms unbound and unchecked in contingency, but each figure for itself lacks the concept of itself. The highest level to which nature drives its existence is life, but as only a natural idea this is at the mercy of the unreason of externality, and individual vitality is in each moment of its existence entangled with an individuality which is other to it, whereas in every expression of the spirit is contained the moment of free, universal self-relation.—Nature in general is justly determined as the decline of the idea from itself, because in the element of externality it has the determination of the inappropriateness of itself with itself.—A similar misunderstanding is to regard human works of art as inferior to natural things, on the grounds that works of art must take their material from outside, and that they are not alive.—It is as if the spiritual form did not contain a higher level of life, and were not more worthy of the spirit than the natural form, and as if in all ethical things what can be called matter did not belong solely to the spirit.—

Nature remains, despite all the contingency of its existence, obedient to eternal laws; but surely this is also true of the realm of self-consciousness, a fact which can already be seen in the belief that providence governs human affairs. Or are the determinations of this providence in the field of human affairs only contingent and irrational? But if the contingency of spirit, the free will, leads to evil, is this not still infinitely higher than the regular behavior of the stars, or the innocence of the plants?

#194.

Nature is to be viewed as a system of stages, in which one stage necessarily arises from the other and is the truth closest to the other from which it results, though not in such a way that the one would naturally generate the other, but rather in the inner idea which constitutes the ground of nature.

It has been an awkward conception in older and also more recent philosophy of nature to see the progression and the transition of one natural form and sphere into another as an external, actual production which, however, in order to be made clearer, is relegated to the darkness of the past. Precisely this externality is characteristic of nature: differences are allowed to fall apart and to appear as existences indifferent to each other; and the dialectical concept, which leads the stages further, is the interior which emerges only in the spirit. Certainly the previously favored teleological view provided the basis for the relation to the concept, and, in the same way, the relation to the spirit, but it focused only on external purposiveness,—(cf. #151) and viewed the spirit as if it were entangled in finite and natural purposes. Due to the vapidity of such finite purposes, purposes for which natural things were shown to be useful, the teleological view has been discredited for exhibiting the wisdom of God. The view of the usefulness of natural things has the implicit truth that these things are not in and for themselves an absolute goal; nevertheless, it is unable to determine whether such things are defective or inadequate. For this determination it is necessary to posit that the immanent moment of its idea, which brings about its transiency and transition into another existence, produces at the same time a transformation into a higher concept.

#195.

Nature is, in itself, a living whole. The movement of its idea through its sequence of stages is more precisely this: the idea posits itself as that which it is in itself; or, what is the same thing, it goes into itself out of that immediacy and externality which is death in order to go into itself; yet further, it suspends this determinacy of the idea, in which it is only life, and becomes spirit, which is its truth.

#196.

The idea as nature is: (1) as universal, ideal being outside of itself, space and time; (2) as real and mutual being apart from itself, particular or material existence,—inorganic nature; (3) as living actuality,—organic nature. The three sciences can thus be named mathematics, physics, and physiology.

I
Mathematics

#197.

(1) The first or immediate determination of nature is the abstract generality of its self-externality,—its unmediated indifference, space. It is the wholly ideal juxtaposition, because it is being outside of itself, and absolutely continuous, because this being apart from itself is still entirely abstract, and has no specific difference within itself.

Much has been said, from different theoretical positions, about the nature of space. I will mention only the Kantian determination that space is, like time, a form of sensory intuition. It has also become customary to establish fundamentally that space must be regarded only as something subjective in representation. Disregarding what, in the Kantian conception, belongs to subjective idealism and its determinations (cf. #5), the correct determination remains that space is a mere form, i.e., an abstraction, that of immediate externality.—To speak of points of space, as if they constituted the positive element of space, is inadmissible, since space, on account of its lack of differentiation, is only the possibility and not the positing of that which is negative and therefore absolutely continuous. The point is therefore rather the negation of space.—This also settles the question of the infinitude of space. Space is in general pure quantity (#53f.), though no longer as a logical determination, but rather as existing immediately and externally. Nature, consequently, does not begin with quality but with quantity, because its determination is not, like logical being, the absolute first and immediate, but essentially a mediated being, a being external to and other than itself.

#198.

Space has, as the concept in general (and more determinate than an indifferent self-externality) its differences within it: (a) in its

143

indifference these are immediately the three dimensions, which are merely diverse and quite indeterminate.

But geometry is not required to deduce that space necessarily has precisely three dimensions, for it is not a philosophical science, and may therefore presuppose space as its object. Moreover, even apart from this, no thought is given to the demonstration of such a necessity. The necessity rests on the nature of the concept, whose determinations, however, because they depict themselves in these first elements of being apart from themselves, in abstract quantity, are only entirely superficial and a completely empty difference. One can also, therefore, not say how height, length, and width differ from each other, because they only ought to be different, but are not yet differences.—Height has its more precise determination as direction according to the center of the earth, but this does not at all concern the nature of space for itself. Following from this point it is equally as indifferent whether this direction is called height or depth, or length or breadth, which is also often called depth.

#199.

(b) But the difference of space is essentially a determinate, qualitative difference. As such it is (a) first, the negation of space itself, because this is immediate and undifferentiated self-externality, the point. (b) The negation as negation, however, is itself spatial, and the relation of the point to space is the line, the first otherness of the point. (c) The truth of the otherness is, however, the negation of the negation. The line, therefore, passes over into the plane, which on the one hand is a determinacy opposed to line and point, and thus is plane in general, but on the other hand is the suspended negation of space, and thus the reestablishment of spatial totality, which, however, now contains the negative moment within itself, an enclosing surface, which splits off an individual, whole space.

That the line does not consist of points, nor the plane of lines, follows from their concepts, for the line is the point existing outside of itself, relating itself to space, and suspending itself, and the plane is just as much the suspended line existing outside of itself.—Here the point is represented as the first and positive entity, and taken as the starting point. The converse, though, is also true: in as far as space is positive, the plane is the first negation and the line is the second, which, however, is in its truth the negation relating self to self, the point. The necessity of the transition is the same.—

The other configurations of space considered by geometry are further qualitative limitations of a spatial abstraction, of the plane, or of a limited spatial whole. Here there occur a few necessary moments, for example, that the triangle is the first rectilinear figure, that all other figures must, to be determined, be reduced to it or to the square, and so on.—The principle of these figures is the identity of the understanding, which determines the figurations as regular, and in this way grounds the relationships and sets them in place, which it now becomes the purpose of science to know.

It may be noted in passing that it was an extraordinary notion of Kant's to claim that the definition of the straight line as the shortest distance between two points is a synthetic proposition, for my concept of straightness contains nothing of size, but only a quality. In this sense every definition is a synthetic proposition. What is defined, the straight line, is in the first place the intuition or representation, and the determination that it is the shortest distance between two points constitutes in the first place the concept (namely, as it appears in such definitions, cf. #110). That the concept is not already given by the intuition constitutes precisely the difference between the two, and is what calls for a definition. That something seems to the representation to be a quality, though its specificity rests on a quantitative determination, is something very simple, and also the case for example with the right angle, the straight line, and so on.

#200.

(2) Negativity, which as point relates itself to space and in space develops its determinations as line and plane, is, however, in the sphere of self-externality equally for itself and appearing indifferent to the motionless coexistence of space. Negativity, thus posited for itself, is time.

#201.

Time, as the negative unity of being outside of itself, is just as thoroughly abstract, ideal being: being which, since it is, is not, and since it is not, is.

Time, like space, is a pure form of sensuousness, or intuition,—but, as with space, the difference between objectivity and a contrastingly subjective consciousness does not matter to time. If these determinations are applied to space and time, then space is abstract objectivity, whereas time is abstract subjectivity. Time is the same principle as the I = I of pure self-consciousness; but the same principle or the simple concept still in its entire externality, intuited mere becoming, pure being in itself as sheer coming out of itself. Time is just as continuous as space, for it is abstract negativity relating itself to itself, and in this abstraction there is as yet no real difference.

In time, it is said, everything arises and passes away, or rather, there appears precisely the abstraction of arising and falling away. If abstractions are made from everything, namely, from the fullness of time just as much as from the fullness of space, then there remains both empty time and empty space left over; that is, there are then posited these abstractions of exteriority.—But time itself is this becoming, this existing abstraction, the Chronos who gives birth to everything and destroys his offspring.—That which is real, however, is just as identical to as distinct from time. Everything is transitory that is temporal, that is, exists only in time or, like the concept, is not in itself pure negativity. To be sure, this negativity is in everything as its immanent, universal essence, but the temporal is not adequate to this essence, and therefore relates to this negativity in terms of its power. Time itself is eternal, for it is neither just any time, nor the moment now, but time as time is its concept. The concept, however, in its identity with itself, I = I, is in and for itself absolute negativity and freedom. Time, is not, therefore, the power of the concept, nor is the concept in time and temporal; on the contrary, the concept is the power of time, which is only this negativity as externality.—The natural is therefore subordinate to time, insofar as it is finite; that which is true, by contrast, the idea, the spirit, is eternal. Thus the concept of eternity must not be grasped as if it were suspended time, or in any case not in the sense that eternity would come after time, for this would turn eternity into the future, in other words into a moment of time. And the concept of eternity must also not be understood in the sense of a negation of time, so that it would be merely an abstraction of time. For time in its concept is, like the concept itself generally, eternal, and therefore also absolute presence.

#202.

The dimensions of time, the present, future, and past, are only that which is becoming and its dissolution into the differences of being as the transition into nothingness, and of nothingness as the transition into being. The immediate disappearance of these differences into individuality is the present as now, which is itself only this disappearance of being into nothingness, and of nothingness into being.

(1) The finite present is differentiated from the infinite in that the finite is the moment now and hence as its abstract moments, as past and future, which is different from the infinite as from the concrete unity. Eternity as concept, however, contains these moments in itself, and its concrete unity is therefore not the moment now, because it is motionless identity, concrete being as universal, and not that which is disappearing into nothingness, as becoming.—Furthermore in nature, where time is now, there does not occur the subsisting difference of these dimensions; they are necessarily only in subjective representation, in memory, fear, or hope. The abstract past, however, and future of time is space, as the suspended space is at first the point and time.

(2) There is no science of time in opposition to the finite science of space, geometry, because the differences of time do not have the indifference of being outside of itself, which constitutes the immediate determinacy of space, and therefore they can not be expressed as spatial configurations. The principle of time only reaches this ability when the understanding has paralyzed it and reduced its negativity to the unit. This motionless unit, as the sheer externality of thought, can be used to form external combinations, and these, the numbers of arithmetic, can themselves be brought under the categories of the truth as intuition or as understanding merely for itself, because the latter is only abstract, whereas the former is concrete. This dead unit, now the highest externality of thought, can be used to form external combinations, and these combinations, the figures of arithmetic, can in turn be organized by the determination of the understanding in terms of equality and inequality, identity and difference. The science which has unity as its principle is therefore constituted in opposition to geometry.

(3) The name of mathematics has moreover been used for the

philosophical observation of space and time, because it lies close to this observation, despite the fact that mathematics, as noted, considers strictly the determinations of magnitude of its objects and not time itself, but only the unit in its configurations and connections. To be sure, time becomes in the theory of movement an object of science, but applied mathematics is generally not an immanent science, precisely because it involves the application of pure mathematics to a given material and its determinations as derived from experience.

(4) One could still, however, conceive the thought of a philosophical mathematics, namely, as a science which would recognize those concepts which constitute what the conventional mathematical science of the understanding derives from its presupposed determinations, and according to the method of the understanding, without concepts. However, since mathematics is the science of the finite determinations of magnitude, which remain fixed in their finitude and valid, and should not change in transit, thus it is essentially a science of the understanding. And since it has the ability to express spatial figures and numbers, which gives it an advantage over other sciences of this kind, it ought to retain this ability for itself and to avoid contamination by either concepts, like time, which are heterogeneous to it, or empirical purposes. It therefore remains open for the concept to establish a more fundamental consciousness than has hitherto been shown, both in terms of the leading principles of the understanding and in terms of order and its necessity in arithmetical operations, as well as in the theses of geometry.—If one wanted to treat the forms of space and the unit philosophically, they would lose on these grounds their particular significance, a philosophy of them would become a matter of logic, or would even assume the character of another concrete philosophical science, according to the ways one imparted a more concrete significance to the concepts.—

It would, however, be a superfluous and thankless task to try to use such an unmanageable and inadequate medium as spatial figures and numbers for the expression of thoughts, and to treat them violently for this purpose. For the specific concept would always be related only externally to them. The simple elementary figures and numbers can in any case be used as symbols, which, however, are a subordinate and poor expression for thoughts. The first attempts of pure thought took recourse to such aids: the Pythagorean system of numbers is the famous example of this. But with richer concepts these means became completely unsatisfactory, since their external juxtaposition and contingent combination are not at all appropriate to the nature of the concept, and make it altogether ambiguous which of the many possible relationships in complex numbers and figures should be adhered to. Besides, the fluid character of the concept is dissipated in such an external medium, in which each determination falls into the indifferent being outside the others. This ambiguity could only be removed by an explanation. The essential expression of the thought is in that case this explanation, and this symbolizing is an empty superfluity.

Other mathematical determinations, such as infinity and its relationships, the infinitesimal, factors, powers, and so on, have their true concepts in philosophy itself. It is awkward to want to take and derive these from mathematics, where they are employed in a non-conceptual, often meaningless way; rather, they must await their justification and significance from philosophy. The truly philosophical science of mathematics as theory of magnitude would be the science of measures, but this already presupposes the real particularity of things, which is only at hand in concrete nature.

#203.

(3) Space and time constitute the idea in and for itself, with space the real or immediately objective side and time the purely subjective side. Space is in itself the contradiction of indifferent being outside of others and undifferentiated continuity, and thereby the pure negativity of itself and the transition into time. Space converts into the individuality of the place. Time is, equally, since its moments held together in unity suspend themselves immediately, the immediate convergence into indifference, into undifferentiated being apart from one another, or into space, so that its place is precisely in that way immediate as sheer indifferent spatiality. This disappearance and regeneration of space in time and of time in space is motion;—a becoming, which, however, is itself just as much immediately the identically existing unity of both, or matter.

The transition from ideality to reality, from abstraction to concrete existence, in this case from space and time to reality, which appears as matter, is incomprehensible to the understanding, and always converts therefore externally for the understanding, and as a given entity. The usual conception is to take space and time as empty and to be filled with matter from the outside. In this way material things are, on the one hand, to be taken as indifferent to space and time, and on the other hand to be taken at the same time as essentially spatial and temporal.

What is usually said of matter is: (a) that it is composite; this refers to its identity with space. Insofar as abstractions are made from time and from all form generally, it is asserted that matter is eternal and immutable. In fact, this follows immediately, but such a matter is also only an untrue abstraction. (b) It is said that matter is impenetrable and offers resistance, is tangible, visible, and so on. These predicates mean nothing else than that matter exists, partly for specific forms of perception, in general for an other, but partly just as much for itself. Both of these are determinations which belong to matter precisely because it is the identity of space and time, of immediate being apart from itself or of becoming.

The transition of ideality into reality is demonstrated therefore in the familiar mechanical phenomena, namely, that ideality can take the place of reality and vice versa; and only the usual thoughtlessness of the representation and of the understanding are to blame that, for them, their identity does not derive from the interchangeability of both. In connection with the lever, for example, distance can be posited in the place of mass and vice versa, and a quantum of the ideal moment produces the same effect as the corresponding real moment.

Similarly, velocity, in the magnitude of motion, the quantitative relationship of space and time, represents mass, and conversely, the same real effect emerges if the mass is increased and the velocity proportionately decreased. By itself a brick does not kill a person, but produces this effect only though the velocity it achieves, in other words, the person is killed through space and time.

It is force, a category of reflection fixed by the understanding, which presents itself here as the ultimate, and therefore prevents understanding and lets it seem superfluous to inquire further after the concept. But this at least appears without thought, namely, that the effect of force is something real and appealing to the senses, and in force there is realized that which is in its expression; indeed, it appears that force achieves precisely this force of its expression through the relationship of its ideal moments, of space and time.

Further, it is also in keeping with this nonconceptual reflection that "forces" are seen as implanted in matter, and as originally external to it, so that this very identity of time and space, which vaguely appears in the reflective category of force, and which in truth constitutes the essence of matter, is posited as something alien to it and contingent, something introduced into it from outside.

II
Inorganic Physics

#204.

Matter in itself holds itself apart from itself through the moment of its negativity, diversity, or abstract separation into parts; it has repulsion. Its being apart from itself is just as essential, however, because these differences are one and the same: the negative unity of this existence apart from itself as being for itself, and thus continuous. Matter therefore has attraction. The unity of these moments is gravity.

Kant has, among other things, through the attempt at a "construction" of matter in his metaphysical elements of the natural sciences, the merit of having started towards a concept of matter, after it had been attributed merely to the deadness of the understanding and its determinations had been conceived as the relations of attributes. With this attempt Kant revived the concept of the philosophy of nature, which is nothing other than the comprehension of nature or, what is the same, the knowledge of the concept in nature. But in so doing he assumed that the reflective categories of attraction and repulsion were ready-made, and further, he presupposed that the category of the reflection itself, out of which matter should emerge, is ready-made. This confusion is a necessary consequence of Kant's procedure, because the former abstract moments can not be conceptualized without their identity; moreover, because the observation of these opposing determinations suspends itself immediately in their identity, there is the danger that they will appear, like attraction, as a mere continuity. I have demonstrated in detail the confusion which dominates Kant's exposition in my system of *Logic,* vol. 1, part 1, pp. 119ff.

#205.

Matter, as having gravity, is only: (1) matter existing in itself, or general. But this concept must: (2) specify itself; thus it is elementary matter, and the object of elementary physics. (3) Particular matter taken together is individualized matter, and the object of physics as the actual world of the body.

A.
Mechanics

#206.

Matter, as simply general, has at first only a quantitative difference, and particularizes itself into different quanta,—masses, which, in the superficial determination of a whole or one, are bodies.

#207.

The body is: (1) as heavy matter the solid identity of space and time, but (2) as the first negation it has in itself their ideality, which differentiates them from each other and from the body. The body is essentially in space and time, of which it constitutes its indifferent content in contrast to this form.

#208.

(3) As space, in which time is suspended, the body is enduring, and (4) as time, in which the indifferent subsistence of space is suspended, the body is transitory. In general, it is a wholly contingent unit. (5) But as the unity which binds together the two moments in their opposition, the body essentially has motion, and the appearance of gravity.

Because the forces have been seen as only implanted onto matter, motion in particular is considered to be a determination external to the body, even by that physics which is presumably scientific. It has thus become a leading axiom of mechanics that the body is set in motion or placed into a condition only by an external cause. On the one hand it is the understanding which holds motion and rest apart as nonconceptual determinations, and therefore does not grasp their transition into each other, but on the other hand only the selfless bodies of the earth, which are the object of ordinary mechanics, appear in this representation. The determinations, which occur in the appearance of such bodies and are valid, are set as the foundation, and the nature of the independent bodies is subsumed under this category. In fact, however, the latter are truly more general and the former is that which is subsumed absolutely, and in absolute mechanics the concept presents itself in its truth and singularity.

#209.

In motion, time posits itself spatially as place, but this indifferent spatiality becomes just as immediately temporal: the place becomes another (cf. #202). This difference of time and space is, as the difference of their absolute unity and their indifferent content, a difference of bodies, which hold themselves apart from each other yet equally seek their unity through gravity;—general gravitation.

#210.

Gravitation is the true and determinate concept of material corporeality, which is thereby just as essentially divided into particular bodies, and which has its manifested existence, the moment of external individuality, in movement, which is thus determined immediately as a relation of several bodies.

General gravitation must be recognized for itself as a profound thought, which constitutes an absolute basis for mechanics if it is conceived initially in the sphere of reflection, though it is so bound up with it through the quantitative determinations that it has attracted attention and credit, and its verification has been based solely on the experience analyzed from the solar system down to the phenomenon of the capillary tubes. Certainly gravitation directly contradicts the law of inertia, for, by virtue of the former, matter strives to get out of itself to another. In the concept of gravity, as has been shown, there are included the two moments of being for itself and of that continuity that suspends being for itself. These moments of the concept now experience the fate, as particular forces corresponding to the power of attraction and repulsion, of being conceived more precisely as the centripetal and the centrifugal forces, which are supposed, like gravity, to act on bodies, and independently of each other and contingently, to meet together in a third entity, the body. In this way whatever profundity was contained in the thought of general gravitation is destroyed again, and the concept and reason will be unable to penetrate into the theory of absolute motion, as long as the vaunted discoveries of forces prevail there.

If one closely considers the quantitative determinations which have been identified in the laws of the centripetal and the centrifugal forces, one very quickly discovers the confusion which emerges from their separation. This confusion becomes even greater if the separation is mentioned in relation to gravitation; gravitation, also called attraction, then seems to be the same as centripetal force, the law of this individual force is taken as the law of the whole of gravitation, and the centrifugal force, which at another time is valued as thoroughly essential, is viewed as something quite superfluous.—In the above proposition, which contains the immediate idea of gravitation, gravity itself, namely, as the concept, which shows itself in the particularity of the body through the external reality of motion, the rational identity and inseparability of these two moments are contained.—The relativity of motion also shows itself in this proposition, which only makes sense in a system of several bodies standing in relation to each other in accordance with a varied determination, so that a different determination will immediately result.

#211.

The particular bodies in which gravity is realized have, as the determinations of their different natures, the moments of their concept. One body, therefore, is the general center of being in itself. Opposing this extreme stands individuality, existing outside of itself and without a center. But the particular bodies are others, which stand in the determination of being outside of themselves and are at the same time, as being in themselves, also centers for themselves, and are related to the first body as to their essential unity.

#212.

(1) The motion of bodies of relative centrality, in relation to bodies of abstract, general centrality, is absolutely free motion, and the conclusion of this system is that the general central body is brought together through relative centrality with dependent corporeality.

As is well-known, the laws of absolutely free motion were discovered by Kepler, a discovery of immortal fame. Kepler proved them, too, in the sense that he found the general expression for the empirical data (cf. #145). Since then it has become a commonplace that Newton first found the proofs of these laws. Not often has fame been more unjustly transferred from the first discoverer to another. Here I only want to point out what has basically already been admitted by mathematicians, namely: (1) that the Newtonian formulas can be derived from Keplerian laws; (2) that the Newtonian proof of the proposition that a body governed by the law of gravitation moves in an ellipse around the central body proceeds in general in a conic section, whereas the main point that was to be proven consists precisely in this, that the course of such a body is neither a circle nor any other conic section, but solely the ellipse. The conditions which make the course of the body into a specific conic section are referred back to an empirical condition, namely, a particular situation of the body at a specific point in time, and to the contingent strength of an impulse which it is supposed to have received at the beginning. (3) Newton's "law" of the force of gravity has likewise only been demonstrated inductively from experience.

On closer inspection it appears that what Kepler, in a simple and sublime manner, articulated in the form of laws of celestial motion, Newton converted into the nonconceptual, reflective form of the force of gravity. The whole manner of this "proof" presents in general a confused tissue of lines of merely geometrical construction to which a physical meaning of independent forces is given, of the empty concepts of the understanding of a force of acceleration, of particles of time, at whose beginning those forces always play a renewed role, and of a force of inertia, which presumably continues its previous effect, and so on. A rational proof of the quantitative determinations of free motion can only rest on the determinations of the concepts of space and time, the moments whose relation is motion.

#213.

(2) The absolute relation of those dependent bodies, which are merely the extreme of the being outside of itself of gravity and therefore lack their own centrality to their relative central bodies, is the residual element of their gravity in them, which because of physical being outside of themselves is mere striving and, therefore, a pressure directed towards the center lying outside of them.

#214.

The separation of the immediate connection in which such a body rests is a contingent condition, which the body, if confronted with an external impediment, suspends as motion,—a relatively free motion in which the distancing from the body is not attributed as dependent, but the motion, if the impediment is removed, is immanent to the body and a manifestation of its own gravity. This motion transforms itself for itself into rest.

The attractive force of the sun, for example towards the planets, or of the earth towards those independent bodies belonging to it, seems to suggest the skewed view that the force would be an activity inhabiting the central body, and that the bodies found in its sphere would behave only passively and externally. Thus absolute motion is also viewed, through the application of terms from common mechanics, as the dead conflict of an independent, tangential force and of a force deriving equally independently from the middle point, from which the body would be passively drawn.

The Galilean law of falling, namely, that traversed spaces behave as the squares of transpired times, shows, in contrast to the abstract, homogeneous velocity of the lifeless mechanism, where spaces are proportional to times, the liberation of the conceptual determinations of time and space. In these terms the former has the determination of the root as the negative moment or principle of one, whereas the latter has the determination of the square as a being outside of itself, more specifically, without another determinacy like that of the root, a coming outside of itself. In this law both moments still remain in the relation, because the freedom of motion in falling, which is also conditioned, is only formal. By contrast, in absolute motion there is the relation in its totality, since this is the realm of free measures in which each determinacy attains its totality. Because the law is essentially relational, time and space are retained in their original difference. Dimensionless time achieves therefore only a formal identity with itself; space, on the other hand, as positive being outside of itself, achieves the dimension of the concept. The Keplerian law is thus the relation of the cubes of the distances to the squares of the times;—a law which is so great because it simply and directly depicts the reason of the thing. The Newtonian formula, however, which transforms it into a law for the force of gravity, exhibits only the perversion and inversion of reflection which has stopped halfway.

#215.

(3) In the extremity of dependent bodies, general gravitation, which bodies have as matter toward each other, is subordinated to the gravitation which they have towards their shared central bodies. Towards each other, then, their motion is external and contingent; the cause of the motion is thrust and pressure. In this common mechanical motion the size of the mass, which has no meaning in the fall, and the resistance, which the size achieves through its particular constitution, are moments of determination. But because this motion contradicts the essential relation of the dependent body, namely, that relation to its central body, it suspends itself through itself in rest. This necessity of the concept appears, however, in the sphere of externality, as an external impediment or friction.

The law of inertia is initially taken from the nature of the motion of dependent bodies, for which the motion, because it involves the difference from themselves for themselves, is external. But precisely for this reason rest is immanent to the bodies, namely, the identity with the center lying outside of them. Their motion converts therefore essentially into rest, but not into absolute rest, rather into the pressure of striving towards their center. This center, if it is to be seen as a striving moment, is at the least the transformation of that external movement into the striving which constitutes the nature of the body.

The individual impediment, or the general one, the friction, is external, to be sure, but also necessary. It is the manifestation of that transition posited by the concept of the dependent body. And precisely this can also be found in consideration of the pendulum, the motion of which, it is said, would continue without stopping if friction could be removed.

For itself the law of inertia expresses nothing but the fixation of the understanding on the abstractions of rest and motion, which state that rest is only rest and motion is only motion. The transformation of these abstractions into each other, which is the concept, is for the understanding something external. This law of inertia, together with thrust, attraction, and other determinations have been inadmissibly transposed from common mechanics into absolute mechanics, where motion is rather to be found in its free concept.

#216.

The difference between central and dependent bodies is in the implicit being of gravity, whose identical nature is its existence. The dependent body has the beginning of the real difference as the being outside of itself of the gravity identical to itself; the dependent body has only a negative center and therefore can only move around the center simply as mass. The determinacy of its motion is not in and for itself, but refers back to a factor which is the mass of the other, so that their sizes can be exchanged, and the motion remains the same.

#217.

This externality of determinate being constitutes the special determinacy of matter. But in this it does not remain limited by a quantitative difference, rather the difference is essentially a qualitative one, so that the determinacy of matter constitutes its being.

The empty abstraction of formless matter contains a merely quantitative difference and views its further determinacy as a form inessential to it. Even the forces of attraction and repulsion are supposed to influence it externally. Since it is the concept positing itself outside of itself, it is so identical to the specific form that the form constitutes its special nature.

B.
Elementary Physics

#218.

Gravity, as the essence of matter existing in itself, only inner identity, transforms, since its concept is the essential externality, into the manifestation of the essence. As such it is the totality of the determinations of reflection, but these as thrown apart from each other, so that each appears as particular, qualified matter which, not yet determined as individuality, is a formless element.

The determination of an element is the being for itself of matter as it finds its point of unity in the concept, though this does not yet have to do with the determination of a physical element, which is still real matter, a totality of its qualities existing in itself.

(a.) Elementary Particles

#219.

(1) Matter in its first elementary state is pure identity, not inwardly, but as existing, that is, the relation to itself determined as independent in contrast to the other determinations of totality. This existing self of matter is light.

#220.

As the abstract self of matter, light is absolutely lightweight, and as matter, infinite, but as material ideality it is inseparable and simple being outside of itself.

In the Oriental intuition of the substantial unity of the spiritual and the natural, the pure selfhood of consciousness, thought identical with itself as the abstraction of the true and the good is one with light. When the conception which has been called realistic denies that ideality is present in nature, it need only be referred to light, to that pure manifestation which is nothing but manifestation.

Heavy matter is divisible into masses, since it is concrete identity and quantity; but in the highly abstract ideality of light there is no such distinction; a limitation of light in its infinite expansion does not suspend its absolute connection. The conception of discrete, simple, rays of light, and of particles and bundles of them which are supposed to constitute light in its limited expansion, belongs among the rest of the conceptual barbarism which has, particularly since Newton, become dominant in physics. The indivisibility of light in its infinite expansion, a reality outside of itself that remains self-identical, can least of all be treated as incomprehensible by the understanding, for its own principle is rather this abstract identity.

Astronomers have come to speak of celestial phenomena which are perceived by us five hundred years and more after their actual occurrence. In this one can see, on the one hand, empirical manifestations of the propagation of light, carried over from a sphere where they obtain into another where they have no meaning, but on the other hand a past which has become present in ideal fashion as in memory.

There is also the conception of light which suggests that from each point of a visible surface beams are emitted in every direction, so that from each point a material hemisphere of infinite dimensions is formed, and that all of these infinitely many hemispheres interpenetrate each other. If this were so a dense, confused mass should form between the eye and the object, and the still-unexplained visibility would rather, on the basis of this explanation, give way to invisibility. The whole conception reduces to an absurdity, somewhat like the conception of a concrete body which is presumed to consist of many substances, with each existing in the pores of the other, in which, conversely, the others exist and circulate. Through this comprehensive penetration the assumption of the discrete materiality of the supposedly real substances is destroyed, and an entirely ideal relationship is established.

The selflike nature of light, insofar as it vitalizes natural things, individualizes them, and strengthens and holds together their unfolding, first becomes manifest in the individualization of matter, for the initially abstract identity is only as return and suspension of particularity the negative unity of individuality.

#221.

Light behaves as a general identity, initially in this determination of diversity, or the determination by the understanding of the moment of totality, then to concrete matter as an external and other entity, as to darkening. This contact and external darkening of the one by the other is color.

According to the familiar Newtonian theory, white, or colorless light consists of five or seven colors;—the theory itself can not say exactly how many. One can not express oneself strongly enough about the barbarism, in the first place, of the conception that with light, too, the worst form of reflection, the compound, was seized upon, so that brightness here could consist of seven darknesses, or water could consist of seven forms of earth. Further, the ineptitude, tastelessness, even dishonesty of Newton's observations and experimentations must be addressed, as well as the equally bad tendency to draw inferences, conclusions, and proofs from impure empirical data. Moreover, the blindness of the admiration given to Newton's work for nearly one and a half centuries must be noted, the narrowmindedness of those admirers who defend his conceptions, and, in particular, the thoughtlessness with which a number of the immediate conclusions of that theory (for example, the impossibility of an achromatic telescope) were dropped, although the theory itself is still maintained. Finally, there is the blindness of the prejudice that the theory rests on something mathematical, as if the partly false and one-sided measurements, as well as the quantitative determinations brought into the conclusions, would provide any basis for the theory and the nature of the thing itself.—A major reason why the clear, thorough, and learned illumination by Goethe of this darkness concerning light has not had a more effective reception is doubtlessly because the thoughtlessness and simplemindedness, which one would have to confess for following Newton for so long, would be entirely too great.—

Instead of these nonsensical conceptions disappearing, they have recently been compounded by the discoveries of Malus, by the idea of a polarization of light, the notion of the four-sidedness of sunbeams, and the idea that red beams rotate in a movement to the left, whereas blue beams rotate in a movement to the right. Such simplistic ideas seem justified by the privilege accorded to physics to generate "hypotheses." But even as a joke one does not indulge in stupidities; thus so much the less should stupidities be offered as hypotheses which are not even meant to be jokes.

#222.

Light shapes the determinate being or the physical meaning of the body of abstract centrality in the determination of its identity. Light is the active identity which posits everything as identical. As this identity, however, is still wholly abstract, things are not yet really identical, but are for an other, positing their identity with the other in the other.

#223.

This abstract identity has its real antithesis outside of itself. As an elementary moment of reflection it falls apart into itself and is as a duality: (a) of corporeal diversity, of material being for itself, of rigidity; (b) of opposition as such, which, existing independently and uncontrolled by individuality, has merely sunken within itself and is thus dissolution and neutrality. The former is the lunar, the latter is the cometary body.

As relative central bodies in the system of gravity these two bodies have their more specific significance, which is based on the same concept as their physical significance and may be stated here: they do not rotate on their axes. The body of rigidity has only a formal being for itself, which is independence comprehended in antithesis and therefore not individuality. Hence it is subservient to another body whose satellite it is, and in which it has its axis. The body of dissolution, on the other hand, the opposite of the body of rigidity, behaves aberrantly, and exhibits contingency in its eccentric path as in its physical existence. One can therefore suspect of these bodies that the proximity of a large planet could change their course. They show themselves to be a superficial concretion, which may just contingently turn itself again into dust.

The moon has no atmosphere and therefore lacks the meteorological process. It shows only high mountains and craters, and the combustion of this rigidity in itself. It has the shape of a crystal, which Heim (one of the few ingenious geologists) has described as the original form of the earth as a merely solid body.

The comet appears as a formal process and unstable mass of vapor; none of them has exhibited anything of a solid nature, such as a nucleus. In contrast to the image of the ancients, that comets are merely meteors, more recent astronomers have not been as inflexible and presumptuous. Until now only the return of some of them has been demonstrated; others were calculated to return, but did not arrive. Suggestions brought forward by astronomers also indicate that the previously held formal view of comets, as crisscross manifestations appearing in conflict with the coherence of the system, should in time be discarded. Then the idea could be accepted that the other bodies of the system protect themselves against comets, that is, that the other bodies of the system function as necessary organic moments of protection. This view would afford better grounds for comfort in regards to the dangers of comets than the reasons which have been adduced so far.

#224.

(3) The antithesis that has gone back into itself is the earth or the planet as such. It is the body of the individual totality, in which rigidity opens up into a separation of real differences, and this dissolution is held together by selflike points of unity.

One is accustomed to seeing the sun and the stars as more excellent natures than the planets, because the first elevation of the reflection above sensory perception sets the abstract as the highest point against that individual element which is not yet conceptualized. The name of a "mad star" has arisen for individual bodies from the immediate view of their motion. In and for itself, however, this motion of the individual bodies as a turning on an axis around itself and also around a central body is the most concrete expression of vitality, and therefore more splendid than both the stillness in the center of the system, and the subservient and extravagant motion of the lunar and cometary bodies. The natural light of the central body is equally its abstract identity, with its truth, like that of thought, in the concrete idea, in individuality.

In regards to the series of planets, astronomy has still not discovered any actual law governing the determination of their proximity, their distancing, or even anything rational—I no longer find satisfying what I tried to show in an earlier dissertation about this issue.—Moreover, the attempts by the philosophy of nature to demonstrate the rationality of the series in its physical constitution, which have until now been merely preliminary attempts to establish basic perspectives, can also be viewed as unsatisfactory. What is irrational is to establish the thought of contingency as the basis, and to see the idea of the organization of the solar system according to the laws of musical harmony, as for example in Kepler's thought, as an imaginative confusion, and not to respect the profound belief that there is reason in this system. For this belief was the sole basis of Kepler's discoveries. Instead, it was the wholly awkward and confused use of the numerical relations of tones, applied by Newton to colors, which acquired fame and remembrance.

(b.) The Elements

#225.

The body of individuality contains the determinations of elemental totality, which have an immediate existence as free, independent bodies, as subordinate moments. As such they constitute general physical elements.

#226.

(1) The element of undifferentiated simplicity is no longer the positive identity with itself, the self-manifestation which is light as such, which constitutes the proper, inner self of the individual body; on the contrary, it is only a negative generality as the selfless moment of an other. This identity is therefore the seemingly harmless but insidious and consuming power of the individual and organic process. This element, air, behaves as a transparent but just as elastic fluid, which absorbs and penetrates everything.

#227.

(2) The elements of the antithesis are (a) being for itself, not the indifferent being of rigidity, but rather being for itself posited in individuality as a moment, and therefore material selfhood, light identical to heat: fire. This element is materialized time, absolutely restless and consuming, and causes the self-consumption of the subsisting body as it conversely destroys the body through its external approach. In consuming another, fire consumes itself.

#228.

(b) The other element is the neutral element, the antithesis which coalesces into itself. Without individuality, however, and thus without rigidity and determination in itself, it is a thoroughgoing equilibrium that dissolves all determinacy mechanically posited in it. It receives its limitation of shape only from outside, and without the unrest of the process in itself, but at the most the possibility of process, namely, solubility. This element, water, can assume a gaseous and a solid form as a state apart from its characteristic state, that of internal indeterminacy.

#229.

(3) Earth, however, the element of the developed difference and its individual determination, is in the first place still indeterminate: earthiness, as such.

(c.) The Elementary Process

#230.

The individual identity, by which the different elements in terms of both their difference from each other and their unity with each other are bound, is a dialectic which constitutes the physical life of the earth, the meteorological process. It is in this process alone that the elements, as dependent moments, have their existence, being generated in it and posited as existent.

Just as the determinations of ordinary mechanics and the dependent bodies are applied to absolute mechanics and the free central bodies, so too, the finite physics of the single individual bodies is taken to be the same as the free, independent physics of the process of the earth. It is seen as a triumph of science that the same determinations are recognized and demonstrated in the general process of the earth as are found in the external and dependent processes of isolated physical corporeality. The demonstration of this likeness is effected by changing the determinations, through abstraction, from their characteristic differences and conditions into superficial generalities like attraction. Thus forces and laws are imaginatively drawn in which the particular, the concrete concept, and the conditions are lacking and are then fantasized as an addition, partly as an external substance and partly by analogy.

A primary difference marks the fixed idea of the substantial, immutable diversity of the elements, which is posited once and for all by the understanding on the basis of the processes of the isolated materials. Where higher transitions occur in these finite processes, where, for example, water is solidified into a crystal, where light and heat vanish, and so on, the obstinacy of formal thought has recourse to the nebulous and to some extent meaningless conceptions of "solution," "becoming bound or latent," and so on. Here, too, essentially belongs the transformation of all relationships in physical phenomena into "substances" and "materials," partly imponderable, so that each physical existence becomes the chaos previously mentioned of materials passing in and out of each other's pores. Such views conflict not only with every concept, but also with reasonable thinking.

#231.

The process of the earth is continuously ignited by its general self, the activity of light, its primordial relationship to the sun. One moment of this process is the diremption of substantial identity, the development of moments of the independent antithesis into a tension between rigidity and selfless neutrality. Through this tension the earth tends towards resolution into, on the one hand, a crystal, a moon, or on the other hand into a fluid body, a comet, and the moments seek to realize their connection with their independent roots.

#232.

The other moment of the process is that being for itself, towards which both sides of the antithesis strive, suspends itself as negativity pushed to its extreme;—it becomes the self-igniting destruction of the different existence sought by the moments. Through this process the substantial identity of the moments is produced, and the earth transforms itself into fertile individuality.

The thunderstorm is the complete manifestation of this process, whereas the other meteorological phenomena are beginnings or moments and undeveloped elaborations of it. Concerning thunderstorms, however, physics has so far been unable to propose a satisfactory explanation—since it limits its perspective to the conditions of the external process—, neither of rain formation (in spite of de Luc's observations and the conclusions drawn from them, and, among the Germans, the arguments made by the clever Lichtenberg against the theory of dissolution, whose conclusions have at least been retained to some extent) nor of lightning and thunder. It has had just as little success with other meteorological phenomena, in particular with meteorites, in which the process progresses as far as the beginning of an earthly core.

#233.

The concept of matter, gravity, sets out its moments in elemental nature, initially in the form of independent realities. The earth is initially the abstract ground of individuality, and posits itself in its process as the negative unity of the abstract, mutually separating elements, and consequently as the real ground and actuality of individualization. Now, in this actuality, the elements present themselves as being unified together in concrete points of unity.

C.
The Physics of Individuality

#234.

The individual body is matter, brought together by the particularity of the elements out of the generality of gravity and into individuality. Thus it is determined in and for itself, and has by virtue of its individuality a characteristic form which constitutes the unity of the differentiation of a body.—This individuality is (a) immediate or at rest, a shape; (b) its separation into the diversity of features and the tension of differences; (c) process, in which the shape dissolves just as much as, in its determinateness in and for itself, emerges.

(a.) Shape

#235.

The individuality of matter in its immediate existence is the immanent form, which gives its own determinate difference to that material of the body which itself has in the first place only a superficial unit, and then one particular determinacy as its essence.

This is the shape, the specific kind of inward coherence of matter and its external border in space;—the individuality of the mechanism.

The specification of matter as an element is at this point shapeless, because it is still only a singularity. Regarding the form of the shape, and individuality in general, it is preferable to avoid the image of an external, mechanical style and composition. It may help in this case to distinguish between the externality of style and the inwardness of the shape's coherence, but the essential point is to remember the peculiar differentiation which arises from this distinction, which at the same time constitutes a determinate, self-identical unity in the relation.

#236.

The abstract specification is the specific gravity or density of matter, the relation of the weight of its mass to the volume. In this relation the material selfhood tears itself away from the abstract, general relations to the central body, ceases to be the uniform filling of space, and opposes a specific being in itself to an abstract being apart from itself.

The varying density of matter is often explained by the assumption of pores;—though "to explain" means in general to refer a phenomenon back to the accepted, familiar determinations of the understanding, and no conceptions are more familiar than those of "composition," "pieces and their details," and "emptiness." Therefore nothing is clearer than to use the imaginative invention of pores to comprehend the densification of matter. These would be empty interstices, though physics does not demonstrate them, despite its attempt to speak of them as at hand and its claim to be based on experience and observation. What is beyond these and is merely assumed is the matter of thought. It does not occur to physics, however, that it has thoughts, which is true in at least two senses and here in a third sense: the pores are only imaginative inventions.

An immediate example of the peculiar specification of gravity offered by physics is furnished by the phenomenon that, when a bar of iron, evenly balanced on its fulcrum, is magnetized, it loses its equilibrium and shows itself to be heavier at one pole than at the other.—The axioms presupposed by physics in its mode of representing density are: (1) that equal amounts of equally large material parts weigh the same;—in this way the formal identity of gravity remains consistent—(2) the measure of the number of parts is the amount of weight, but (3) also of space, so that bodies of equal weight occupy equal amounts of space; (4) consequently, when equal weights are found in different volumes, the equality of the spaces is preserved by the assumption of pores which fill the space.—

Kant has already contrasted intensity to the quantitative determination of the amount, and, instead of positing that the heavier body contains more particles in a certain space, he has assumed that in the heavier body the same number of particles fill space to a greater degree. In this way he created "dynamic physics." At least the determination of the intensive quantum would be just as correct as that of an extensive quantum; but this distinction (cf. #56) is empty and in itself nothing. Here the intensive determination of size, however, has this advantage: that it points to the category of measure and indicates initially a being in itself, which as a conceptual determination is an immanent determinacy of form, and only existent as quantum. But to distinguish between extensive or intensive quantum differences,—and dynamic physics goes no further than this—does not express any reality.

#237.

Density is at first only a simple determinacy. The simple determinacy is, however, essentially a determination of form as a unity split apart from itself. Thus it constitutes the principle of brittleness, the shaping relation of its consistently maintained points.

The previously mentioned particles, molecules of matter, are an external determination of reflection. The real significance of the determination of the unit is that it is the immanent form of shaping.

#236.*

The brittle is the subjective entity existing for itself, but it must deploy the difference of the concept. The point becomes the line and posits itself as an opposed extreme to the line; the two are held by

---

*This numbering is in the original.

their middle term and point of indifference in their antithesis. This syllogism constitutes the principle of shaping in its developed determinacy, and is, in this abstract rigor, magnetism.

Magnetism is one of the determinations which inevitably became prominent when thought began to recognize itself in determinate nature and grasped the idea of a philosophy of nature. For the magnet exhibits in a simple, naive way the nature of the concept. The poles are not particular things; they do not possess sensory, mechanical reality, but rather an ideal reality; the point of indifference, in which they have their substance, is the unity in which they exist only as determinations of the concept, and the polarity is an opposition of only such moments. The phenomena revealed by magnetism as merely particular are merely and repeatedly the same determinations, and not diverse features which could add data to a description. That the individual magnetic needle points to the north, and thus to the south as well, is a manifestation of general terrestrial magnetism: in two such empirical magnets the poles named similarly repel each other, whereas the poles named differently attract. And precisely this is magnetism, namely, that the same or indifferent will split apart and oppose each other in the extreme, and the dissimilar or different will posit its indifference. The differently named poles have even been called friendly, and the similarly named poles have been called hostile.

The statement, however, that all bodies are magnetic has an unfortunate double meaning. The correct meaning is that all real, and not merely brittle, figures contain this concept; but the incorrect meaning is that all bodies also have this principle implicitly in its rigorous abstraction, as magnetism. It would be an unphilosophical thought to want to show that a form of the concept is at hand in nature, and that it exists universally in its determinacy as an abstraction. For nature is rather the idea in the element of being apart from itself, so that, like the understanding, it retains the moments of the concept as dispersed and depicts them so in reality, but in the higher organic things the differentiated forms of the concept are unified as the highest concretion.

#239.

At the opposite end from magnetism, which as linear spatiality and the ideal contrast of extremes is the abstract concept of the shape, stands its abstract totality the sphere, the shape of the real absence of shape, of fluid indeterminacy, and of the indifferent elasticity of the parts.

#240.

Between the two actually shapeless extremes contained within magnetism as the abstract concept of the figure there appears, as an immanent form of juxtaposition distinct from that determined by gravity, a kind of magnetism transformed into total corporeality, cohesion.

#241.

The common understanding of cohesion merely refers to the individual moment of quantitative strength of the connection between the parts of a body. Concrete cohesion is the immanent form and determinacy of this connection, and comprehends both external crystallizations and the fragmentary shapes or central shapes, crystallization which displays itself inwardly in transparent movement.

#242.

Through external crystallization the individual body is sealed off as an individual against others, and capable of a mechanical process with them. As an inwardly formed entity the body specifies this process in terms of its behavior as a merely general mass. In terms of its elasticity, hardness, softness, viscosity, and abilities to extend or to burst, the body retains its individual determinacy in resistance to external force.

#243.

As density, however, is at first only simple determinacy by virtue of the relation of volume to mass, cohesion is this simplicity as the selfhood of individuality. The self-preservation of the body during the vibration from a mechanical force is, therefore, also an emergence of its individual, pure ideality, its characteristic motion in itself through its whole cohesion. It is the specific determination of its ideal externality in itself through its self-identified time. In this vibration, the product of real force and external pressure which the body survives in the form of its specified ideality, this simple form achieves independent existence.

But entities without cohesion—which are inflexible and fluid—are without resonance and in their resistance, which is merely an external vibration, make only a noise.

#244.

This individuality, since it is at first here only immediate, can be suspended by mechanical force. The friction, which brings together that difference of corporeality held apart by cohesion in the negativity of a temporal moment, causes an initial or concluding self-destruction of the body to break forth. And the body exhibits its specific nature, in the relationship between the inner change and the suspension of its cohesion, through the capacity for heat.

(b.) The Particularization of Differences

#245.

Shaping, the individualization of the mechanism or of weight, turns into elemental particularization. The individual body has the totality of the elements within itself; as the subject of the same the body contains the elements in the first place as attributes or predicates, but in the second place these are retained only in immediate individuality, and thus they exist also as materials indifferent to each other. Thirdly, they are the relations to the unbound elements and the processes of the individual body with those elements.

In connection with the ancient, general idea that each body consists of the four elements, or with the more recent view of Paracelsus that it consists of mercury or liquid, sulphur or oil, and salt, and with many other ideas of this kind, it is to be remarked first that it is easy to refute these names if one understands by them only the particular empirical substances that they primarily denote. It is, however, not to be overlooked that these names were meant much more essentially to contain and to express the determinations of the concept. Thus we should rather wonder at the vehemence with which thought recognized only its own determination in such sensory things and held fast to its general significance. On the other hand, such a conception and determination, since it has reason as its source—which neither loses its way in the sensory games of phenomena and their confusion, nor allows itself to be brought to forget itself—is elevated infinitely far above the thoughtless investigation and chaotic narrative of the bodies' attributes. Here it is counted as a service and praiseworthy to have made yet another particular discovery, instead of referring the many particulars back to generality and the concept, and recognizing the latter in them.

#246.

The body individualizes: (a) the external self of light in its darkness into its specific opacity, color; (b) air, as abstract, selfless generality into the simplicity of its specific process, or, as odor, is rather the specific individuality of the body in its simplicity, itself only as process; (c) water, the abstract neutrality, is individualized into the determinate neutrality of saltiness, acidity, and, immediately, into taste.

#247.

These particularized bodies are, in their general earthly totality, in the first place only superficially related to one another and preserve their independence by being isolated from each other. But as individuals they also stand in relation to each other and, to be sure, outside of the mechanical relationship as particular individualities.

#248.

At first these bodies relate to each other as independent entities, but they then become manifest as a mechanical relationship in an ideal movement, in the internal reverberation as sound. Now, however, in real selfhood, they emerge as an electrical relationship to each other.

#249.

The being for itself of these bodies, as it is manifested in physical contact, is posited in each by the difference from the other. Thus this being is not free, but rather an antithetical tension, in which, however, it is not the nature of the body which emerges: only the reality of its abstract self, a light, is produced and, in fact, as a light set in opposition. The suspension of the diremption, the other moment of this process, has an undifferentiated light as its product, which disappears immediately as incorporeal. Apart from this abstract physical manifestation, the process has only the mechanical effect of shaking as a significant outcome.

It is well-known that the earlier distinction between vitreous and resinous electricity, determined as a part of sensory existence, was idealized by empirical science into the conceptual distinction between positive and negative electricity. This is a remarkable instance of the way in which empiricism, which initially attempts to grasp and retain generality in sensory form, suspends itself.

Although there has been much discussion recently of the polarization of light, it would have been more appropriate to reserve this expression for electricity than for the phenomena observed by Malus, where transparent media, reflecting surfaces, and their various reciprocal inclinations, as well as a determinate corner of light, are actually so many different kinds of situations, which produces no difference in light itself, but does show itself in light's shining.

The conditions under which positive and negative electricity emerge, in relation to smoother or rougher surfaces, for example, a breath of air, and so on, are proof of the superficiality of the electrical process, and show how little the concrete, physical nature of the body enters into it. Similarly, the weak coloration of the two electrical lights, and the smell and the taste of them, show only the beginning of a physicality in the abstract self of the light in which the process is maintained. Negativity, the suspension of the antithetical tension, is mainly a shock. The self-positing, self-identical self remains as such and consistent in the ideal spheres of space, time, and mechanism. Light has scarcely begun to materialize itself as warmth, and the combustion which can arise from the "discharge" is (Berthollet, *Statique chimique,* partie I, sect. III, not. XI) rather a direct effect of shock than the consequences of the realization of light as fire.

Galvanism is the electrical process made permanent; it is permanence as the contact between two different, nonbrittle bodies, which, as part of their fluid nature (the "electrical conductive potential" of metal), their entire immediate difference towards each other, and the surface qualities of their relationship, maintain their tension mutually. The galvanic process occurs only through this particular specificity of bodies of a more concrete and corporeal nature, and subsequently undergoes a transition to the chemical process.

#250.

The individuality of the body is the negative unity of the concept, which is not self-positing simply as an immediate entity and an unmoved generality, but only in the mediation of the process. The body is therefore a product, and its shape a presupposition, for which the end that it will ultimately achieve is also presupposed. The particularization of the body, however, does not stop at either mere inert diversity or the opposition between different attributes and their tension within the body's pure selfhood. Rather, since the particular attributes are only the reality of this simple concept, the body of their soul, of light, the entire corporeality moves into tension and the process which is the development of the individual body, a process of isolation;—the chemical process.

(c.) The Process of Isolation

#251.

The chemical process has its products as a presupposition, and therefore begins (1) from the immediacy of their presupposition. In accord with the concept, the particular body is immediate insofar as its attributes or material components are unified together into a simple determination and become equal in the simplicity of specific gravity, thickness. Metals are solid, but in terms of their particularity become fluid and capable of maintaining a determinate difference towards each other.

#252.

The middle term, through which the concept with its reality unites these solid differences as the unity of both terms and the essence of each in itself,—or posits the difference of one with the difference of the other into a unity, and therefore becomes real as the totality of their concept—is initially opposed to the immediate solidity of the extremes as an abstract neutrality, the element of water. The process itself is the decomposition of water into opposed moments through the presupposed difference of the extremes; they thereby suspend their abstraction and complete themselves as the unity of their concept.

#253.

The moments into which water decomposes or, what amounts to the same thing, the forms under which it is posited, are abstract, because water itself is only a physical element and not an individual physical body;—the chemical elements of the antithesis are oxygen and hydrogen. The metals, however, which have been integrated in the process, also receive only an abstract integration from that abstract middle term, a reality which is only a positing of their difference, an oxide.

The condition of lime as an oxide lies closest to the condition of metals, due to the inner indifference of their solid nature. But nature's inability to hold on to the specific concept also allows individual metals to change so far in the opposite direction that their oxide immediately comes to resemble acids. It is well known that chemistry can portray, as amalgamations at least, the metallic components of lime and potash, but also ammonia, strontium, barytes, and indeed, even of different soils, and thereby depict these bodies as oxides. To be sure, the chemical elements are such abstractions that when they are in the form of gases, in which they become manifest for themselves, they interpenetrate like light and, notwithstanding their ponderability, their materiality and impenetrability reveal themselves here to be raised to immateriality. Furthermore, oxygen and hydrogen have a determination so dependent upon the individuality of the body that the components of oxygen are determined in oxides, as a base in general, and, in the opposite direction, as an acid, just as, by contrast, the acidic determination in hydrochloric acid reveals itself as hydrogenization.

#254.

In contrast to the solid indifference of the particular corporeality stands physical brittleness, the being of particularity grasped together in the unity of selfhood (brass represents the totality, as the unification of sulphur and metal). This brittleness is the real possibility of combustion, the reality of which is itself the self-devouring being for itself, fire, and remains an external entity. Fire mediates the inner difference of the combustible body through the physical element of abstract negativity, air, with a being as posited or reality, and enhances it to acidity. Air, however, decomposes in its negative principle into this, oxygen, and a dead positive residuum, nitrogen.

#255.

The chemical elements are: nitrogen, the abstraction of indifference; oxygen, the element of self-subsistent difference, the burning element; hydrogen, the element belonging to the opposition or self-subsistent indifference, the combustible element; and carbon, as the abstraction of their individual element.

#256.

(2) The two products of the abstract processes, acids and bases or alkalis, are now no longer merely but actually diverse, and (concentrated acids and alkalis enhanced caustically) are therefore incapable of subsisting for themselves. In a state of restlessness they suspend themselves, and are posited as identical to their opposites. This unity, in which their concept is realized, is the neutral body, salt.

#257.

(3) In salt the concrete and shaped body is the product of its process. The relation of such diverse bodies to each other involves to some extent the more precise particularization of the bodies, from which "elective affinities" derive. In general, however, these processes are for themselves more real, since the extremes occurring in them are not abstract bodies. More specifically, they are the dissolved particles of the neutral bodies into abstractions, the processes from which they are produced, retrogressions back to oxides and acids, and further, both immediately and in abstract forms, back to the indifferent bases, which manifest themselves in this way as products.

Empirical chemistry deals mainly with the particularity of the products, which are then ordered according to superficial and abstract determinations. Metals, oxygen, nitrogen, and many other bodies, earth, sulphur, phosphorous appear in this order together; just as chaotically, the more abstract and the more real processes are posited on the same level. If a scientific form is to come from this mixture, then each product should be determined according to the level of the process from which it results and which gives it its particular significance. It is just as essential to distinguish the levels of the abstraction or the reality of the process. Animal and vegetable substances belong in any case to an entirely different order, and so little of their nature can be comprehended through the description of the chemical process that much more is destroyed than saved, and only the course of its death is grasped. These substances, however, should serve to work against that metaphysics dominant in both chemistry and physics, namely, the thought or empty idea of the unchangeability of matter, its composition and subsistence in matter. We see admitted in general, however, that chemical substances lose those attributes in combination which they demonstrate separately. Nevertheless the idea remains that these substances are the same things with the attributes as without, and as things with these attributes they are not only products of the process.

An important step towards simplification of the particularities in the elective affinities is the law discovered by Richter and Guiton Morveau, which states that neutral compounds suffer no change regarding their state of solution when they are mixed in solution and the acids exchange bases with each other. The quantitative scale of acids and alkalis has been constructed on the basis of this law, according to which each individual acid has a particular relation for its saturation to each alkali; so that, however, for every other acid whose quantitative unity is only different from the others, now the alkalis have among each other the same relation to their saturation as to the other acids, and similarly, acids display a constant relation among each other and relative to all the different alkali.

Since, moreover, the chemical process has its determination in the concept, the empirical conditions of a particular form, as for example electricity, are not as fixed as sensory determinations and not as abstract moments as is represented for example by an elective affinity. Berthollet, in his famous work *Statique chimique,* has brought together and investigated the circumstances which produce changes in the results of chemical action, results often attributed only to the conditions of the affinity, which are taken as constant and fixedly determined laws. He says: "The superficiality which these explanations bring into science is prominently regarded as progress."

#258.

The chemical process is, to be sure, in general terms, life, for the individual body in its immediacy is suspended and brought forth by the process, so that the concept no longer remains an inner necessity, but becomes manifest. But the body also achieves a mere appearance, and not objectivity. This process is finite and transient, because the individual body has immediate individuality, and therefore a limited particularity, so that the process has immediate and contingent conditions. Fire and differentiation are extinguished in the neutral body, and it does not break apart sufficiently in itself to divide. Similarly, difference exists at first in indifferent independence, but does not stand for itself in relation to the other, nor does it activate itself.

Certain chemical phenomena have led chemists to apply the determination of purposiveness in explaining them. An example is the fact that an oxide is reduced to a lower degree of oxidation than that at which it can combine with the acid working on it, and a part of it is more strongly oxidized;—here the self-determination of the concept lies in the realization.

#259.

In the chemical process the body thus displays the transiency of its immediate individuality both in its emergence and its passing away, and presents itself as a moment of generality. In this immediate individuality the concept has the reality which corresponds to it, a concrete generality which derives from particularization, and at the same time contains in itself the conditions and moments of the total syllogism which fall apart from each other in the immediate chemical process;—the organism.

III
Organic Physics

#260.

The real totality of the individual body, in which its particularity is made into a product and equally suspends itself, elevates itself in the process into the first ideality of nature, but an ideality which is fulfilled, and as self-related negative unity has essentially attained selfhood and become subjective. With this accomplished, the idea has entered into existence, initially as an immediate existence, life. This is: (a) as shape, the general image of life, the geological organism; (b) as particular or formal subjectivity, vegetable nature; (c) as individual, concrete subjectivity, animal nature.

A.
Geological Nature

#261.

The general system of individual bodies is the earth, which in the chemical process initially has its abstract individuality in particularization, but as the totality it has an infinite relation to itself, as a general, self-dividing process,—and is, immediately, the subject and its product. As the immediate totality, however, presupposed by subjective totality itself, the body of the earth is only the shape of the organism.

#262.

The members of this organism do not contain, therefore, the

generality of the process within themselves, they are the particular individuals, and constitute a system whose forms manifest themselves as members of the unfolding of an underlying idea, whose process of development is a past one.

#263.

The powers of this process, which nature leaves behind as independent entities beyond earth, are the connection and the position of the earth in the solar system, its solar, lunar, and cometary life, the inclination of its axis to the orbit and the magnetic axis. Standing in closer relation to these axes and their polarization is the distribution of sea and land: the compact spreading of land in the north, the division and sharp tapering of the parts towards the south, the further separation into an old and a new world, and the further division of the former into continents distinguished from one another and from the new world by their physical, organic, and anthropological character, to which an even younger and more immature continent is joined;—mountain ranges, and so on.

#264.

The physical organization of the earth shows a series of stages of granitic activity, involving a core of mountains in which the trinity of determinations is displayed, and leads through other forms which are partly transitions and modifications, though its totality remains the existing foundation, only more unequal and unformed within itself. This is partly also an elaboration of its moments into a more determinate difference and more abstract mineral moments, such as metals and fossil objects generally, until it loses itself in mechanical stratifications and alluvial terrains lacking any immanent formative development.

#265.

This crystal of life, the inanimate organism of the earth which has its concept in the sidereal connection but possesses its own process as a presupposed past, is the immediate subject of the meteorological process, which as an organized whole is in its complete determinateness. In this objective subject the formerly elementary process is now objective and individual,—the suspension of immediacy takes place, through which general individuality now emerges for itself and life becomes vital or real. The first real vitality, which the fructified earth brings forth, is vegetable nature.

B.
Vegetable Nature

#266.

The generality and individuality of life are still immediately identical in immediate vitality. Consequently the process by which the plant differentiates itself into distinct parts and sustains itself is one in which it comes out of itself and falls into pieces as several individuals, for which the whole plant is more the basis than a subjective unity. A further consequence is that the differentiation of the organic parts is only a superficial metamorphosis, and one part can easily pass into the function of the other.

#267.

The process of shaping and reproduction of the single individual coincides in this way with the process of genus formation. And because self-like generality, the subjective unit of individuality, does not separate itself from real particularization but is only submerged in it, the plant does not move from its place, nor is it a self-interrupting individualization, but a continually flowing self-nourishment. It does not relate itself to individualized inorganic nature, but to the general elements. Nor is it capable of feeling and animal warmth.

#268.

Insofar, however, as life is esentially the concept which realizes itself only through self-division and reunification, the plant processes also diverge from each other. (1) But their inner process of formation is to be seen partly as the positive, merely immediate transformation of nourishment supplies into the specific nature of plants. On the one hand, and for the sake of essential simplicity, this is the division into abstract generality of an implicitly inseparable individuality, as into the negative of vitality, becoming wood. But on the other hand, on the side of individuality and vitality, this is the process specifying itself in an outward direction.

#269.

(2) This is the unfolding of the parts as organs of different elementary relations, the division partly into the relation to earth and into the air and water process which mediates them. Since the plant does not hold itself back in inner, subjective generality against outer individuality, it is equally torn out of itself by light, from which it takes the specific confirmation and individualization of itself, knotted and multiplied into a multiplicity of individuals.

#270.

Since, however, the reproduction of the individual vegetable as a singularity is not the subjective return into itself, a feeling of self, but inwardly becomes wooden, the production of the self of the plant consequently moves in an outward direction. The plant brings forth its light as its own self in the blossom, in which the neutral color green is determined as a specific coloration, or, too, light is produced as a white color, purified from the dark.

#271.

Since the plant in this way offers itself as a sacrifice, this exteriorization is at the same time the concept realized by the process, the plant, which has produced itself as a whole, but which in the process has come into opposition with itself. This, the highest point of the process, is therefore the beginning of the process of sexual differentiation which occurs in the process of genus formation.

#272.

(3) The process of genus formation, as distinct from the processes

of formation and reproduction of the individual, is an excess in the actuality of plant nature, because those processes also directly involve a dissolution into many individuals. But in the concept the process is, like subjectivity which has converged with itself, that generality in which the plant suspends the immediate individuality of its organic life, and thereby grounds the transition into the higher organism.

C.
The Animal Organism

#273.

Organic individuality exists as subjectivity insofar as its individuality is not merely immediate actuality but also and to the same extent suspended, exists as a concrete moment of generality, and in its outward process the organism inwardly preserves the unity of the self. This is the nature of the animal which, in the reality and externality of individuality, is equally, by contrast, immediately and inwardly self-reflected individuality, inwardly existing subjective generality.

#274.

The animal has contingent self-movement because its subjectivity is, like light and fire, ideality torn from gravity,—a free time, which, as removed at the same time from real externality, determines its place on the basis of inner chance. Bound up with this is the animal's possession of a voice in which its subjectivity, existing in and for itself, dominates the abstract ideality of time and space, and manifests its self-movement as a free vibration within itself. It has animal warmth, as a permanent preservation of the shape; interrupted intussusception; but primarily feeling, as the individuality which in its determinacy is immediately general for itself and really self-differentiating individuality.

#275.

The animal organism, as living generality, is the concept which passes through its three determinations, each of which is in itself the same total identity of substantial unity and, at the same time and as determined for itself by the form, is the transition into others, so that the totality results from this process. It is only as this self-reproducing entity, not as an existing one, that the animal organism is living.

#276.

The animal organism is therefore: (a) a simple, general being in itself in its externality, whereby real determinacy is immediately taken up as particularity into the general, and is thereby the unseparated identity of the subject with itself;—sensibility;—(b) particularity, as excitability from the outside and, on the other hand, the countereffect coming from the outward movement of the subject;—irritability;—(c) the unity of these moments, the negative return to itself through the relation of externality, and thereby the generation and positing of itself as an individual,—reproduction. Inwardly, this is the reality and foundation of the first moments, and outwardly, this is the articulation of the organism and its armament.

#277.

These three moments of the concept have their reality in three systems, namely, the nervous system, the circulatory system, and the digestive system. The first is in the systems of the bones and sensory apparatus, whereas the second turns outwardly on two sides in the lungs and the muscles. The digestive system is, however, as a system of glands with skin and cellular tissue, immediate, vegetative, reproductive, but as part of the actual system of the intestines it is the mediating reproduction. The animal thus divides itself in the center (*insectum*) into three systems, the head, thorax, and the abdomen, though, on the other hand, the extremities used for mechanical movement and grasping constitute the moment of the individuality outwardly positing and differentiating itself.

#278.

The idea of the living organism is the manifested unity of the concept with its reality; as the antithesis of that subjectivity and objectivity, however, this unity exists essentially only as process. It exists at the same time as the movement of the abstract relation of the living entity to itself, which dissolves itself into particularity, and, as the return into itself, it is the negative unity of subjectivity and totality. Each of these moments is itself a process, however as a concrete moment of the living, and the whole is the unity of the three processes.

#279.

(1) The abstract process of living individuality is the process of inner formation in which the organism converts its own members into a nonorganic nature, into means, and feeds on itself. Thus it produces precisely this totality of its self-organization, so that each member is reciprocally the end and the means, and maintains itself through the others and in opposition to them. It is the process which has the simple feeling of self as a result.

#280.

(2) The self-feeling of individuality is, in its negative return into itself, immediately exclusive and in a state of tension with inorganic nature as with real and external nature. (3) Since animal organization is immediately reflected into itself in this external relation, this ideal relationship is the theoretical process and, indeed, the determinate feeling, which differentiates itself into the multiple sensory qualities of inorganic nature.

#281.

The senses and the theoretical processes are therefore: (1) the sense of the mechanical sphere—of gravity, of cohesion and its variation, of heat, and feeling as such; (2) the senses of antithesis, of the particularized principle of air, and of equally realized neutrality, of water, and of the antitheses of its dissolution;—smell and taste; (3) the sense of the pure, essential, but exterior identity, of the side belonging to the materials of gravity: fire, light, and color;—and (4) the sense for the depiction of subjective reality, or of the independent inner ideality of the body standing in opposition, the sense of hearing.

The threefold moments of the concept therefore convert here into a fivefold number, because the moment of particularity or of the antithesis in its totality is itself threefold. Another reason for the transition is that the animal organism is the reduction of inorganic nature split apart from itself, but at the same time it is its developed totality. Because it is still natural subjectivity, the moments of nature's developed totality exist separately, but as an infinite unity. The determinations of this subjectivity, therefore, have the sense of touch as their particular sense, the most fundamental, general sense, which thus could also better be called feeling. Particularity is the antithesis, and this is the identity and the antithesis itself. Thus the sense of light belongs to this particularity, an identity which constitutes one side of the antithesis, as abstract, but precisely therefore determines itself. Also belonging here are the two senses of the antithesis itself as such, air and water, both like the others in their embodied specification and individualization. To the sense of individuality belongs that subjectivity which, as purely self-demonstrating subjectivity, is tone.

#282.

The real process of inorganic nature begins equally with feeling, namely, the feeling of real externality, and with this feeling the negation of the subject, which is at the same time the positive relation to itself and its certainty in contrast to its negation. It begins with the feeling of a lack, and the drive to suspend the lack, which is the condition of being stimulated externally.

Only what is living feels a lack, for it alone in nature is the concept, the unity of itself and of its specific opposite; in this relation it is a subject. Where there is a limitation, it is a negation only for a third, an external reflection. It is lack, however, insofar as in one sense the overcoming of the lack is also at hand, and the contradiction is posited as such. A being which is capable of having and enduring the contradiction of itself in itself is the subject; this constitutes its finitude.—Reason proves its infinitude precisely at that point when reference is made to finite reason, since it determines itself as finite. For negation is finitude and a lack only for that which is the suspended being of itself, the infinite relation to itself. Thoughtlessness, however, stops short at the abstraction of the limitation, and in life, too, where the concept itself enters into existence, it fails to grasp the concept, but remains fixed on the determinations of representation: drives, instincts, and needs.

An important step towards a true representation of the organism is the substitution of the category of stimulation by external forces for the category of the intervention of external causes. This latter contains the beginning of idealism, the assertion that nothing at all can have a positive relation to the living if the living being is not in and for itself the possibility of the relation itself, that is, not determined by the concept, and thus in general not immanent to the subject.

But perhaps the most unphilosophical of any such scientific concoctions of the reflective categories is the introduction of such formal and material relationships into the theory of stimulation, which has long been regarded as philosophical. This includes for example the entirely abstract antithesis of receptivity to active capacity, which supposedly stand to each other as factors in inverse relations of magnitude. The result of this is to reduce all differences in the organism to the formalism of a merely quantitative differentiation, involving increase and decrease, strengthening and weakening, in other words, removing all possible traces of the concept. A theory of medicine built on these arid determinations of the understanding is complete in half a dozen propositions, and it is no wonder that it spread rapidly and found many adherents.

The cause of this philosophical confusion, which initiated the tendency to befriend nature, lay in the basic error of initially determining the absolute as the absolute indifference of subject and object, and then treating all determinations as only quantitative differences. It is the case, rather, that the absolute form, the concept and the principle of life, has for its soul only the qualitative difference which consumes itself in itself. But because this truly infinite negativity was not recognized, it was believed that the absolute identity of life, as the attributes and the modes in the external understanding are for Spinoza, can not be fixed without making the difference into a merely external difference of the reflection. In this way, however, life is left altogether lacking the salient point of selfhood, the principle of self-movement, the differentiation of the self and the principle of individuality in general.

Another crude and utterly unphilosophical procedure is the one which attempted to give the formal determinations a real meaning by replacing the conceptual determinations with carbon and nitrogen, oxygen and hydrogen, and determined the difference previously characterized as intensive as now more or less of the one or another substance, whereas the active and positive relation of the external stimulus would be the addition of a lacking substance. One example is the assertion that in an asthenia, or a nerve fever, nitrogen has the upper hand in the organism because the brain and nerves are supposedly in general intensified nitrogen, since chemical analysis has shown this to be the principal ingredient of these organic structures. The ingestion of carbon is therefore supposedly indicated in order to restore the balance of these substances, in other words, in order to restore health. The remedies which have been shown to work empirically against nerve fever are, for this same reason, regarded as belonging to the side of carbon, and this superficial compilation and opinion are presented as explanation and proof. The crudity of this procedure consists in taking the external *caput mortuum,* the dead substance, a dead life which chemistry has already destroyed a second time, for the essence of a living organ, and indeed, for its concept.

This last argument gives rise to that highly facile formalism which replaces the determinations of the concept with sensuous materials like chemical substances, as well as relationships belonging to the sphere of inorganic nature, like the north and south polarity of magnetism, or the differences between magnetism and electricity. This is a formalism which conceives the natural universe and develops its conception in such a way that it attaches a ready-made schema of north and south or east and west polarities externally to the spheres and differences it uses. For this purpose there is a great variety of forms possible. For it remains a matter of choice whether one employs the determinations of the totality for the schema, as they appear for example in the chemical sphere, oxygen, hydrogen, and so on, and transfers them to magnetism, mechanism, electricity, and the masculine and the feminine, contraction and expansion, and so on, then applies them to the other spheres.

#283.

Need and excitement are connected to the relation between the universal and the particular mechanism (sleeping and waking), the relation to air (breathing and skin processes), water (thirst), and the individualized earth, namely, the particular forms of the earth (cf. hunger, #275). Life, the subject of these moments of totality, develops inwardly a tension between itself as concept and the moments of a reality external to itself, and is the ongoing conflict in which it overcomes this externality. Because the animal can only exist as an essentially individual entity, and this only individually, this objectification is not adequate to its concept and therefore turns back constantly from its satisfaction to the condition of need.

#284.

The mechanical seizure of the external object is only the beginning of the unification of the object with the living animal. Since the animal is hence a subject, the simple negativity of the punctured unity, the assimilation can be neither of a mechanical nor a chemical nature, for in these processes both the material substances as the conditions and the activity remain externally in opposition to each other, and lack living, absolute unity.

#285.

In the first place, because the living organism is the general power over the nature external and opposed to it, assimilation is the immediate fusion of the ingested material with animality, an infection by the latter and simple transformation (cf. #278). Secondly, since the power of the living organism is the relation of itself to itself in mediation, assimilation is digestion. It is the opposition of the subject to its immediate assimilation, so that the former stimulates itself on the other hand as a negative, and emerges as the process of the antithesis, the process of animal water (of stomach and pancreatic juices, animal lymph as such) and of animal fire (of the gall, in which the accomplished return of the organism into itself from its concentration in the spleen is determined as being for itself as active consumption).

#286.

This animal stimulation is turned at first against the external potency, which, however, is placed immediately on the side of the organism by the infection (#277). But this stimulus, as the antithesis and the being for itself of the process, has at the same time the determination of externality over against the generality and simple self-relation of the living organism. Both aspects together, initially appearing on the side of the subject as means, actually constitute therefore the object and the negative side in conflict with the organism, which has to overcome and to digest.

#287.

This inversion of attitude is the reflection of the organism into itself, the negation of its own negativity of outwardly directed activity. As a natural being it combines the individuality which it reaches in the process with its generality as disjunctive, in such a way that on the one hand it separates from itself the first negation, the externality of the object and its own activity, on the other hand, and as immediately identical with this negation, with this means reproduces itself. Thus the outward moving process is transformed and transposed into the first formal processes of reproduction from its own self.

The primary moment in digestion is the immediate action of life as the power over the inorganic object, which it sets against itself and presupposes as its stimulating attraction only insofar as it is itself identical with it. This action is infection and immediate transformation. It has been empirically demonstrated and shown to accord with the concept, by the experiments of Spallanzani and others and by recent physiology, that this immediacy, which the living organism has as a generality, continues itself into its food without any further mediation, by its mere contact with it and simply by taking it up into its own warmth and sphere. This is a refutation of both the theory of a mechanical, fictitious sorting out and separating of parts already homogeneous and useful, and the theory of mediation conceived as a chemical process. But the investigations of the mediating actions have not found more specific moments in this transformation (as appears, for example, in vegetable substances as a series of fermentations). On the contrary, they have shown for example that a great deal of food moves straight from the stomach into the mass of gastric juices, without passing through other mediating stages, that the pancreatic juice is further nothing more than saliva, that the pancreas could quite as well be dispensed with, and so on.

The last product, the chyle, which the thoracic duct takes up and which is discharged into the blood, is the same lymph which is secreted by each intestine and organ, effects the skin and lymphatic system in the immediate process of transformation, and is everywhere found already prepared. The lower organisms of animal life, which, moreover, are nothing more than lymph coagulated into a membranous point or tube—a simple intestinal canal—do not go beyond this immediate transformation. The mediated digestive process in the higher organizations of animal life is, in respect of its characteristic product, just such a superfluity as, in the plant, the generation of seeds mediated by "sexual difference." The *faeces* often show, especially in children, in whom after all the increase of material is most apparent, the greatest part of the food unchanged, mixed mainly with animal substances, bile, phosphorus, and the like, and the primary action of the organism to be to overcome and to eliminate its own products.

The syllogism of the organism is not, therefore, the syllogism of external purposiveness, for it does not stop at directing its activity and form against the outer subject but makes this process, which because of its externality is on the verge of becoming mechanical and chemical, into an object itself. And since it is nature, in the uniting of itself with itself in its outward process, it is no less a disjunctive activity, which rids itself of this process, abstracts itself away from its anger towards the object, from this one-sided subjectivity, and thereby becomes for itself what it is in itself: the identity of its concept and its reality. Thus the end and the product of its activity are found to be that which it already is originally and at the beginning. In this way the satisfaction accords with reason: the process outward into external differentiation is converted into the process of the organism with itself, and the result is not the mere production of a means, but of the end.

#288.

Through the process with external nature the animal achieves self-certainty and its subjective concept, truth and objectivity as a single individual. And it is the production of itself just as much as its self-preservation, or reproduction as production of its first concept. Thus the concept joins together with itself, and is, as concrete generality, genus. The disjunction of the individual finding itself in the genus is the sexual difference, the relation of the subject to an object which is itself such a subject.

#289.

This relation is the drive: the individual as such is not adequate to its genus, nor does this adequacy fall into an external reflection. The individual is at the same time, in this limitation of the genus, the identical relation of the genus to itself in one unity. The individual thus has the feeling of this lack and exists in the natural difference of the sexes.

#290.

(3) The process of genus formation has, as in the inorganic process of chemism, taken the general concept as the essence of individuals to a general extreme. The tension between the individual and the inadequacy of its single actuality drives each to have its self-feeling only in the other of its genus, and to integrate itself through union with the other. Through this mediation the concrete generality joins together with itself and yields individual reality.

#291.

This product is the negative identity of the differentiated individuals and is, as realized genus, an asexual life. But on the side of nature the product is only implicitly this genus and distinct from the individuals which have perished in it. It is thus itself an individual which has in itself the determination of the same difference and transiency. But at the same time, in this new life in which individuality is suspended, the same subjectivity is retained positively and in this, its return into itself, the genus as such has emerged for itself in reality, and has become a higher being than nature.

#292.

Underlying the various orders and structures of the animals lies the general type of the animal determined by the concept, which nature manifests partly in the different steps of its development from the simplest organization to the most complete, in which it is the instrument of the spirit, and partly in the different circumstances and conditions of elementary nature.

The concept of the animal has the concept itself as its essence, because it is the actuality of the idea of life. The nature of its generality enables it to have a simpler and more developed existence which corresponds more or less to it. Thus the concept in its determinacy can not be grasped from existence itself. The classes, in which it emerges developed and manifested completely in its moments, appear as a particular existence in contrast to the others, and can also have a bad existence in them. The concept is already presupposed for the judgment of whether the existence is bad. If, as usual, existence is presupposed, then it will undoubtedly be used in an empirical way to reach no fixed determination, and all particular attributes will also seem to be lacking. Acephalous animals, for example, have been used as proof that people can live without brains.

Zoology, like the natural sciences generally, has concerned itself primarily with discovering more certain and simpler signs for subjective cognition. Only since this goal of an "artificial" system for classifying animals was given up has the way been opened for a broader view, and among the empirical sciences there is hardly one which in recent times has expanded as much as zoology, particularly through its auxiliary science of comparative anatomy. This expansion has not occurred solely in the sense of more observations, for none of the sciences lacks these, but in the sense of arranging its material to accord with reason.

Partly it is the habits of individual animals, viewed as a coherent whole determining the construction of every part, which have become the main point, so that the great founder of comparative anatomy, Cuvier, could boast that he could recognize the essential nature of the entire animal from a single bone. Partly it is that the general type of the animal has been traced in the various, still apparently incomplete and disparate forms, and its importance recognized in the hardly noticed suggestion, as well as in the mixture of organs and functions, and in this way has been raised above and beyond its particularity into its generality. A primary feature of this method is the recognition of how nature shapes and adapts this organism to the particular element in which it is placed, an environment which can also be one particular species of plant or another of animal. It is due to the immediacy of the idea of life that the concept, whether or not it is only determined in and for itself, does not exist as such in life. Its existence is therefore subjected to the manifold conditions and circumstances of external nature, and can appear in the most inadequate forms. The fecundity of the earth causes life to break out in every way. Even perhaps less than the other spheres of nature, therefore, can the animal world present in itself an independent, rational system of organization, or retain a hold on forms determined by the concept and preserve them against the imperfection and mixture of conditions, from confusion, degeneration, and transitional forms. This weakness of the concept, which exists in the animal though not in its fixed, independent freedom, entirely subjects even the genus to the changes that are shared by the life of the animal. And the environment of external contingency in which the animal must live exercises perpetual violence against the individual. Hence the life of the animal seems in general to be sick, and the animal's feeling seems to be insecure, anxious, and unhappy.

#293.

Due to the externality of its existence, the individual organism can not accord with its determination. It finds itself in a state of disease when one of its systems or organs, stimulated to conflict with an organic power, establishes itself for itself and persists in its particular activity against the activity of the whole. For the fluidity and pervasive process of the activity is thus obstructed.

#294.

The characteristic manifestation of disease is, thus, when the identity of the entire organic concept, as the successive course of life's movement through its different moments, sensibility, irritability, and reproduction, presents itself as fever. This fever is to the same extent both the isolated activity in opposition to the course of totality, and the effort towards and beginning of healing.

#295.

Medicine provokes the organism to remove the inorganic power with which the activity of the individual organ or system is entangled and thereby isolated. Essentially, however, the irritation of the formal activity of the particular organ or system is suspended, and its fluidity is restored within the whole. The medicine achieves this as an irritant, but one which is even more difficult to assimilate and to overcome, and against which the organism is compelled to exert its entire strength. While it acts in this way against an external entity, the organism steps out of the limitation with which it had become identical and in which it had become involved.

Medication must in general be viewed as an indigestible substance. But indigestibility is only a relative category, though not in the vague sense in which it is usually taken, as if it really meant something easily digestible by weaker constitutions. On the contrary, such an easily digestible substance is indigestible for stronger individuals. The true relativity, that of the concept, which has its actuality in life, consists, when expressed in the quantitative terms which count as valid here, in homogeneity being greater, the more the opposed terms are intrinsically self-subsistent. The highest qualitative form of relativity in the living organism has manifested itself as the sexual relation, in which independent individualities are identical to each other.

For the lower forms of animal life, which have not achieved a difference within themselves, the digestible substance is the substance without individuality, such as water for plants. For children, the digestible substance is partly the completely homogeneous animal lymph, mother's milk, a substance which is already digested or rather has further differentiated within itself, and partly the least individualized of mixed substances. Substances of this kind, on the other hand, are indigestible for stronger natures. These natures digest more easily individualized animal substances, or plant juices which sunlight has matured to a more powerful self and are therefore "spirituous," instead of, for example, the vegetable products still in their merely neutral color and closer to the chemical process proper. Through this more intensive selfhood the former substances form an even stronger contrast, but for that very reason they are more homogeneous irritants. Taken together, medications are negative irritants, poisons, a stimulant and at the same time an indigestible substance, to the extent that the organism alienated from itself in disease must gather up its strength, turn against the medication as an external, foreign body, and thereby achieve again the self-feeling of its individuality.

But Brownianism, regarded as a complete system of medicine, is merely an empty formalism, especially in its determination of diseases and the actions of medications according to sthenic or asthenic body types, the latter further divided into direct and indirect asthenia.* Brown's theory is, moreover, too often limited by formulations derived from the natural sciences, such as his recourse to the factors of carbon and nitrogen, oxygen and hydrogen as explanations, or magnetic, electrical, and chemical moments. Nevertheless, his theory did have two important consequences: through him, the view of merely particular and specific issues, both in diseases and medications, was expanded to the general in them as essential elements; and through his opposition to the previously used method, which was even more fixed on asthenic and asthenizing questions than the subsequent phases, he showed that the organism does not react to the most antithetical kind of treatment in such an opposite way, but that frequently, at least in the final results, it reacts in a similar and hence general way. Thus the simple identity of the organism with itself as its true essence is demonstrated in opposition to a particular entanglement of one of its systems with specific irritants.

#296.

The animal individual, in overcoming and moving beyond particular inadequacies in conflict with its concept, does not suspend the inadequacy in general which it has within it, namely, that its idea is the immediate idea, or that the animal stands within nature. Its subjectivity is only the concept in itself but not itself for itself, and exists only as an immediate individuality. That inner generality is thus opposed to its actuality as a negative power, from which the animal suffers violence and perishes, because its existence does not itself contain this generality within itself.

#297.

As abstract, this negative generality is an external actuality which

*Cf. J. Brown, in his *Elementa medicinae,* 1780.

exerts mechanical violence against the animal and destroys it. As its own concrete generality it is the genus, and the living organism submerges its different individuality partly in the process of genus formation. Partly, however, the living organism directly suspends its inadequacy in relation to the genus, which is its original sickness and the inborn seed of death, since it imagines the individuality of its death. But because this generality is immediate, the individual achieves only an abstract objectivity, it blunts its activity, grows ossified, and thus kills itself by itself.

#298.

But the subjectivity of the living organism is just as essentially in itself identical to concrete generality and the genus. Its identity with the genus is thus only the suspension of the formal antithesis, of immediacy, and of the generality of individuality. Since this subjectivity is, moreover, the concept in the idea of life, it is in itself the absolute being in itself of reality. Through this suspension of its immediacy subjectivity coalesces itself absolutely with itself, and the last self externality of nature is suspended. In this way nature has passed over into its truth, into the subjectivity of the concept, whose objectivity is itself the suspended immediacy of individuality, the concrete generality, the concept which has the concept as its existence,—into the spirit.

C.

The Philosophy of Spirit

Preliminary Concepts

#299.

Spirit has for us nature as its presupposition, of which it is truth. In this truth, its concept, nature has disappeared; spirit has therefore produced itself as idea, of which the concept is both the object and the subject. This identity is absolute negativity, because in nature the concept has its completely external objectivity. But it has suspended its articulation, and in this it has become identical with itself. It is this identity only insofar as it is a return from nature.

#300.

The essence of the spirit is therefore freedom, the identity of the absolute negativity of the concept with itself. It can distance itself from everything external and from its own externality as well as from its being, and thus bear infinite pain, the negation of its individual immediacy; in other words, it can be identical for itself in this negativity. This possibility is its self-contained being in itself, its simple concept, or absolute generality itself.

#301.

This generality is also, however, its determinate sphere of being. With a being of its own the general is self-particularizing, yet remains self-identical. The nature of the spirit is therefore manifestation. The spirit is not determinate as a being in itself and against its externality, nor does it reveal something. Instead, its determinacy and content are this revelation itself. Its possibility is therefore an immediate, infinite and absolute reality.

#302.

The revelation is the positing of its objectivity, which is in the abstract idea as the immediate transition or becoming of nature. But the revelation of the spirit, which is free, is the positing of nature as its world; a setting forth, which as reflection is at the same time the presupposition of the world as a nature existing independently. But the true revelation is revelation in the concept, the creation of the world as its being, a being in which the spirit has the positivity and truth of its freedom.

The absolute is the spirit; this is the highest definition of the absolute.—To find this definition and to comprehend its content was, it can be said, the absolute tendency of all education and philosophy. It was the point on which all religion and science turned, and world history is to be comprehended on the basis of this point alone.—But the essence of the spirit is the concept. The word and the representation of the spirit were found at an early period, and the content of the Christian religion is to reveal God as spirit. To grasp what is given here as representation, and the essence in itself in its own element, the concept, is the task of philosophy. But this task is not truly and immanently solved as long as the concept and freedom are not the issue and the soul of philosophy.

#303.

This idea is the concept of the spirit; or it is this in itself, as a universal entity. But it is only spirit absolutely insofar as it is the concept for itself, or as individuality; and it is essentially for itself only as it is separated from itself, has its concept as a presupposition, and relates to itself as to its immediacy. This is nature, as the being of the spirit, which is therefore its beginning.

#304.

This beginning is the first moment of its concrete concept, which in its totality: (1) grasps the subjective spirit in itself; (b) as objective spirit realizes this concept; and (c) as absolute spirit is itself the unity of its concept and its objectivity.

#305.

The two first parts of the doctrine of the spirit embrace the finite spirit. Spirit is the infinite idea, and finitude here means the disproportion between the concept and reality, with the qualification that it is a shining within itself,—an appearance that the spirit itself posits as a barrier, in order, by its suspension, to have and to know freedom for itself as its essence. The different steps in the activity of the spirit are steps towards its liberation, and in the absolute truth of this liberation these three steps are one and the same: finding a world presupposed, the generation of the world as a world posited by the spirit, and gaining freedom from the world.

The category of finitude is primarily fixed by the understanding in relation to the spirit and reason. It is held not only as a matter of strict logic, but also treated as a moral and religious concern, so that to recognize it as a standpoint of modesty and to adhere to it as a last step, or the wish to go further, are taken as an audacity of thought, even as a mark of insanity.—In fact, however, such a modesty of thought is the worst of virtues, for it treats the finite as an absolute, and remains fixed in untruth and an ungrounded type of knowledge. The category of finitude was not only developed and explained at different points (cf. nos. 15, 34, 45, and so on), but logic must, for the simple thought forms of finitude, as the rest of philosophy will for concrete forms, only show that the finite is not fixed, but exists above all only as transition. It can, therefore, least of all be said that reason and the spirit are finite. There are finite spirits: this is the expression of the imagination which remains at the level of the untruth of immediate appearance, of that which is meant, of a being which the abstract understanding fixes through the form of abstract generality or identity. But the finite spirit is least of all just any finite entity, or being itself, and infinitely less, since other finite entities have their cessation through another; the spirit itself, however, the concept and eternity, complete this nullification of nullity, the vanity of the vain. By contrast, the modesty alluded to is not only this vanity itself, but the greater vanity, the fixation of vanity against truth. In the course of the development of the spirit, this vanity shall appear as wickedness at that turning point when mind has reached its extreme immersion in subjectivity, and its most central contradiction.

I.
The Subjective Spirit

#307.*

Spirit can be called subjective insofar as it is in its concept. Since, however, the concept is the reflection of its generality originating from its differentiation in itself, the subjective spirit is (a) immediate, the spirit of nature—the object usually treated by "anthropology" as "the soul"; (b) spirit as the identical reflection into itself and into others, relationship or differentiation—consciousness, the object of the *Phenomenology of the Spirit;* (c) spirit existing for itself or as subject—the object of "psychology." Consciousness awakes in the soul; consciousness posits itself as reason; and subjective reason frees itself for objectivity through its activity.

A.
The Soul

#308.

Spirit came into being as the truth of nature which has translated and suspended itself. But spirit is, then, not merely true and primordial: its transition into the realm of the concept is not only reflection into others and reflection into itself, but it is also free judgment. The becoming of spirit in this way indicates that nature suspends itself in itself as untruth, and that spirit no longer presupposes itself as immediacy self-externalized in physical individuality, but as general and as that immediacy, simple in its concreteness, in which it is soul.

---

*This numbering is in the original.

#309.

The soul is not only immaterial for itself, but the general immateriality of nature and its simple, ideal life. The soul is also the
absolute substance, as the immediate identity of self-subsisting subjectivity and corporeality, whose identity remains, as general essence, the absolute basis of its differentiation and individuation. In
this abstract determination, however, it is only the sleep of the spirit.

The question of the immateriality of the soul can only be of
interest if matter is represented as true, on the one hand, and on the
other hand, if spirit is represented as a thing. Even physicists,
however, have in recent times dealt with imponderable substances,
such as warmth, light, and so on, to which they could also add space
and time. Otherwise these imponderables still have a sensory existence, a self-externalized being. Yet living matter, which can be
found included among such substances, lacks not only gravity, but
every other aspect of existence which would allow us to treat it as
material. The fact is that in the idea of life the self-externality of
nature is already in itself suspended, along with the concept and its
substance. But in the spirit, the concept exists in freedom as absolute negativity and not as immediate individuality, so that the object
of the intelligible unity is the unity itself. Thus self-externality, as the
fundamental characteristic of matter, is completely dissolved and
transformed into generality.

Another related question concerns the interdependence of the soul
and the body. It was assumed as a fact, and the only remaining
problem was how to comprehend it. The usual answer was that it
was an incomprehensible secret. And indeed, if we take them to be
absolutely antithetical and absolutely independent, body and soul
are just as impenetrable to each other as every part of matter is to
another. In this view they respond to each other only in the pores,
their reciprocal being where the other is not. But this answer is not
the same as the one given by all other philosophers since the relation
was first questioned. Descartes, Malebranche, Spinoza, and Leibniz
have all seen God as this relation, especially in the sense that the
finite soul and matter have no truth, so that God is not merely
another word for that incomprehensibility, but rather its true identity.—Either this identity, however, is not yet grasped immediately as
God, for it does not yet have this determination, or the soul itself is

seen as a general soul, in which matter exists in its truth, as a simple thought or a generality.—This soul must not, however, become fixed again, for example as the world soul, for then it is only the general substance which merely has actual truth as individuality.

#310.

Spirit is at first this immediate submergence in nature: (a) the soul in its determination as nature; (b) as the soul is particularized, it emerges in antithesis to its lack of consciousness; (c) in the process it acquires corporeality, and thus becomes real.

(a.) The Natural Determinacy of the Soul

#311.

Spirit as the abstract soul of nature is simple, sidereal, and terrestrial life. It is the *nous* of the ancients, the simple, unconscious thought, which (a) as this general essence is the inner idea and would have its reality in the underlying externality of nature. But since it, as soul, is immediate substance, its existence is the particularization of its natural being, an immediate and natural determinacy, which has its presupposed reality in the individual earth.

#312.

The general planetary life of the nature spirit has the diversity of the earth as immediate differentiation within it; it then dissolves into particular spirits of nature, which wholly express the nature of the geographic parts of the world and constitute racial diversity.

The contrast between the earth's poles, by which the northern land is more compressed and more heavily weighted than the sea, whereas the southern hemisphere separates and disperses into widely distant peaks, introduces into the differences between continents a further modification which Treviranus (*Biology,* part 2) has exhibited in the case of the plants and animals.

#313.

This diversity is transformed by the contingency of nature into particularities, which may be called local spirits, and manifests itself in outward forms of life and occupation, physical development and disposition, but even more in the inner tendency and capacity of intellectual and moral character.

#314.

The soul, as the concept in itself in general, isolates itself as the individual subject. But this subjectivity is here considered only as the individuation of natural characteristics; it is the mode of the different temperaments, characters, physiognomies, and other dispositions of families or single individuals.

#315.

(b) Immediate judgment is the awakening of the individual soul, which confronts its unconscious natural life, in the first instance as one natural characteristic and condition confronts another, namely, sleep. This transitional phase of individuality connects with the earth as the general body of individuality.

#316.

Waking is neither externally nor for us intrinsically different from sleep; rather, waking is itself the judgment of the individual soul, and thus the differentiation of itself from its undifferentiated generality. All self-conscious and rational activity of the spirit occurs in the waking state.—Sleep is an invigoration of this activity, though not in the sense of rest (the power of living action actually becomes sluggish due to the lack of its expression), but as a return from the world of specialization, from dispersion into details where it has become rigidified, into the general essence of subjectivity, which is the substance of those specialized energies and their absolute master.

#317.

Insofar, however, as the entire being of the individual is an awakened being, its particularization is the natural development of an age.

#318.

(c) Real individuality as the reflection of the soul in itself is its waking being for itself in self-contained, organic physicality. It also involves a self-feeling determined in and for itself and still identical with its corporeality, external and internal sensation.

The progress of the general soul to an individuality which is still immediate is above all the progress of the natural idea, from ideal generality to vitality, that is, organic individuality. In any case this has no further meaning than that it contains the spirit in itself, and this is its individual and natural existence, which, however, exists here only in external representation. As in the previous case, therefore, what can be said more precisely about wakefulness as a specific waking of the spirit, and about the course of an age in the unique meaning of its intellectual development, must be seen as anticipated or as taken from representation.—On the natural side of this immanence of the individual spirit in its physicality falls in general the healthy and sympathetic sense of community. Belonging here, then, are not only the external feelings of the senses considered above (#279), but also the sensations, determined more precisely as immediately symbolic, including colors, smells, sounds, either immediately attractive or repulsive, either in a more general or in a more idiosyncratic manner. Under this rubric would also be found not only the inner sympathy of the parts of the body, but also certain mental qualities, such as the passions or the emotions. It is important to include here the line of connection by which anger and courage are felt in the breast, the blood, desire in the reproductive system, irritation, and contemplation, intellectual activity in the head, which is also considered the center of the sensible system.

(b.) The Antithesis of the Subjective Soul to Its Substance

#319.

The soul, which lives at first immediately in its substantial identity, is in its individuality as a negative self-relation, and the division of its subjectivity is set against its substantial life, which is incompatible with its concept. This first reflection into itself is at the same time a reflection into another; it stands at first, therefore, only in relation to its natural determination.

#320.

The subject is (a) in an abstract and general relation to its natural life; the soul is, to be sure, the subject from this perspective, but its predicate in this general relation is still its substance, an impotent, merely formal being for itself, a sense of foreboding and dreaming of its more general natural life, the feeling of the nature spirit.

This relation rests on the dividing line of the spirit from itself as soul. Spirit as such has generality for its object as a thought entity, pure, that is, with its abstract subjectivity, identical with its selfhood, and its relationship to it is itself this thought. This certain substantiality is freedom, the pure negativity of all immediacy. Such free substantiality is already a part of pure self-consciousness and the actual spirit.

Thus the present, unfree matter is a reduction of free self-consciousness,—a disease in which the soul, which according to Plato delivers prophecies in the liver, or more definitely in the ganglia than in the brain or the belly. Spirit in this instance has sunken back into the spirit of nature.—In history this magical relation, which can occur in isolated individuals as a diseased condition, constitutes a phase of transition from substantial spirituality to self-consciousness and understanding.—Forebodings, prophecies, the many miraculous aspects of dreams, and other tendencies, somnambulism and animal magnetism: all these belong more or less to the realm of dream in general, where the spirit hovers between natural spirits and its rational reality, and produces thereby a representation of its more general connection in a larger natural sphere than the sort of consciousness which has understood and reasoned about itself. But since real generality, namely that of thought, only adheres to this consciousness, then that expansion of sympathetic life which emerges as representation is limited absolutely to a particular circle, and what this soul sees and predicts is only its particular interiority, not that of a general essence. But this magical circle is ultimately an incantation, a form of subjugation, a dependency, because the soul is reduced from its free generality to particularity. Thus the image of humanity's primitive condition, in which nature and the spirit do not appear externally to inner intuition but with pure immediacy, becomes diminished daily, as with few aspects of the tradition, and dwindles into an ever-weaker position. It becomes an empty assumption, by which the general nature of the idea as a reasonable thought, which belongs only to the spirit in its free subjectivity, remains unobserved.

#321.

(b) The subjective soul itself, however, breaks the immediate, substantial identity of its relation with particular, natural being. Its antithesis, which is at the same time an identity, is a relation of contradiction: a condition of disruption, in which both aspects of the relation emerge in reality against each other and corporeal reality becomes the reality of the soul, or conversely, the soul constructs its own reality as corporeal.

This relation is the condition of madness in general. It should at the same time be remarked that: (1) this relation, like the magical relation, exists merely as ideal moments, as untrue relations, and thus persists only as conditions or diseases of the spirit. Precisely as everything finite persists, and, more specifically, just as the formal judgment and the formal syllogism exist without truth and apply only to the abstract moments of the objective concept, thus it has only a violent existence and is grounded in destruction,—a destruction which the understanding causes as it transforms the concrete into abstractions solely through its reality. Thus the relations which have now emerged are only the ideal moments of the spirit free in being, and still dominated by the hypothetic judgment. They are still substantially related to their substance in their self-differentiating subjectivity, and just as essentially the contradiction in this relation, their being is above all not their being, but exists rather as the being of their other.

(2) On this level of the relation the spirit is determined as a thing, and more precisely, as that which is understood as soul. To the ancients, for whom the antithesis of thought and being had not yet been as fully actualized, the soul had the more indeterminate meaning of spirituality. By contrast, in more recent metaphysics and other representations the spirit as soul has become a thing of many characteristics and powers, fixed as a specter, or more precisely as an angel, and even decorated with a color as a sensory entity. Metaphysics has generally held to the abstract determination of a thing, and the soul therefore has in and for itself the determinations of being, of quality and quantity, and is subordinated to the reflective categories of individual substances, causes, and so on. Here the question of the location of the soul, of the connection between this thing and the other thing, the body, has been of interest.

It is a contribution of Kant's to have weighed the metaphysics of spirit and soul as things and, what is the same, to have freed the spirit from this metaphysics and representation and to have posited the self in its place. For the spirit as thing can only be spoken of in a relation, that is, on the level of reflection, where the spirit of course loses its immediate substantiality or its subsisting universailty, and determines itself as difference and as subject, although it has not yet achieved true reality.

(3) The different forms of madness,—insanity, wildness, raving, nonsense, are shadings which contain many indeterminate qualities, concerning the determinations which they have in contrast to each other, just as they themselves confront conditions which common sense accepts. As important as this differentiation is for the treatment of these diseases, it is at the same time a perversion to want to create an awareness of human beings on that basis, as well as on the basis of crimes and other depravities and disturbances of humanity. To recognize these disorders presupposes in fact a concept of what the human being should be.

Moreover, in all forms of disease it is not only possible to observe a lack of understanding, but also to see what is actually called madness. For it is the absolute unhappiness of contradiction that the spirit, which is the free identity of subjective and objective, exists in its selfhood not as absolute ideality, but as an actual thing, and exists just as much as an objective entity in contrast to the thing as its pure identity. As such it is the relation of necessity or of finite reciprocal effect, of immediate transformation and reversal. This madness, in other words, grasps fate purely as blind fate, that is as absolute alienation from the concept, and as such it is after all identical with itself, knowing itself at once to be and not to be itself.—Distraction can be seen as the beginning of madness; in it is the spirit in itself, and it has no present in its corporeality, though it does exist in it, and mistakenly reverses the situation. The highest level is anger, whereby the singularity of selfhood fixes arbitrariness in its pure abstraction against the objective idea into a static reality, and exchanges itself with pure will.

Psychic treatment rests on the insight that madness is not the loss of reason, from the side of both the intellect and the will, but is only madness, and presupposes therefore the treatment of the sick as reasonable beings, thereby providing a fixed basic assumption on which the rest can build.

#322.

(c) The soul is substantial, however, as the general concept for itself, the overarching power and fate of the other reality which is essentially its own immediacy. The soul's relation to judgment is, therefore, a suspension of its form and the positing of the form as its own.

#323.

Because it is originally identical to this corporeality, and has its reality in it, the soul's activity is not directed against the body as against an external and antagonistic object. To injure organic life and to foster an antagonistic, destructive treatment of corporeality would instead make this into a negative objectivity aimed against the subject, producing thereby a power and a fate, and would derange the standpoint of the spirit.

#324.

The activity of the soul against the body is, rather, to establish its self-subsisting identity with its corporeality, only to suspend the form of the immediacy of this unity, and to posit as general the pervasive soul in its body for itself.

#325.

The soul forms itself, then, in the body which it has from nature (#318). It builds up, in this immediate being, its generality through the repetition of actions purposively determined, through induction. Thus it remembers itself in the body in such a way, on the one hand, that its identity with the body is determined by the soul and forms its subjective unity with itself. On the other hand, it achieves being in the body, a being as a general habit, a determinate habit, and as historical authenticity. In this way, as a thoroughly formed instrument, it dominates the body.

(c.) The Reality of the Soul

#326.

The soul, in its thoroughly formed corporeality, exists as an individual subject, and the corporeality is an externality which stands as a predicate of the subject, which in this way only relates to itself in itself. This externality thus does not represent itself, but the soul, of which it is the sign. In this identity of interior and exterior the soul is actual, and has only in its corporeality its free shape, its human, pathognomonic and physiognomic expression.

Under the heading of human expression are included, for example, the upright figure in general, the formation of limbs, especially the hand, as the absolute instrument, of the mouth, of laughter, weeping, and so on, and the intellectual tone diffused over the whole, which immediately announces the body as the exteriority of a higher nature. This tone is a slight, indefinite, an inexpressible modification. For the spirit is identical with its general exteriority and thus free, whereas the shape is immediate and natural, and can therefore only be an indefinite sign for the spirit, for it represents the spirit as an other, and not for itself in its generality. For the animal, then, the human figure is the highest form in which the spirit appears. But for the spirit it is only its first appearance, because it is reality still sunken in the sphere of immediacy.—Spirit is, therefore, absolutely finite and isolated in the human figure as sign. It is, to be sure, its existent form, but at the same time the human figure is something entirely contingent in its physiognomic and pathognomonic determinacy for the spirit. Thus to want to raise physiognomy and, above all, cranioscopy (phrenology) to the level of sciences is one of the emptiest ideas there could be, emptier than a *signatura rerum*, which supposed that the shape of a plant would reveal its true medicinal uses.

#327.

In and for itself, spirit as the general soul shows the untruth of matter. Corporeality, which is at first nothing but a form of immediacy, can therefore achieve its formation in general and without any resistance. Through this first formation of being in itself the spirit, which will be against it, is suspended, has lost its own determinate meaning of the soul, and becomes an "I."

#328.

This infinity of the spirit as the relationship of itself to itself in its immediacy is its own suspension, which has been produced first and is therefore still a moment, though against and in this infinity. What is included here with itself in otherness is also determinate individuality, which is the subject for itself, and contains itself as this negativity. The judgment, in which the subject becomes "I" in contrast to an object, as if in contrast to a foreign world, is thus reflected immediately into itself. Thus the soul becomes consciousness.

B.
Consciousness

#329.

Consciousness constitutes the reflected or relational level of the spirit, the level of its appearance. The self is the infinite relation of the spirit to itself, but a subjective relation, as self-certainty. As this absolute negativity it is identity in its otherness; the self is itself and extends over the object, it is one side of the relation and the whole relation;—the light, which manifests both itself and the other.

#330.

But the identity is only formal. The spirit as soul is in the form of substantial generality; as self-subsisting gravity, it is related as subjective reflection in itself to darkness. And consciousness is, like relationship in general, the contradiction between the independence of the two sides and their identity in which they are suspended.

#331.

The object, as it is released by the infinite reflection of the spirit in its judgment, has this finite relation to itself as its essence, and is a subsisting and a given entity in contrast to the being for itself of the self.

#332.

Since the self does not exist as the concept, but only as a formal identity, the dialectical movement of consciousness does not seem to it to be its own activity, but seems to occur in itself, that is, as a change in the object. Consciousness appears differently, therefore, according to the differences in the given object, and the ongoing development of consciousness appears as a development of the object. The observation of its necessary changes, however, the concept, falls, because it is still as such interior, within us.

Kantian philosophy may be most accurately described as having conceived of the spirit as consciousness, and as containing only determinations of the phenomenology, not the philosophy, of spirit. Kant views the self as the relation to a "thing in itself" lying somewhere beyond, and it is only from this perspective that he treats the intellect and the will. Though with the concept of reflecting judgment he does speak of the idea of the spirit, subject-objectivity, an intuitive understanding, and so on, and even the idea of nature, this idea is itself demoted to an appearance again, namely, to a subjective principle. Reinhold, it may therefore be said, correctly understood Kantianism, when he treated it as a theory of consciousness, under the name of the faculty of imagination. Fichtean philosophy adheres to the same point of view, for his "not-I" is only an object of the "I," only determined as in consciousness; it remains an infinite impulse, that is, a thing in itself. Both philosophies show, therefore, that they have not clearly reached the concept or the spirit as it is in and for itself, but only as it is in relation to something else.

#333.

The aim of the spirit as consciousness is to make its appearance identical with its essence, to raise the certainty of itself to truth. The existence of the spirit in consciousness is formal or general as such; because that is determined only abstractly, or it is only self-reflected as an abstract self, its existence retains a content which is not yet its own.

#334.

The levels of this elevation of certainty to truth are: (a) consciousness in general, which has an object as such; (b) self-consciousness, for which the self is the object; (c) the unity of consciousness and self-consciousness, where the spirit sees itself as the content of the object and as in and for itself determinate;—as reason, the concept of the spirit.

(a.) Consciousness as Such

#335.

Consciousness is: (1) immediate consciousness, and its relation to the object is accordingly the simple, unmediated certainty of it. The object itself is subsisting, but as it is reflected in itself it is determined further as immediately individual. This is sensory consciousness.

To sensory consciousness belongs the categories of feeling as content, external or internal, and spatial and temporal experience as form. But these both belong to the spirit in its concrete form, both as feelings and as intuitions. Consciousness as a case of relation comprises only the categories belonging to the abstract self, and these it treats as features of the object. Sensory consciousness therefore apprehends the object immediately as subsisting, a something, an existing thing, an individual entity, and its immediacy as determined in and for itself. What the object is otherwise in its concrete form concerns the spirit; the self as a concrete entity is the spirit. Even the categories of feeling are only sensory in the form of immediacy; their contents can be of a quite other nature. In consciousness, the self is still abstract thought and has initially as object, therefore, the abstract categories of thought. Spatial and temporal singularity is the here and the now, and the object of sensory consciousness, as I determined in my *Phenomenology of Spirit* (*Werke* 2 p. 73). More essentially, the object is to be taken only according to the identity of the relation by which it has its determination. In this way it exists for consciousness only as an external entity, neither externally for itself nor a being external to itself. The other can achieve this freedom only through the freedom of the spirit.

#336.

The sensory as something becomes an other; the reflection of something in itself, the thing, has many qualities, and as a single individual it exists in its immediacy as manifold predicates. The many individual moments of sensory consciousness become therefore a broad field, a multiplicity of relations, categories of reflection, and generalities. As the object is so changed, sensory consciousness becomes sense perception.

#337.

(2) Consciousness, having passed beyond the sensory level, wants to grasp the object in its truth, not as merely immediate, but as mediated, reflected in itself, and general. Such an object is a combination of sensory qualities and categories of thought; consciousness here combines concrete relations and reflection into itself. In this way its identity with the object is no longer the abstract one of certainty, but now the determinate identity of knowledge.

The particular level of consciousness at which Kantian philoso-

phy conceives the spirit is perception, which is in general the standpoint of our ordinary consciousness, and more or less of the
sciences. The sensory certainties of individual apperceptions or
observation form the starting point. These are in turn supposed to
be elevated to truth by being observed in their relations, reflected
upon, and according to categories of the understanding turned
at the same time into something necessary and general, into
experiences.

#338.

This linkage of the individual and the general is a mixture,
because the individual remains basically hardened being, whereas
the general by contrast is reflected in itself. It is, therefore, a many-
sided contradiction—between the individual things of sense apperception, which supposedly constitute the ground of general experience, and the general, which supposedly has a higher claim to be the
essence and the ground—between the individuality of things themselves, which constitutes their independence, and their manifold
qualities, which are free from this negative bind and from one
another, and are independent, general materials.

#339.

The truth of perception is the contradiction, instead of the identity of the individual object and the generality of consciousness, or
the individuality of the object itself and its generality. The truth is
thus that the object is appearance, and that its reflection into itself is
an interior subsisting for itself. The consciousness which receives
this object, into which the object of perception has been transferred,
is the understanding.

#340.

(3) For the understanding the things of perception count as appearances; their interior, which the understanding has as an object,
is, on the one hand, their suspended multiplicity, and in this way it is
the abstract identity, but, on the other hand, it also contains the
multiplicity, but as internal, simple difference, which remains self-
identical in the changes of appearance. This simple difference is, in

the first place, the realm of the laws of phenomena, a copy, but brought to rest and general.

#341.

The law, at first as the relation of general, lasting determinations, has, insofar as its difference is the inward one, its necessity in itself; the one of the determinations, as not externally different from the other, lies immediately in the other. But in this way the interior difference is what it is in truth, namely, the difference in itself, or the difference which is none.

#342.

Consciousness, which as understanding has at first only an abstract interior, then takes the law as its object, and has now found the concept. But insofar as consciousness and the object are still a given, it observes the object as a living entity,—an interiority, which is in and for itself determinate generality, or truth.

#343.

Self-consciousness is sparked, however, by the consciousness of life; for as consciousness has an object, as an entity different from itself, it is also true in life that the difference is no difference. For the immediacy in which the living entity is the object of consciousness is precisely the appearance, or the mode reduced to negation which now, as inner difference, or concept, is the negation of itself against consciousness.

(b.) Self-consciousness

#344.

The truth of consciousness is self-consciousness, and the latter is the ground of the former, all consciousness of another object being as a matter of fact also self-consciousness. The expression of this is I = I.

#345.

In this form, however, it is still without reality: as it is its own object, there is strictly speaking no object as such, for it contains no distinction between it and the object. The self, however, the concept for itself, is the absolute diremption of judgment. In this way self-consciousness is for itself the drive to suspend and to realize itself.

#346.

Since abstract self-consciousness is itself immediate, and the first negation of self-consciousness, it is subsisting and sensually concrete in itself. Self-determination is, therefore, on the one hand negation as a moment posited by itself in itself, whereas on the other hand it is an external object. Or the whole, which is its object, is the preceding level, consciousness, and it remains this itself.

#347.

The drive of self-consciousness is thus to suspend its subjectivity in general; more precisely, to give to abstract knowledge content and objectivity from itself, and conversely, to free itself from its sensuality, to suspend objectivity as a given, and to posit itself as identical with itself, or to equate its consciousness with its self-consciousness.—Both are one and the same.

#348.

(1) Self-consciousness in its immediacy is a singularity and a desire: the contradiction, implied in its abstraction, which should be objective, or in its immediacy, which should be subjective. As against I = I, the concept is in itself the idea, the unity of itself and its reality.—Its immediacy, which is determined to be suspended, has at the same time the shape of an external object, which determines that self-consciousness is consciousness. But, for the self-certainty arising from the suspension of consciousness, the object is determined as null in itself. Self-consciousness, therefore, is in itself in the object, and in this way conforms with the drive. In the negation, as the proper activity of the self, it becomes this identity for the self.

#349.

To this activity the object, which implicitly and for self-consciousness is selfless, can offer no resistance: the dialectic, which is its nature, is to be suspended, and is here an activity which the self perceives at the same time as external. The given object thereby becomes just as subjective as the subjectivity which externalizes itself and becomes objective to itself.

#350.

The product of the process is that the self in this reality joins itself with itself; but this return yields at first only existence as an individual, because it relates itself only negatively to the selfless object and the object is thereby merely consumed. Thus desire is in its satisfaction always destructive and selfish.

#351.

But self-consciousness has in itself already the certainty of itself in the immediate object, the feeling of self, which it acquires in the satisfaction and which thus is not abstract being for itself or merely its individuality, but is an objective entity. For the satisfaction is the negation of its own immediacy, and the diremption of this immediacy thus occurs in the consciousness of a free object, in which the self knows of itself as a self.

#352.

(2) It is a self-consciousness for a self-consciousness, at first immediately, as an other for an other. I immediately perceive myself in the other as "I," and yet also an immediately existing object, another "I" absolutely independent of me. This contradiction, that I am only I as the negativity of immediate existence, yields the process of recognition.

#353.

The process is a struggle. For I can not know of myself in the other as myself, insofar as the other is an immediate other existence for me. I consequently concentrate on the suspension of this immediacy. But this immediacy is at the same time the existence of self-consciousness, in which as in its sign and instrument self-consciousness has its own feeling of self and its being for others, and has the general means of entering into relation with them. In the same way I can not be recognized as immediate, except insofar as the "I" suspends the immediacy in myself, and thereby brings my freedom into existence.

#354.

The struggle for recognition is thus a matter of life and death: either self-consciousness imperils the life of the other and brings itself into danger—but only into danger, for each is no less determined to preserve its life as the essential moment. Thus the death of one, which from one perspective solves the contradiction—though by the abstract, therefore crude negation of immediacy—is yet, from the essential perspective or the existence of recognition, the greater contradiction.

#355.

Since life is as essential as freedom is, the struggle ends in the first place—for in this sphere the immediate individuality of the two self-consciousnesses is presupposed—as in inequality: whereas one of the fighters prefers life and retains its abstract or individual self-consciousness, but surrenders its claim for recognition, the other holds fast to this universality, and is recognized by the former as inferior. Thus arises the relation of master and servant.

The struggle for recognition and the subjugation under a master are the phenomena in which the social life of people emerges. Force, which is the basis of this phenomenon, is thus not a basis of law, but only the necessary and legitimate moment in the transition from the state of self-consciousness mired in appetite and selfish isolation into the suspension of immediate self-hood. This other, however, overcomes the desire and individuality of sunken self-consciousness and transforms it into the condition of general self-consciousness.

#356.

This relation is in the first place and according to its identity a shared feature of the need, the desire, and the concern for satisfaction. In place of the crude destruction of the immediate object there follows the acquisition, preservation, and formation of it, as of the intermediary by which the two extremes of dependence and independence are welded together.

#357.

According to the distinction between the two, the master has in the servant and its servitude the intuition of the objectivity of his individual being for itself, in its suspension, but only insofar as it belongs to an other.—The servant, however, in the service of the master, works off his individual or self-will, suspends his inner immediacy, and through this externalization learns fear of the master and beginning of wisdom,—the transition to general self-consciousness.

#358.

(3) General self-consciousness is the positive knowledge of self in another self: each self as a free individuality has absolute independence, though in virtue of the negation of its immediacy without distinguishing itself from that other. Each is thus general self-consciousness and objective; each has real generality in such a way as it recognizes itself in the free other, and knows this insofar as it recognizes the other and knows it to be free.

This general reappearance of self-consciousness, the concept, which knows itself in its objectivity as a subjectivity identical with itself and therefore general, is the substance of all true spiritual life, of the family, the fatherland, the state, and of all virtues,—love, friendship, bravery, honor, fame.

#359.

This unity of consciousness and self-consciousness has in the first place individuals existing in contrast to each other as beings for themselves. But their difference in this identity is entirely indeterminate diversity, or rather it is a difference which is none. Hence its truth is the unmediated generality subsisting in and for itself and the objectivity of self-consciousness,—reason.

(c.) Reason

#360.

The essential and real truth which reason is, exists in the simple identity of the subjectivity of the concept with its objectivity and generality. The generality of reason has, therefore, the meaning of the object given in consciousness as well as the self in consciousness.

#361.

Reason has, therefore, as the pure individuality of the certainty that the categories of self-consciousness are just as objective, categories of the essence of things as its own thoughts.

#362.

As this identity reason is the absolute substance, which is truth. The unique determinacy which it has here, after the object presupposed against the self has suspended its one-sidedness as much as the self set against the object,—is the substantial truth, whose determinacy is the concept itself subsisting purely for itself, I,—the certainty of itself as an infinite generality. This knowing truth is the spirit.

C.
Spirit

#363.

Spirit has shown itself as the unity of the soul and consciousness,—the former a simple immediate totality, and the latter is knowledge which is not limited by any object, and no longer stands in relation to it, but is knowledge of the simple, neither subjective nor objective totality. Spirit originates, therefore, only from its own being, and only relates itself to its own determinations.

#364.

The soul is finite, insofar as it is immediate or determined by nature; consciousness is finite, insofar as it has an object; and spirit is finite, insofar as it immediately has determinacy in itself, or insofar as the determinacy is posited by spirit. In and for itself it is absolutely infinite objective reason, which is defined as its concept and its reality, knowledge, or intelligence. Hence the finitude of spirit consists more precisely in the fact that knowledge has not grasped the being of reason in and for itself. This is infinite, however, only insofar as it is absolute freedom, and thus presupposes itself as the immediate determinacy of its knowledge. It thereby reduces itself to finitude, and appears as the eternal movement of suspending this immediacy and comprehending itself.

#365.

The progress of the spirit is development, because its existing phase, knowledge, involves consciousness in and for itself as the purpose or rationale. Thus the action of translating this purpose into reality is strictly only this formal transition into manifestation. Insofar as knowledge is infinite negativity, this translation in the concept is creativity in general. Insofar as knowledge is only abstract or formal, the spirit in it does not conform to its concept, and its purpose is to bring forth the absolute fulfillment and the absolute freedom of its knowledge.

#366.

The way of the spirit is: (a) to be theoretical: it has to do with its immediate determinacy and the positing of this determinacy as its own;—or, it has to free knowledge from its presuppositions and therefore from its abstractions, and make the determinacy subjective. Since the knowledge in itself is determined in and for itself, or exists as free intelligence, it is immediately: (b) will, practical spirit, which in the first place is immediately willed, and its determination of will is to be freed from its subjectivity, so that it exists as free will and objective spirit.

#367.

The theoretical and the practical spirit still fall in the sphere of the subjective spirit in general; this knowledge and will are still formal. But as spirit it is above all the unity of subjectivity and objectivity. As subjective spirit it is thus just as productive, though its productions are primarily formal. The production of the theoretical spirit is only of its ideal world, whereas the production of the practical spirit is of formal material and the content of its own world.

The doctrine of the spirit is usually treated as empirical psychology, with the spirit considered as a collection of powers and faculties which find themselves thrown together in a coincidental fashion. Thus it seems that one or the other faculty could just as well exist or not, a view which does not occur in physics, for example, where it is clear that nature would lose quite a bit if such a feature as magnetism did not exist.—The relation of the faculties to each other is of course seen as extremely necessary or purposeful, but this utility of the faculties appears often to be very remote, or even at times in bad taste.

Psychology belongs, like logic, among those sciences which in modern times have derived the least use from the more general intellectual culture and the deeper concepts of reason. It thus finds itself in a dreadful condition. To be sure, the turn taken by Kantian philosophy has given it greater importance: it has even been claimed that in its empirical condition it constitutes the foundation of metaphysics, for metaphysics is to consist of nothing but the empirical apprehension and the analysis of the facts of human consciousness, above all as facts, just as they are given. But this view of psychology, which mixes the standpoint of consciousness with anthropology, has actually changed nothing of its condition. It has only meant that, both for the spirit as such and for metaphysics and philosophy generally, all attempts to recognize the necessity of what is in and for itself have been abandoned, along with the effort to realize the concept and the truth.

(a.) Theoretical Spirit

#368.

Intelligence finds itself determined; as knowledge, however, intelligence consists in treating what is found as its own. Its activity is to be reason for itself, because it is reason in itself, and to make subjective its objectivity subsisting in and for itself. Intelligence is therefore not receptive, but rather essentially active, suspending the pretence of finding reason, or raising the purely formal knowledge, which it is as the self-discovery of reason, to a determinate knowledge of itself. The manner of this elevation is itself rational, because it is reason, and a necessary, conceptually determined transition of one determination of its activity into the other.

(1) The distinction of intelligence from will is often incorrectly taken to mean that each has a fixed and separate existence, as if will could exist without intelligence, or the activity of intelligence could be without will. But this would miss the truth of the will, for only free self-determination is will, as the will is intelligence, and freedom itself exists only as self-certainty in the immediate determination subsisting in itself. Thus the truth of intelligence manifests itself as will, or rather, intelligence shows itself in the will as truth. The will of the spirit to be intelligence is its self-determination, by which the purposes and interests posited by the spirit are abstracted so that it does not relate to itself as will.

The most trivial form of that false distinction is the imagined possibility that the understanding could exist without the heart, and the heart without the understanding. Such a view is the abstraction of the observant understanding, which holds fast to such distinctions. Just as it is the actual understanding in the individual which makes this kind of separation, ushers in the untruth of intellectual thought and remains fixed there, thus it is an understanding which is just as much will. But it is not philosophy which should take such untruths of thought and the imagination for truth.—A number of other phrases used for intelligence, namely, that it receives and accepts impressions from outside, that ideas arise through the causal operations of external things upon it, and so on, belong to a point of view which mixes sensory and rational determinations (#336), a standpoint that is alien to the spirit and even less appropriate for philosophy.—That the intelligence appears determined in infinitely multiple, contingent ways is equally the standpoint of entirely finite individuality, and the extreme untruth of empirical observation.

(2) A favorite form of reflection deals with forces and faculties of the soul, the intelligence, or the spirit. In regards to a faculty—the dynamics of Aristotle have an entirely different meaning—it characterizes being for itself and is different from the entelechy, from the activity of being for itself and from reality. Faculty, like force, is the fixed determinacy of any thought content, conceived as reflection into self. Force (#85) is, to be sure, the infinity of form, of inside and outside; but its essential finitude constitutes the indifference of the content in contrast to the form (ibid. note). In this lies the irrational element which by this form of reflection and observation of the spirit, treating the spirit as a number of forces, is brought into the spirit as it is also brought into nature. What can be distinguished in this activity is stereotyped as an independent determinacy, and the spirit is made in this way into a skeletonlike, mechanical collection. If a force of the spirit, that is, its contents, the particular determinacy which it contains, is considered, it proves again to be determinate, that is, dialectic and transitory, not independent. Thus it is precisely the used form of a force that suspends itself, which should be the reflection into self or determinacy, and is affixed to independence. In this way the concept emerges, in which the forces disappear.

This concept and the dialectic are intelligence itself, pure subjectivity of the self in which the determinations as fluid moments are suspended, and for which the absolute concrete is the night of the self, where there is intelligence as well as the determinations of their activity which are taken as forces. As the simple identity of this multiplicity it determines itself as the simplicity of a determinacy, understanding, the form of a force, of an isolated activity, and grasps itself as intuition, the power of imagination, the faculty of understanding, and so on. But this isolation, the abstractions of activities and the opinions of them are not the concept and the rational truth themselves.

#369.

As the soul, intelligence is immediately determined, as consciousness it is related to this determinacy as to an external object; as intelligence it finds itself thus determined. It is therefore: (1) feeling, the inarticulate weave of the spirit into itself, in which it is to some extent palpable, and contains the whole material of its knowledge. For the sake of the immediacy in which the spirit is as feeling or sensation, it exists above all only as individual and subjective.

#370.

The form of sensation is, to be sure, a determinate affection, but this determinacy is simple and in it the differentiation of both their content against other contents, and the externality of it against the subjectivity which is still not posited.

It is commonly enough assumed that the spirit has in its sensation the material of its representations, but this thesis is more usually understood in a sense antithetical to that which it has here. In contrast with the simplicity of feeling, it is usual rather to assume that the primary mental phase is judgment generally and the distinction of consciousness into subject and object, and the particular quality of sensation is derived from an independent object, external or internal. Here in the sphere of the spirit, this standpoint of consciousness opposed to idealism has been submerged. The feeling or the sensation are, by their form, resembling content, since it is this immediate, still implicitly undifferentiated, dull knowledge of the spirit.

Aristotle, too, recognized the determination of sensation, for he saw that the sentient subject and the sensed object, separated by consciousness, only exist as the sensation of the possibility, though he said of the sensation that the entelechy of the sentient and the sensed are one and the same.—No prejudice is probably more false than the thesis that nothing exists in thought which does not exist in the senses,—and indeed, in the usual sense which is attributed to Aristotle. His actual philosophy, however, is the exact opposite of this idea.

Another equally familiar prejudice as this historical one is the idea that there is more in feeling than in thought; this point is often made in regards to moral and religious feelings. Now it has happened that the material which itself is the feeling spirit is the being determined in and for itself of reason. But this form of simplicity is the lowest and the worst, in which it can not be as spirit, as the free entity or the infinite generality which is its essence. It must, rather, above all go beyond this untrue manner of its being, because it exists in immediacy as determinate, and in any case is only a contingent, subjective, and particular entity. If someone refers on any topic not to the nature and the concept of the issue, least of all to reasons or to the generalities of common sense, but to one's own feeling, the only thing to do is to leave them alone, because by their behavior they reject the community of rationality, and shut themselves up in their own isolated subjectivity, their private and particular selves.

#371.

The abstract identical direction of the spirit in sensation, as in all other of its further determinations, is attention: the moment of the formal self-determination of the intelligence.

#372.

This self-determination is, however, essentially not abstract; as an infinitude it dissolves the simplicity of its determinate being and thereby suspends its immediacy. Thus it posits itself as a negative, the felt entity, distinct from the intelligence as reflective into itself, and from the subject, in which feeling is suspended. This level of reflection is the representation.

#373.

(2) The representing activity of the intelligence is: (a) recollection. With its simple, dissolving sensation and its determination as a negative extreme set against the reflection into itself, recollection posits the content of the sensation as subsisting outside of itself. Thus it throws content into space and time, and is intuitive. The intuition is immediate, insofar as the abstract alienation and the intelligence are not all reflection into themselves and set against this externality.

#374.

This positing, however, is the other extreme of the diremption: the intelligence posits the content of its feeling in its own inwardness, in a space and time of its own. In this way the content is an image or representation in general, freed from its initial immediacy and abstract individuality among other things, and taken up, at first abstractly and ideally, into the form of the self's generality.

#375.

Recollection is the relation of both, the subsumption of the immediate, individual intuition under this formal generality, the representation which is the same content. Thus the intelligence in the determinate sensation and its intuition are inward, recognize themselves thus, no longer require the intuition and possess it as their own.

#376.

(b) The intelligence which is active in this possession is the reproductive imagination, the production of images from the interiority of the self. The concrete images are in the first place related to the external, immediate space and time which are treasured along with them.—But since the image in the subject, where it is treasured, only has the negative unity in which it is carried and receives its concretion, thus its originally concrete condition, by which as a unit of sensation and intuition or in consciousness it is determined, has been broken up. The reproduced content, belonging as it does to the self-identical unity of the intelligence, and emerging from its interior into the representation, is a general representation, which supplies the link of association for the images which according to circumstances are either more abstract or more concrete representations.

The "laws of the association of ideas" were of great interest, especially during that outburst of empirical psychology which occurred at the same time as the decline of philosophy. In the first place, it is not "ideas" which are associated. Secondly, these modes of association are not laws, just for the reason that there are so many laws about the same thing that they suggest an arbitrariness and a contingency which are the very opposite of a law. The ongoing sequence of images and representations suggested by association is in general the play of thoughtless representation, in which the determination of the intelligence is still an entirely formal generality, a content given in the images.—Image and idea are only distinguished by the fact that the former is more concrete; representation, the content, may be an image, concept, or idea, but always has the character, though belonging to intelligence, of being given and immediate in terms of its content.—Otherwise it appears, since intuition is immediate relation, the self an ideal one, and thus its self-reflection is an external generality, which is not yet the determination of the content, whereas representation and its production are a determinate generality—that intuition, representation, and imagination are essentially thinking, although they are not yet liberated thought, and their content is not a thought.—

Abstraction, which occurs in the representative activity, by which general representations are produced, is frequently explained as the incidence of many similar images one upon the other, and is supposed to be thus made intelligible. If this superimposition is to be no mere accident or without principle, a force of attraction in similar images must be assumed, or something of the sort, which at the same time would have the negative power of rubbing off the still-dissimilar elements against each other. This force is in fact intelligence itself, the self as a general entity that by its memory gives the images generality directly.

#377.

Thus even the association of representations is a subsumption of the individual under a single generality. This generality is at first a form of the intelligence. But it is in itself just as much determinate, concrete subjectivity, and its own content can be a thought, concept, or idea. As the subsumption of images under a specific content, intelligence recollects them in themselves as determinate, and forms them into their content. In this way it is creative imagination, imagination which symbolizes, allegorizes, or poeticizes.

#378.

Intelligence has been so far perfected in the determinate recollection of creative imagination that its self-generated content has a pictorial existence. Yet the material of the pictorial creation is given, and the product does not have the immediacy of existence. Intelligence must give the creation this immediacy: as intelligence in the creation forms the totality of the representation, it has turned back from its particularization in subjective representation and external intuition to the free, identical relation to itself. This recollection of the intuition is memory.

#379.

(c) Memory (Mnemosyne, muse) is the unity of the independent representation and the intuition, with the former as a free attempt to utter itself immediately.—This immediacy is, because the intelligence is not yet practical, immediate, or given; but in this identity the intuition does not count positively or as self-representing, but as a representative of something else. It is an image, which has received as its soul and meaning an independent representation of the intelligence. This intuition is the sign.

The sign is any immediate intuition, but representing a totally different content from what it has for itself;—it is the pyramid, into which a foreign soul is conveyed and preserved. The sign is different from the symbol, an intuition which according to its essence and concept is determined to be more or less the thought which it expresses as symbol. Intelligence, therefore, gives proof of a freer choice and authority in the use of intuitions when it treats them as signifying rather than symbolic.

Usually, language and the sign are relegated somewhere into the appendix on psychology, or even logic, with no recognition of their necessity and connection in the system of intelligent activity. The true place for the sign is the one just mentioned: where intelligence, which intuitively generates time and place, now gives its own independent representations a determinate existence, a filled place and time, treating the intuition which it has as its own material of sensation, eliminating its immediate and unique representation, and giving it another as its meaning and soul.—This sign-creating activity may justifiably be called memory, or "productive memory," since memory, which is often used in ordinary life as interchangeable and synonymous with recollection, and even with representation and imagination, above all has only to do with signs. And even if it is used in this more precise sense, it is otherwise thought of as only the reproductive memory: the intelligence essentially produces, however, what it reproduces.

#380.

The intuition, which is used for a sign is in its immediate phase given and spatial. But since it exists only as suspended, and the intelligence is its negativity, the true form of the intuition as a sign is its existence in time,—but this existence vanishes in the moment of being, and its tone is the fulfilled manifestation of its self-proclaimed interiority (#279). The tone which articulates itself further to express specific representations—speech and its system, language— gives to sensations and intuitions a second and higher existence than they immediately possess, and invests the images with existence in the realm of representation.

#381.

The identity of intuition in the sign and its meaning is primarily a single production; but as a unity with the intelligence it is just as essentially general. The activity of recollecting this and thereby making it general, as well as reproducing it, is the outwardly retentive and reproductive memory.

#382.

There are many signs in general, and as such they are absolutely contingent in juxtaposition to each other. The empty bind which fixes such sequences and holds them in this order is the entirely abstract, pure power of subjectivity,—the memory, which is called mechanical for the complete externality in which the members of such sequences are juxtaposed.

#283.*

The name is thus the thing, as it exists and has validity in the realm of representation. But it also has an externality brought forth from the intelligence, and it is the intuition which is inessential for itself, standing in the use of intelligence and subjectively made, so that it only has value through the meaning given to it by the intelligence, which is the determinate representation in and for itself, and the thing or the objective entity. Mechanical memory is the

*This numbering is in the original.

formal suspension of that subjectivity, whereby the contradiction of the sign falls away and the intelligence makes itself for itself in the habit of language a thing, as an immediate objectivity. In this way, through the memory, it makes the transition to thought.

#384.

(3) Through the recollection of its immediate determinacy and the manifestation of its subjective activity of determination, the unity and truth of intelligence are achieved: the thought. The thought is the thing, the simple identity of subjective and objective. What is thought, is; and what is, is only insofar as it is thought.

#385.

Thought is in the first place formal: generality as generality, and just as much being as the simple subjectivity of intelligence. In this way it is not determinate in and for itself; the recollected representations brought to thought are, insofar as they are still content,—a content which in itself is only the determinate being in and for itself of reason.

#386.

Thought, however, as the free generality which it is only as pure negativity, is therefore not: (a) only the formally identical understanding, but (b) essentially diremption and determination,—judgment, and (c) the identity which finds itself in this particularization, the concept and reason. Intelligence has determinate being in comprehension, though it existed at first as immediate material, and in itself it is absolutely only its own, thereby it exists not as determinate being, but as the act of determination.

In logic there is thought, in the first place as it is in itself, then as it is for itself and in and for itself,—these have been viewed as being, reflection, concept, and as idea. In the soul it is alert self-possession; in consciousness it also occurs as a phase. Thought thus recurs again and again in these different parts of philosophy, because they are different only through the element and the form of the antithesis they are in, but thought is this one and the same center, to which as to their truth the antitheses return.

#387.

Thought, as the free concept, is also free in terms of the content. The determinacy of reason is the proper determinacy of subjective intelligence, and as determinate it is its content and existence. Thinking subjectivity is thereby actual; its determinations are purposes; it is free will.

(b.) Practical Spirit

#388.

The spirit as intelligence is primarily, however, abstract for itself; as free will it is fulfilled, because it exists as concept, as self-determining. This fulfilled being for itself or individuality constitutes the side of existence or reality, the idea of the spirit, whose concept is reason.

#389.

This existence of the self-determination of spirit is in the first place immediate, where spirit finds itself, and as inward in itself or through nature it is self-determining individuality. It is therefore: (1) practical feeling.

#390.

Free will is the individuality or the pure negativity of the self-determining being for itself, which is simply identical with reason and therefore general subjectivity itself, the will as intelligence. The immediate individuality of the will in practical feelings thus has this content, but as immediately individual, hence contingent and subjective.

An appeal is sometimes made to the feeling of right and morality which the person has in himself, to his benevolent dispositions and so on, and to his heart in general, that is, to the subject, insofar as the different practical feelings are all united in it. As far as this appeal implies: (1) that these determinations are immanent in themselves, and (2) that when feeling is opposed to the logical understanding, it, and not the partial abstractions of the understanding, may be the totality, the appeal has a legitimate meaning. But on the other hand, feeling too may be one-sided, inessential, and bad; through the form of the immediacy it is essentially contingent and subjective. The rational, which exists in the shape of rationality when it is apprehended by thought, has the same content as the practical feeling has, but depicted in its generality and necessity, in its objectivity and truth.

Thus it is foolish, on the one hand, to suppose that in the transition from feeling to law and duty there is any loss of content and excellence; it is this transition which first brings feeling to its truth. It is equally foolish to consider intellect as superfluous or even harmful to feeling, heart, and will; the truth and, what is the same thing, the rationality of the heart and will can only find a place in the generality of the intelligence, not in the individuality of feeling.

On the other hand, however, it is suspicious and even worse to cling to feelings and the heart as against intelligent rationality, because all that the former holds more than the latter is only particular subjectivity, vanity and caprice.—For the same reason it is out of place in an observation of feelings to deal with anything beyond their form and to discuss their content; for the latter, when thought, is precisely what constitutes the self-determinations of the spirit in its generality and necessity, its rights and duties.

#391.

The practical feeling, as the self-determination of the thinking subject in general, contains the "ought" in relation to its subsisting individuality, which is in itself worth nothing, and is determinate only in its identity with generality as a true being subsisting for itself. But the practical feeling, in its immediate individuality with the "ought," exists only in relation to determinacy; and since in this immediacy it still has no necessary identity, it only yields the feeling of pleasantness or unpleasantness.

(1) Delight, joy, pain, and so on, shame, repentance, contentment, and so on, are partly only modifications of the formal practical feeling in general, but also partly different in the content which constitutes the determinacy of their "ought."

(2) The celebrated question of the origin of evil in the world, at least insofar as evil is understood merely as unpleasantness and pain,

finds its answer here. For evil is nothing other than the incongruity between the "is" and the "ought." This "ought," however, has many meanings, indeed, infinitely many, since contingent purposes also have the form of the "ought." In the case of these casual aims, evil only practices what is rightfully due to their vanity and nullity. They are themselves the evil, and that there are such and numerous other individuals inadequate to the idea derives from the necessary indifference of the concept towards immediate being in general: the concept, as free reality, relates to being essentially as determinate nullity in itself, although being is also given access to free reality through the concept;—a contradiction which is called evil. In death there is neither evil nor pain; for in inorganic nature the concept does not confront its existence. But in life, and still more in the spirit, there is this distinction at hand, and this negativity, activity, self, freedom, are the principles of evil and of pain.—Jacob Boehme viewed selfhood as pain and torture, and as the source of nature and the spirit.

#392.

The practical "ought" is (2) a real judgment. The immediacy of feeling is, for the self-determination of the will, a negation; it thus constitutes the subjectivity of the will, which should be suspended in order for the will to be identical for itself. Since this activity of the form is not yet liberated and is therefore formal, the will is still natural will, drive and inclination, and with the more precise determinacy that the totality of the practical spirit places itself into an individual one of the limited determinations, namely, passion.

#393.

Inclinations and passions have as their contents the same self-determinations as the practical feelings. Because the ones, like the others, are immediate self-determinations which do not yet have the form of rationality, they are multiple particularities. They have, on the one hand, the rational nature of the spirit as their basis, but on the other hand they belong to the subjective, individual will; they are thus essentially infected by contingency, and stand to the individual and to each other in a relation marked by external, confining necessity.

The same holds for the inclinations as for the feelings: although they are self-determinations of the free will in itself, in terms of content they are not free for themselves, nor have they reached generality and objectivity. To be sure, passion already contains this in its determination, though it is limited to a particularity of the will and the subjectivity of the individual, be the content what it may. But with regard to the inclinations the question is raised: which are good, and which are bad; up to what degree will the good continue to be good; and, as there are many, each with its own particularities, how have they, since they are after all located within one subject and according to experience can not all be gratified, suffered at least a little reciprocal restriction? In the first place, as regards these many drives and inclinations, the case is much the same as with the psychic forces, the aggregate of which is the theoretical spirit;—a collection which is now increased by the number of drives. The formal rationality of the drive and the inclination consists merely in the general drive not to be subjective, but rather to be realized. Yet their true rationality can not reveal itself from a perspective of external reflection, partly because it presupposes that a number of independent natural determinations and immediate drives are fixed, partly because the immanent reflection of spirit itself goes beyond their particularity and immediacy, and gives them a rationality and objectivity in which they exist as necessary relations, rights, and duties. It is this objectification which reveals their content, their relation to each other, and above all their truth. As Plato showed, the full reality of justice can only be presented in the objective figure of justice, namely, the construction of the state as ethical life.

The answer to the question, then, of which are the good and rational inclinations, and how they are to be subordinated to each other, transforms itself into the exposition of the laws and forms of common life produced by the relations of the spirit as it suspends its subjectivity and realizes itself;—an objectivity in which precisely its self-determinations in general lose the form of inclinations, just as the content loses subjectivity, contingency, or caprice.

#394.

The general moment in these drives is the individual subject, the act of satisfying impulses or formal rationality, namely, the translation from subjectivity into objectivity. In the latter the former returns to itself: that the thing which has emerged contains the moment of subjective individuality, is called the interest.—Since the activity is the individual subjectivity in that dialectical movement, nothing is brought about without interest.

#395.

Here, however, interest does not yet exist as the merely formal activity or pure subjectivity, but has as drive or inclination a determinate content from the immediate will. The dialectic of this multiple and particular content is, however, the simple subjectivity of the will itself, which raises the contradiction of the drives in the first place as reflecting will into formal generality, and itself makes (3) happiness its goal.

#396.

Happiness is the confused representation of the satisfaction of all drives, which, however, are either entirely or partly sacrificed to each other, preferred and presupposed. Their mutual limitation, on the one hand, is a mixture of qualitative and quantitative determinations; on the other hand, since the inclination is a subjective and immediate basis for determination, it is the subjective feeling and good pleasure which must have the decisive vote as to where happiness is to be placed.

#397.

The will, which as passion is abstract understanding and converges into a unity of its determinacies, is liberated in the general purpose of happiness from this individualization. The many particular inclinations, however, still taken as immediate, independent determinations, are at the same time suspended in the unity of purpose of happiness, and as such are dependent. The will stands as this indeterminate generality, reflected into itself over the individual inclination; the generality is initially that of the will, since the two converge and thereby produce determinate individuality and reality; the will exists from the standpoint of having to choose between inclinations, and involves choice.

#398.

The will is in this way free for itself, since it is, as the negativity of its immediate determinate being, reflected into itself; however, insofar as the content that it includes with this individuality and reality remains a particularity, it is only real as subjective and contingent will. As the contradiction of realizing itself in particularity and yet finding satisfaction in the generality from which it at the same time derives, the will is in the first place the process of dispersion and the suspension of an inclination through the other, and the partial gratification which it entails, through another to infinity.

#399.

.The truth, however, of the particular aim of the will, of the particularity which is just as much determinate as suspended, and of the abstract individuality, of choice, which yields just as much of a content in such a purpose as it does not yield, is the unity in which both are only a moment; the absolute individuality of the will, its pure freedom, which determines itself for itself in and for itself. The spirit in this truth of self-determination, which is itself the goal as the pure reflection into itself, is thus, as general, objective will, the objective spirit.

II
The Objective Spirit

#400.

The objective spirit is the unity of the theoretical and the practical spirit: a free will which for itself is free will, once the formalism, contingency, and subjectivity of its practical activity are suspended. By the suspension of this mediation the objective spirit is the immediate, self-posited individuality, which in this way is general and freedom itself. The will exists only in this way for itself, in that it thinks itself and is will as free intelligence.

#401.

The spirit, which in this way is the idea of reason subsisting in and for itself and is for itself as such, is the concept of the absolute spirit. The existing side of subjective reason is the individual will as the knowledge of this concept, which constitutes its content and purpose and is only its formal activity.—This identity: (1) as a simple, immediate concept is the law; (2) as reflection or judgment is morality; (3) as reality in accord with its concept, or the totality of the syllogism, it is the ethics of everyday life.

A.
Law

#402.

Spirit, in the immediacy of its absolute freedom, is individual, but one that knows its individuality as an absolute free will: it is (1) a person, the abstract and insofar subjective self-knowledge of this freedom.

#403.

(2) For the personality, since it is subjective and therefore as immediate a person, negation or reality in its abstraction is an external existence which is found at hand. But in its immediate form this reality is devoid of will, and the thing, which is objective in contrast to the subjectivity of the intelligence and choice, is, in contrast to subjectivity insofar as it is a person, a nullity in and for itself, which the person takes as an accident, the external sphere of freedom;—possession.

#404.

By the judgment of possession, in the first place through external appropriation, the thing acquires the predicate of "mine." But this predicate has the meaning here that "I" invest my personal will into it, which is absolute. With this meaning possession is property, which as possession is a means, but as existence of the personality is an end.

#405.

My will is thus in the first place external and for others. In that I am, as a person, the infinite relation of myself to myself, I am the absolute repulsion of myself from myself, have my realization only in the being of other people, and only then am I a real person for myself.

#406.

The thing is the mean by which the extremes meet. These extremes are the people who, in the knowledge of their identity with others, are simultaneously mutually independent. For them my will has its definitely recognizable existence in the thing through the immediate bodily act of taking possession, through the formation of the thing or, it may be, the mere designation of the thing.

#407.

(3) The subjective and contingent side of property is the thing, in general an external, immediate thing, and that I place my will in this thing. The side of the predicate of the "mine" which I give to the thing is the interest, insofar as my will is arbitrary, so that I can just as well put it in it as not, and just as well withdraw it as not;—the law, in its absolutism and at the same time from the side of reality, is a formal one.

#408.

But insofar as my will lies in a thing, it is only "I" who can withdraw it, and it is only with my will that the thing can pass to another, whose property it becomes similarly only with his will;—contract.

#409.

The two wills in the contract are as an internal state of mind different from their realization, the performance. The comparatively ideal utterance of the contract (#406) in the stipulation contains the surrender of property by one, the transition and assumption by other wills. It is therefore in and for itself valid and does not need the performance of one or the other to become so, which would include an infinite regress or infinite division of thing, work, and time. But since the will in this sphere is at the same time still formal and arbitrary (#407), it can exist either in a way corresponding to its concept or not.

#410.

Only for the externality of the possession can "I" be wounded and forced; but since the possession, in contrast to me as a person, exists essentially as an external entity, no damage of personality and no coercion can or should (#390) occur in and for themselves.

#411.

The property of many is, on the one hand, the absolutely identical relation of persons in recognition;—on the other hand, it is mediated by the arbitrary judgment of each individual, which makes a certain thing into their property as against the others'. Recognition is recognition not only of the abstract, but of the real personality of others, that is, of their judgment, and what is or could be my property is dependent on them as well as on their judgment of what is mine.

#412.

Because of the external relation in this judgment it has contingency, in the first place, in such a way that the general substance of the predicate, namely, the free will of the personality is recognized, but the thing is subsumed under one law by the particular will of these several people. This is a simple negative judgment expressing the civil suit, whose settlement requires a third judgment which is disinterested in the thing.

#413.

Secondly, however, people themselves relate to each other in the syllogism of the law as immediate extremes reflected into each other, and their actual recognition is only through the suspension of the immediacy of each through its free self-determination, not through coercion. The reflection of the individual into its subjective immediacy, and the negation of the general side of the predicate of possession, namely, the negation of the free personality of the other, is an infinite judgment which as an action is the crime.

#414.

This action, whereby the abstract individuality of the person posited for itself is realized, is null in and for itself. But in it the acting entity establishes itself as rational, yet formally and only by itself as a recognized law, has subsumed itself through the action, and been at the same time subsumed under it. The manifested nullity of this action and the elaboration of this formal law through a subjective individual will is revenge, which, because it derives from the interest of the immediate, subjective personality, is at the same time only a new injury, and so on to infinity. This progress suspends itself equally in a third judgment which is disinterested, punishment.

#415.

The reality of the law, which the personal will gives itself in an immediate way, has developed itself in general as a contingency; it shows itself to be mediated by subjective caprice, and this as an essential moment which on the one hand sets the power above the law, but on the other hand in its abstraction for itself is a nullity and essentially has truth and reality only in the identity with the general will: morality.

The phrase "law of nature," which until now has been customary for the philosophical doctrine of law, contains the ambiguity that it may mean either the law as something existing already formed in nature, or law as governed by the nature of things, that is, by the concept. The former used to be the common meaning, so that at the same time a "condition of nature" was poetically created, in which the law of nature should dominate; whereas the condition of society and the state actually required a limitation of freedom and a sacrifice of natural rights. In fact, however, the law and all its determinations are based on free personality alone, a self-determination which is much rather the opposite of the determination of nature. A natural condition is therefore a condition of violence and injustice, of which nothing truer may be said than that one ought to depart from it. Society, by contrast, is the condition in which only the law has reality; what is to limit and to sacrifice are precisely the caprice and violence of the state of nature. The formalism of law consists in the fact that it is the abstract and hence precisely immediate determination of the free personality. The subsumption of the particular existence under this is therefore something contingent, and the question of which objects are my property is a matter of arbitrariness and chance.—The transition of the law into morality is made thus by the necessity of subjectivity, which is at the same time however the suspension of its contingency, whereby it becomes a general and determinate entity in and for itself.

B.
Morality

#416.

The particularity of the person becomes an essential moment through the judgment of the free personality. The subjective interest and the particular well-being become thereby on the one hand purposive; on the other hand the general will subsisting in and for itself reaches its reality through subjectivity, insofar as it has the disposition, insight, and intention of the good through the sacrifice of its immediacy.

#417.

The moral standpoint is thereby the reflective judgment of freedom, or the relation in which personal subjectivity fixes itself absolutely as independent, and thus pushes the moments of the will to independent extremes,—to the general rational will and to an external, independent world. Subjectivity is its mean, and is just as immediately identical with them as they, because they are independent, are posited with each other in a merely relative relation.

#418.

The general conclusion is that the moral subject, as the unity of the antithesis subsisting for itself, which is equally as independent in the extremes, is this inner contradiction and identity, as the activity and the drive to suspend them, that is, to act, and to realize the goal in one, and to make the external world conform to the goal.

#419.

Action is, to be sure, the absolute determination of selfless objectivity set against the free subject through its purpose. But since this objectivity is also independent, it can reverse the action of the individual and bring something else to light that lay in it. Although all change as so posited by the activity of the subject is its deed, the subject does not for that reason recognize it as its action, but only admits as its own and its guilt that element in the deed which lay in its knowledge and will;—because it values itself only as absolutely subjective will subsisting for itself.

#420.

But this general transition, which is action in general, still contains other multiple relative identities: (a) the general will subsisting in and for itself, which is the law and the substance in which the immediate individuality of the subject, as well as the external reality in general, are suspended. It is therefore the absolute final aim, the good in and for itself, the subject's duty and the final purpose of the world.

#421.

But (b) the good contains in its concept, as the general moment of the will, the moment of reality, which, however, lies in the individuality that is different from this generality and in the subjectivity of the self-reflective "I" and its self-determining activity;—the subject ought to have insight into the good, and make this its intention, and bring it about by its activity.

#422.

(c) The good is in the first place an abstract, general quality, but as an essential element of the will it is negative in itself and therefore a particular element. Thus it produces many forms of good and many forms of duty, whose differences occur dialectically in opposition to each other, and bring them into collision.

#423.

They ought, however, to stand in agreement, since each is absolute as a duty and a good, because they have the general will as their essence. For this very reason the individual should, since the action is the activity of subject and has individuality as a principle, know them especially in their diversity, as well as the many sides of the objectivity presupposed by the subject as individual, and the many sides of the case, which is a concrete instance and in itself multiple; as well as the many kinds of duties which are related to these many kinds of sides. Further, the individual should be the true dialectic that recognizes the subordination of these elements under each other, and resolves a single one of them or a combination of them with the exclusion of the other or its absolute value.

#424.

(d) To the subject, who in the subsisting sphere of freedom exists essentially as a particular, their interest and welfare must be an essential aim and therefore a duty. But at the same time in aiming at the good, which is not the particular but only the general will, the particular interest ought not to be a constituent moment. On account of this independence it is a matter of chance whether they harmonize. And yet they ought to harmonize, because the subject as individual and general is one identity in itself.

#425.

(e) This inward side ought in general to be joined through the action, through the activity of the subject, with objectivity. Since objectivity, however, as the other independent extreme, constitutes a unique world for itself, it is coincidental whether it corresponds to the subjective aims, whether the good is realized, and the wicked, which is essentially an aim and actually null, is realized in it: it is no less a matter of chance whether the subject finds in it their well-being, and more precisely, whether in the world the good subject is happy and the wicked unhappy.—But at the same time the world ought to allow the good action to be carried out in it, as it ought to grant the good subject the satisfaction of their particular interest, and refuse it to the wicked, just as it ought to nullify the wicked itself.

#426.

The all-round contradiction expressed by this repeated "ought" is the most abstract analysis of the spirit, its deepest descent into itself. The pure relation of the self-contradictory determinations is the abstract certainty of themselves, the infinity of subjectivity, for which the general will, the good, right, and duty no more exist than not, and which knows itself as choosing and deciding.

#427.

Since this choosing self-certitude is the reflection of the abstract will, which is infinite in its immediate individuality, it yields the two directly interchanging forms of conscience and evil. The former is the will of goodness, but a goodness which to this pure subjectivity is the nonobjective, the nongeneral, the unutterable, and about which the subject knows that their individuality has the decision, and thereby perceives and enjoys their particular excellence. Evil, however, is this same knowledge of the individual as the decisive agent, insofar as it does not merely remain in this abstraction, but takes up the content of a subjective interest contrary to the good.

#428.

This highest peak of the phenomenon of the will, which dissolves itself into absolute vanity, to a nonobjective but purely self-aware goodness, and to a self-assurance which involves the nullification of the general, collapses immediately into itself. Evil, as the pure reflection of subjectivity itself in opposition to the objective and general, is entirely abstract appearance, the immediate reversal and annihilation of itself. For it is rather immediately pure identity with itself;—the action of evil, which is crime (#414), the presentation of this reversal, in which the moments of the concept have the shape of external reality in contrast to each other.

#429.

The purely abstract, good disposition is, inside of itself, the suspension of the mediation of this reflection, with the result, on its negative side, that the nullification of the will would hold its own against the good,—the nullification of nullity. This generality has at the same time, in its concept and in this consciousness, the meaning of the unutterable or of the absolutely immediate good, and thereby of the objective. Subjectivity, in this its identity with the good, has thus suspended the standpoint of the relation, and has passed into ethics.

C.
Ethics

#430.

Ethics are the completion of the objective spirit, not only the truth of law and of morality as their unity, but of the subjective and objective spirit. It is, namely, freedom as the general rational will, which dissolves itself in the pure thought of the antithesis to individual subjectivity, and has its self-knowledge and disposition, its practical operation and immediate, general actuality at the same time as custom—where self-conscious freedom has become nature.

#431.

The free substance, in which the absolute "ought" is no less an "is," has reality as the spirit of a people. The abstract diremption of its negativity towards existence is the separation into persons, whose immediate independence it controls as the inner power and necessity. The person, however, as a thinking intelligence, recognizes the substance as his own essence, and ceases to be when reminded of being a mere accident; the person looks upon it as absolute final aim. In reality the person does not see an achieved present, but rather something brought about by action, something which actually exists. Thus, without any selective reflection, the person performs his duty as his own and as something which subsists, and in this necessity the person has himself and his freedom.

#432.

Because the substance is the absolute unity of the individuality and generality of freedom, it follows that the reality and activity of each individual to protect and to be oneself, while it is on the one hand conditioned by the presupposed total in whose complex it alone exists, it is on the other hand a transition into a general product.—In the same way the substance and the general work are the independence of the individuals which are thereby produced. The disposition of individuals is the knowledge of this identity of all their interests with the whole, and that the other individuals know each other mutually and are real in this identity,—trust,—the genuinely substantial ethical disposition.

#433.

General work, which is the substance itself, separates itself and its work into the differences which are the estates: the general, the activity of the substance as such; the particular, whose work involves the needs of the particular existence and whose closest aim is the particular subjectivity, but whose accomplishment at work presupposes all others, and equally reaches into them. The social position of the isolated figure is individuality, insofar as it is for itself a totality, to be sure, a natural one, but through spirituality is just as much raised into the ethics of the elevated whole, the family.

#434.

These relations between individuals in relationship to their substance constitute their ethical duties. To the individual, on the one hand, identity with the totality of the family is the natural substantiality. On the other hand, however, the individual ought to attend to the possibility of having an estate and a position in the entire social substance. The individuals should educate themselves in general, and really become something only insofar as they are recognized as a particular colleague on a general project, and really work on the project.

#435.

The ethical personality, that is, the subjectivity which is permeated by substantial life, is virtue. In relation to external immediacy, to destiny, a relation as to a being, to a non-negative and thereby a quiet repose in itself: in relation to substantial objectivity, to the whole of ethical reality, it exists as trust, as deliberate effort for the community, and the capacity of sacrificing oneself for the community; whereas in relation to the incidental relations of social circumstance it is in the first instance justice and then benevolence. In the latter sphere subjectivity expresses its particular character, temperament, and so on, as personal virtues.

#436.

The general work of the substance consists in relation to the extreme of individuality in the two-sided task: on the one hand to maintain them as persons, along with the law as a necessary reality, to transform the revenge of the damaged existence into punishment, and then to support the well-being of the people who at first attend only to themselves, but above all have a general aspect. On the other hand, however, the task is to take both, the whole disposition and activity of the individual who strives to be a center for himself, and to lead him back into the life of the general substance, and in this sense as a free power to interrupt those initial spheres.

#437.

The laws express the nature and the determinations of the general substance; they are, in the first place, immediate, and thus restrictions on the independent self-will and the particular interest of the individual; in the second place, however, they are the absolute final purpose and the general work: hence they are a product of the functions of the various estates which separate themselves more and more from the general particularization (#433), are brought forth through all the activity and private concerns of individuals, and are presented as current custom.

#438.

The abstract essence of the laws is the general will subsisting in and for itself, its actuality as living custom. Insofar, however, as the extreme of individuality is partly immediate naturalness of the will, the drive, the inclination, and partly caprice in general, but also the moral abstraction of pure subjectivity and vanity subsisting for itself, which it reflects into itself, thus it is by contrast the other extreme, namely, the will subsisting in and for itself, determinate as much as individual reality and the active subjectivity of the general;—the government and its personal, determining and deciding head, the prince.

#439.

The constitution contains the determinations by which the rational will, insofar as it is only the general will in itself of individuals found and understood, is maintained in reality by the efforts of the government and its particular branches, and protects equally against its contingent individuality and against the contingency of separate individuals.

#440.

The external moment which the government has, as the general form of individual reality in contrast to the extreme of individuality, general in its abstract determination as the merely collective form of an aggregate of many, and which at times then bears the misleading name of "the people," gives the false impression that the constitution is a contract, namely, the arbitrary agreement of different persons over an arbitrary and contingent thing. The connection is, on the contrary, substantial and absolute: from it, in the first place, all rights and their reality proceed, and the constitution is rather the moment when arbitrariness is taken from the self-comprehension and activation of the substance.

#441.

That the ethical spirit, which exists here as substance, comprehends itself, and grasps and produces its general essence and its organization, can be attributed to the wisdom and the knowledge of the general estate, to a higher sphere in general than the one of its substantial being. In this way the disposition of individual ethics and its relation to the reality of the substance, as to one differentiated by its individuality and reflection, is trust (#431). Insofar, however, as abstract moral persons ought to recognize their expressive, individual will (#435) in general, this participation is to be regulated, because it is partly appearance and partly real and a guarantee, so that the recognition, establishment, and activation of the general will become fixed, primarily against the personal particularity and the orientation of the individual towards private interests.

#442.

The ethical spirit is itself (1) an individual spirit which achieves its reality in a particular, determinate people. As such a determinte being, immediate naturalness exhibits its totality in the form of geographical and climatic determinacy. Above all it exists in a particular developmental stage of its intellectual life, and only in this stage does it comprehend, grasp, and write itself.

#443.

(2) As such an isolated individual the spirit is exclusive against other like individuals. In their mutual relations, arbitrariness and contingency have a place: for the general law, which is only posited for the sake of the autonomous independence of those people who form a real totality in themselves, and who have no further need nor ought to be, is not a reality.

#444.

This independence reduces any dispute between them to a relation of violence, a condition of war, for which the general estate determines itself with the particular purpose of preserving the independence of the state against others, and becomes the estate of bravery.

#445.

This condition shows the omnipotence of the state in its individuality, an individuality that extends to abstract negativity. Country and fatherland then appear as the power through which the particular independence of individuals and their absorption in the external existence of possession and in natural life come to feel their own nullity,—as the power which maintains the general substance by the sacrifice of this natural and particular existence, and which mediates itself with itself in the disposition of freedom and the defeat of the frivolous.

#446.

Through the condition of war, however, either the mutual recognition of free national individualities may result, or the people who prefer the infinite honor of freedom and bravery over the finite subsistence of particular existence may reach what they desire, namely, the subjugation of the other and the end of their independence. But, in the former case, peace is reached by a convention which ought to last forever.

#447.

External civil rights rest partly on the positive treaties which settle the claims of people against each other, but to that extent contain only rights which fall short of true reality (#443); partly on "international law," whose general principle is its presupposed recognition by the states, and thus limits the otherwise unlimited actions of the states against each other in such a way that the possibility of freedom remains. On the other hand, it distinguishes individuals as private persons from the state. In general, international law rests on social customs.

#448.

(3) As the spirit of a particular people is real and its freedom exists under natural conditions, it exists finally in time, and as regards its range and scope, its reality has essentially a particular principle of development,—a history. But as a limited spirit it passes into universal world history, the events of which exhibit the dialectic of the particular national spirits, the judgment of the world.

#449.

This movement is the path of liberation for the ethical substance from its particularities, in which it is real in the individual peoples,—the act whereby the spirit itself becomes general, the world spirit. Since this is the development of the spirit's self-consciousness in time, its several moments and stages are the national spirits, each of which, however, as single and natural can complete only one level and only one task in the whole deed.

#450.

This freedom and its task are the highest and absolute law. The self-consciousness of a particular people is the vehicle for the contemporary development of the collective spirit in its existence, and the objective reality in which that spirit invests its will. Against this absolute will the will of the other particular national spirits has no rights; yet the general will strides on over a particular level, then delivers it over to its chance and trial.

#451.

To the extent that this business appears as an action, a resolution, and therefore a work of individuals, these individuals, as regards the substance of their work, are instruments, and their subjectivity, which is what is particular to them, is the empty form of activity. What they therefore have gained personally, through the individual share which they have gained in substantial business, is fame, which is their reward.

#452.

Intellectual substance, which liberates its content as well as its individual reality or its self-consciousness from the limitation of the fear of death, also elevates these to infinity, and in this way becomes objective as general spirit, known by self-consciousness as its substance, is thereby liberated from fear, and becomes reality in accordance with its concept.

III
Absolute Spirit

#453.

The concept of the spirit has its reality in the spirit. If this reality is in completed identity with that concept as the knowledge of the absolute idea, then the necessary aspect is that the implicitly free intelligence liberates itself for its concept, in order for it to be a shape worthy of it. The subjective and the objective spirit can therefore be seen as the path on which this side of reality or existence forms itself (#304). Conversely, this path also has the significance that the subjective spirit is seen as the first entity which exists in its immediacy without the concept, grasps its essence and forms itself from there, and thereby reaches its free identity with the concept, its absolute reality.

#454.

Since the subjective individuality in its free development is essentially a process that begins with immediate life, the highest identity which being has, and therefore observes all the determinate beings in the world as a nullity and entities to be sacrificed, the ethical substance has the significance of absolute power and the absolute soul, and contains the significance of the essence of nature and of the spirit.

#455.

The diremption of this general and pure substance of the spirit is therefore the judgment in itself and the knowledge for which it exists as such.

(a.) The Religion of Art

#456.

The immediate shape of this knowledge is that of the intuition and representation of the absolute spirit as the ideal.

#457.

The significance of the ideal is the substantiality as the identical and concrete essence of nature and of the spirit, a concrete essence which is called God. The proof that this significance is the absolute truth is the mediation by which nature is suspended into the spirit, and the spirit suspends its subjectivity through its activity into the absolute spirit, thereby placing itself as its final ground in such a way that this mediation is in itself just as much the suspension of the mediation, of the antithesis (#72, 74, 105, and so on), and knows itself as the absolute first principle.

#458.

As this consciousness of the absolutely first takes shape, its immediacy produces the factor of finitude in art, and is also the determinate shape of God for itself, at first as the abstract of an immediate existence, of an elementary or concrete natural being, or of the opposite, pure thought.

#459.

The truth, however, of that immediate shape and its shapeless negativity, of the here and now and of the beyond, is the concrete shape born from the spirit. In this ideal the natural immediacy appears only as the sign of thought, liberated from its contingency and transfigured through thought to express the idea, so that the shape shows it and it alone:—the shape of beauty.

#460.

Insofar as beauty in general is the penetration of the intuition or of the image by thought, and exemplary thought, it is something formal, and the content of thought, as well as the material which it uses for its imagination, can in the first place be of the most various types.

#461.

Insofar, however, as the form has its true content, that penetration itself, the spiritual substance in its absolute significance (#457), it is, however, for the sake of the immediacy in which this knowledge is intuition or imagistic representation, the shape, to a certain extent finite, as being is immediate and thereby external material, the content is partly therefore only a particular spirit of the people.

#462.

That this existence is a product of the subject, which grasps the idea and brings it to external presentation, is not because of its finitude; for the subject is only purely formal activity, and the work of art is only then an expression of God when there is no sign of subjective particularity in it, and the indwelling spirit of the people is conceived and born into the world unmixed and unspotted by its contingency.—The mediation, which has gone through the pain and the activity of a subject and has taken shape, is immediately suspended. The work presents the substance of the subject, and the labor pains are precisely this absolute manifestation and negativity of the subjective particularity.

#463.

Insofar, however, as the image of the God is at hand as immediate, thus the relation of the others, driven by their self-subsisting essences in the act of worship through devotion and the act of lowering in thoughts, relinquishes their own subjectivity, symbolically sacrifices their particular reality, and becomes conscious in the enthusiasm and in the enjoyment of their identity with the substance. Thus the relation loses its external shape and, to the same extent, transfers its subjectivity, which is inward in substance only as general knowledge, into existence.

#464.

In world history, however, the absolute spirit suspends the finitude of its knowing reality and the limited existence of its idea in and for itself into generality, as well as the form of the intuition, of the immediate knowledge and existence, into self-mediating knowledge and an existence which is itself knowledge, and passes into revelation.

(b.) Revealed Religion

#465.

Absolute spirit at this level of the suspended immediacy of its shape, and its knowledge as well at the level of reflection, is, on the one hand, the general spirit of nature and of the spirit subsisting in and for itself; but on the other hand, it exists for the representation. The subjectivity of knowledge, because it is reflection, lends independence to the moments of its life, whose totality it essentially is, making them presuppositions of each other, and phenomena which succeed each other; it makes a complex of events according to finite reflective categories.

#466.

In this separation the reflection separates the form from the content, and in the form the different moments of the concept are separated into particular spheres or elements, in each of which the absolute content manifests itself.

#467.

(1) In the moment of generality, the sphere of pure thought or the abstract element of the essence, it is therefore the absolute spirit which is in the first place the presupposed principle, and as a substantial power in the reflective determination of causality is creator of heaven and earth. But in this eternal sphere the spirit only generates itself as its son, whose generation or positing is equally, however, suspended and the eternal being of the concept; just as its

determination to be different from the general essence eternally suspends itself, and, through this mediation of the self-suspending mediation, the first substance is only concrete individuality—is the spirit.

#468.

(2) In the moment of particularity, however, as judgment, in which individuality in general is included or becomes itself again in the moment of reflection, it is this concrete eternal essence which is presupposed. Its movement is the actual creation or disintegration of the eternal moment of mediation, of the only son, who is divided into the independent antithesis. On the one hand, namely, are heaven and earth, elemental and concrete nature, and on the other hand, standing in relation to such nature, the spirit, which therefore is finite. That spirit, as the extreme of self-subsisting negativity, completes its independence until it becomes wickedness, becomes directly an extreme through its relation to an opposing nature and through its own naturalness thus posits it.

#469.

(3) In the moment of individuality as such, namely, of subjectivity and of the concept itself, in which the antithesis of general and particular has sunk to its identical ground, the place of presupposition (a) is taken by the general substance, as actualized out of its abstraction into an individual self-consciousness. This individual is also as such identical with the essence, and thereby evil in and for itself is suspended. Further, this immediate concreteness expires in the absolute pain of negativity, in which it, as concreteness, is identical with itself, and thus, as absolute return from that negativity and as general unity of the general and individual essentiality for itself, has realized its being as the idea of the spirit, eternal, but living and real.

#470.

(b) This totality, since it exists in the sphere of reflection, is the self-subsisting totality or presupposition, and in opposition to this totality stands the division and finite immediacy of individual subjectivity. For this subjectivity the initial presupposition and its movement are at first an other and an object of contemplation; the intuition of its self-subsisting truth, through which this finite subject, on account of its immediate nature, at first determines itself as nullity and evil. It is, therefore, according to the example of its truth, the movement to relinquish its immediate natural determinacy and its own will, and to unify itself with that example in the pain of negativity, in general abstraction. In this way the subject recognizes itself as identical with the essence, which (c) through this mediation brings about its own dwelling in self-consciousness, and is the real, general spirit.

#471.

The revelation of the absolute, whose life is presented in a cycle of concrete shapes of representation, follows from its separation into independent parts with a temporal and external sequence, and in this last result it gathers itself as the true and the real in the general, simple, and eternal spirit. In this form of truth, truth is the object of philosophy.

(c.) Philosophy

#472.

Philosophy is the unity of art and religion, as the simple intuition and substantial production of art are elevated to self-conscious thought through the separation into parts and the mediation of religion. In this element the self-conscious idea purifies itself just as much from its first immediacy as from the appearance of the event, from the contingency, the externality, and the sequential nature which its content has in religion. This knowledge is thus the concept of art and religion in which the diverse elements of the content are recognized as necessary, and this necessity and immediacy are recognized as free.

#473.

This recognition of the necessity in the content of the absolute representation, as well as of the necessity of both forms, on the one hand, immediate intuition and its poetry, and on the other hand, the presupposed representation, the objective and external revelation, and the subjective retreat and inner identification of faith with representation. This recognition of the content and the form and the liberation of these forms completes itself when philosophy in the end grasps its own concept, that is, looks back on its knowledge.

#474.

This concept of philosophy is the self-thinking idea, truth aware of itself (#183), or logic with the significance that it is generality preserved in concrete content. In this way science returns to its beginning, with logic as the result. The presupposition of its concept, or the immediacy of its beginning and the aspect of its appearance at that moment, are suspended.

#475.

This initial appearance is formed by the syllogism, which has logic basically as its starting point, with nature for the middle term and is linked ultimately to spirit. Logic becomes nature, and nature becomes spirit. Nature, which stands between the spirit and its essence, divides itself, though not to the extremes of finite abstraction. For the syllogism is in the idea and nature is essentially determined as a transition point and negative moment. But the mediation of the concept has the external form of transition, and science takes the form of being.

#476.

In the second syllogism this appearance is suspended, for the spirit is the mediating factor. This is a syllogism which is already the standpoint of the spirit itself, presupposes nature and joins it with logic. It is the syllogism of reflection on the idea; science appears as subjective cognition.

#477.

These appearances are suspended in the idea of philosophy, which has self-knowing reason, the absolutely general, for its middle term: a middle which divides itself into spirit and nature, with the former as its presupposition, and the latter as its general extreme. Thus immediate nature is only a posited entity, as spirit is in itself, not a presupposition, but rather totality returning into itself. In this way the middle term, the self-knowing concept, has as its reality primarily conceptual moments and exists in its determinacy as general knowledge, persisting immediately by itself.

Translated by Steven A. Taubeneck

SOLGER'S POSTHUMOUS WRITINGS AND CORRESPONDENCE

Edited by Ludwig Tieck and Friedrich von Raumer
First Volume 780 P. Preface XVI P.,
Second Volume 784 P. Leipzig, 1826

In: *Jahrbücher für wissenschaftliche Kritik 1828,* No. 51/52,
53/54, 105/106, 107/108, 109/110.

First Article

With writings of such rich and varied content, also touching upon many situations immediately surrounding us, the demand for a review to follow shortly after their appearance is all the more appropriate. Whatever lies in the observations and opinions of an important man about significant most recently occurring events, individualities and their works, or those still engaging our interest in the present, and in the discussion of them within a circle of friends, men for the most part still living among us, could be drawn to the attention of general interest or constitute a topic of curiosity. The need to engage curiosity is now generally waning. But aside from the piquant details, there lie still more solid points of view in the determination of this collection to be a monument to the estimable individuality of the man and to show the public the final points of his philosophical formation in his last and posthumous works.

The first part of the collection contains, to begin with, excerpts from a diary of Solger from his earlier years and then about the progress of the latter up until his death, the rich treasure of a letter collection that remains locked within the circle of intimate friendship and bears the character of such conversation and communication throughout. The editors, from whom also the larger part of the transmitted letters of Solger's friends stem, supplement the context through the insertion of brief historical notes and have more or less rounded out the collection to a biographical whole by an introduction and a conclusion. The overall picture of Solger's character could not be projected more accurately than by these men so intimately and long acquainted with him. We select this depiction, which concludes their undertaking in a worthy manner: "In his youth he was slender and flourishing, of average height. His eye, of the clearest blue, somewhat protruding, good-naturedness and nobility the foremost expression of his face. Whenever the subject matter was important enough, a sublime anger could wipe out this good-naturedness which even won over children. The expression of his physiognomy was in seriousness a completely different one than when he smiled; his friendliness was endearing. Following the nervous disease that fatally attacked him in the year 1807, his sense of humor changed somewhat, and little by litte even his build. He became stouter and fuller, the expression of manly power and equanimity took the place of the lively youth."—"Only a few human beings have been endowed with this magic of language. Even to the uninitiated he spoke clearly and intelligibly about difficult subjects. Just like his entire life, his marriage was exemplary and as happy as is seldom the case. As husband, father, friend, teacher, and citizen, one will always be able to mention and praise his name as a model for imitation."

We believe it will not be disagreeable for the reader to survey briefly the main data of his life history:

Carl Wilhelm Ferdinand Solger was born on November 28, 1780, in Schwedt, where his father was the director of the then still existent margravian House—in both office and within family circles and among his friends, a highly honorable and esteemed true German character. A few anecdotes from the early youth of the son have been imparted, from which we want to repeat an apparently characteristic one. For a long time Solger called himself by the formal form of address, "Sie" (you), with his younger brother, which in their childish quarrels often gave their relationship a comical solemnity. With his early talent for cutting out animals and human figures from paper, he knew how to entertain the latter often. Whenever this one, however, pestered him on this account at an inconvenient time, he tended to make a very serious face and reject his inadmissible demand with great vehemence and call out: "Do you, sir, think that I have nothing else to do but cut out dolls for You?" This "comical solemnity," this seriousness which destroys itself in itself, the triviality that takes itself seriously, can be seen as an image of the caprice, the childishness of which has disappeared by itself through maturity and solidity of character, but which followed Solger's consciousness throughout his entire life as the principle of irony.

Solger first attended school in Schwedt, then from the age of fourteen the Gymnasium of the Gray Monastery in Berlin, at nineteen the University of Halle, where he studied law, for whom, however, the study of ancient languages, even more powerfully stimulated by Wolf's witty lecturing, was at the same time his favorite pastime.* He thereby acquired an extraordinary fluency in English and Italian, began to learn Spanish, and by knowing how to manage all of this, took the most cheerful interest in these delights. Here the circle of friends elucidated in the correspondence became linked. At Michaelmas, 1801, he went to Jena for half a year, especially to hear Schelling lecture. No further details about this turning point in his scholarly interest and studies there has been cited other than Karl Schelling's later theses (p. 88), which Solger opposed in the animatedly conducted Disputatorium organized by his brother.† These were similar to theses Solger also drew up in the metaphysically speculative manner of the times for purposes of debate. In the year 1802 he took a trip to Switzerland and France, about which inter-

---

*Friedrich August Wolf (1759–1824). Famous classical philologist of the time.
†Karl Eberhard von Schelling (1783–1854). Chief medical counsel.

esting excerpts are given in the diaries. With the beginning of 1803 Solger was appointed to the House of War and Domains in Berlin, but he continued his studies, especially in Greek, with the greatest zeal and in the year 1804 had the translation of Sophocles' *Oedipus Rex* published. Only on p. 159 does an explanation of the view that guided him occur about the work of the translation of the entire Sophocles, which still maintains itself as the most superior. The substantial preface to this translation is reprinted in the second volume of this collection, p. 445 ff.* In the year 1804 Solger attended Fichte's course of lectures on the Doctrine of Knowledge "with infinite pleasure and profit, as I hope" (he writes, p. 131). "Whoever wants to be pulled together, trained, and given a complete workout, he should go to him." And, p. 134: "I admire his strict philosophical discourse. . . . No one else seizes hold of his listener with such power, no one leads him that way without mercy into the keenest school of reflection. It is a genuine delight to have made the acquaintance of both great men in this discipline, him and Schelling, and to compare them." In the year 1806 he bade farewell to the chamber in order to be able to devote himself entirely to scholarship. The position was left vacant for a long time yet, so that he could immediately step into it again in the event he were to make this decision. From here, where the diaries cease, the excerpts and notes from the writings begin. Compilations on history, especially for a work on Greek mythology, about Indian religious teaching and philosophy, on Pausanias, Plato, and the Greek tragedians now begin. One marvels (like the editors, who have the mass of his papers before them, rightly say referring to that) at the diligence of the man. One sees that he made his object comprehensive scholarship, which at the same time was also supposed to serve as material and filling for his higher philosophical interests and views, to which he always returns from those extrinsic works, or rather does not cease to cling to his occupation with them. Extending through the entirety of his intellectual and life-engaged attitude is a basic feature of his disposition which expresses itself like this on p. 143 in a letter to Krause (p. xvi of the preface), one of the best friends of the deceased, who distinguished by integrity, knowledge, discern-

---

*All P.'s refer to the edition of *Solger's Posthumous Writings* by Tieck and Raumer cited at the beginning.

ment, and solid judgment, esteemed by all who knew him, was snatched up in his best years: "So I now wish to admit that for me the most urgent, yes, the only truly serious necessity, is your society. In reality, there is no firm ground and foundation other than this intimate association with friends. . . . It is only in this way that I am able to stand fast, if need be, to lift, and support others." This feeling for communication with his friends and for their participation in his works dominates throughout the entire correspondence and strengthens and consoles him up to the end about the discords that life otherwise offered him. The misfortune of the state in the year 1806 deeply distressed the patriotic Solger. Yet there is nothing more detailed to be found about Solger's views and relationships in this course of events. In the year 1808 he became a doctor of philosophy (p. 158) without its being indicated where and how. In the fall of 1809 he departed as such for Frankfurt on the Oder, where he soon became professor extraordinarius, held partly philological, partly philosophical lectures there, and as one sees, brought a significant revival to these studies. Even the citizenry of this city gained such confidence in him that in the year 1810 the city commissioners elected the professor of philosophy, who was not yet paid a salary and who did not see himself provided for by other means of subsistence for long, lord mayor, with a salary of 1,500 taler. Seen superficially, one could be reminded with this of Democritus' fellow citizens. But in order to earn the reputation of the Abderites through a behavior towards a philosopher, there is more to it than that. For according to Diogenes Laertius, the Abderites honored the philosopher of their city after listening to his work *Diakosmos* with a gift of about five hundred times 1,500 taler, aside from additional displays of high esteem.* Moreover, one sees that those city commissioners took their election and their offer solemnly extended to Solger by a delegation seriously and that they had indeed not just wanted to make a pleasant gesture towards philosophy. But one really should not compare remote times of such different circumstances and characters to each other. Solger found a conscientious occupation in the office that was offered to him incompatible with the work in what constituted the most characteristic and innermost

---

*Diogenes Laertius: Philosopher of late antiquity (second or third century B.C.), who wrote a history of philosophy in ten books with the title *On the Lives of the Philosophers*.

of his intellect. With due consideration, he declined the position, soon received some salary from the government, and shortly thereafter (in the summer of 1811), he was drawn to the newly established university at Berlin, where he now devoted his brilliant teaching talent as well as his literary activity, mainly to philosophy, up until his death (October 25, 1819; on p. 778 there are printing errors about this date).

The larger part of the correspondence transmitted in the first volume and probably all of the hitherto unpublished essays of the second volume fall into this last period of Solger's life. One sees that for him the letter conversation with his absent friends was an important detailed business. His facility in expressing himself in a refined manner made the composition of the many and copious letters possible without spending too much time on it. In the wealth of subjects discussed, this report must limit itself to a few anyhow. It is only meant to emphasize what characterizes more general tendencies of Solger and the times. Right at the beginning, it becomes noticeable that Solger acquired a fluency of expression, maturity of style and judgment very early. It is already excellent in the first essays of the twenty-year-old youth. The transmitted excerpts from the diary of these years carry the imprint of the already-present mature bearing. The critiques and travel annotations through Switzerland and France are not products of an enthusiasm of youth, youthful superficiality and liveliness, but results of a prudent reflection. The literary judgments are mostly concerned with belletristic writings, critiques that, properly selected, would have surely distinguished themselves in a public journal. Already the first deal with writings of one of the editors, *Zerbino, Blond Eckbert,* the *Tannhäuser.** One already sees there the inclination towards this later friend's literary criticism and style (the first personal acquaintance falls into the last period of Solger's sojourn in Frankfurt) and the young man immediately steeped in the new characteristic tone and direction of that time in the first expressions of his awakened interest. In contrast to the commonplace of youthful opinion, subject and content are less powerful, not of predominant influence upon his criticism. This delights chiefly in the formal and subjective features, the extraordinary profusion of imagination, of mood, etc. While he overlooks the

---

Zerbino, Blond Eckbert, Tannhäuser: Poetic works by Ludwig Tieck.

old shriveled up women in which more of the fantastic is supposed to have resided, etc., in the Schillerean rewriting of *Macbeth* and the witches, the newly arisen partiality for Holberg* (p. 101, 102), to whom an enchantment is attributed supposedly resting upon the very cheerful and extremely good-natured Nordic mood, is not lacking and is found especially excellent there where almost all characters of the play are certain fools and therefore say an enormous amount of splendid nonsense: "the complete silliness of his servants" are especially praised as "irredeemable."

So we see ourselves transferred into the midst of the view of one of the remarkable epochs that can be regarded as the crises in German literature and from which points of comparison we want to select a few. The one occurs during Goethe's youth. We find it depicted in its entire characteristic range in his life by Goethe himself, who participated so much in its execution. After describing "the perplexity" into which criticism led, the confusion into which "young minds felt themselves displaced by its dislocated maxims, half-understood laws and splintered teachings," Goethe indicates the manner in which he saved himself from this chaotic state and this distress. In order to gain a true foundation, feeling, or reflection for his poems, he had to reach into his bosom, and for the observation of an object or occurrence, for poetic depiction, first of all, keep himself within the circle that was capable of touching him—of instilling an interest within him. One ingredient in this powerful conduct is his acquaintance with Shakespeare, whose great influence is further depicted especially in *Wilhelm Meister's Apprenticeship*,† where the poet has Wilhelm proclaim that these Shakespearean dramas are not poems; one rather imagines oneself standing before the opened, colossal books of fate in which the storm winds of the most agitated life howl and strip it violently of all its leaves. All presentiments he ever had about the human race and its fates which accompanied him from youth onward he had found fulfilled and developed without his noticing it. In this way Shakespeare had lent a helping hand to the expanded life experience of the poet and done his part to carry the circle of imagination beyond the merely immediate objects and relationships as beyond the reflections limited to this and to gain

---

*Ludwig Holberg (1684–1754). The originator of the Danish Comedy.
†Book 3, chapter 11.

deeper content, but always out of the well of one's own bosom. Because, and this is an important word that Goethe adds in the intially mentioned connection: "The inner content of the treated object is the beginning and the end of art." He then adds further that he and the friends who shared this enthusiasm did not deny the possibility of recognizing the merits of Shakespeare more closely, of understanding them, of evaluating them with insight, but they kept this in reserve for later epochs. At present, they wanted only to participate happily and reproduce actively.

The other crisis has expanded our literary horizon beyond yet additional phenomena and contributed not only to disseminating knowledge about Dante, Holberg, the Nibelungs, Calderón, but also prompted, besides a renewed enthusiasm for Shakespeare, the study, admiration, and imitation of these remote and heterogeneous configurations. As, however, the first crisis in boredom with the formal dug for content and brought it to the surface, so it was connected inversely with this expansion of taste for forms and foreign characteristics that the sense for content and substance concentrated itself in subjective abstraction, in a formless weaving of the mind within itself, that it even had to yield to the enjoyment and appreciation of humor and common wit. Earlier, mention was made of the splendid nonsense and the marvelous silliness, and there are probably still admirers of Shakespeare who cannot recover from the aesthetic enthusiasm for Corporal Nym and Lieutenant Pistol.* Thus content and substance, each of its own accord, then made itself sober, thin, without seriousness in its own productions. It was intentionally sacrificed in order to float up into emptiness and consciously, in ironic fashion, pass off the inner truthlessness of the material as the best. On the one hand, we saw the theory of the poetry of poetry, on the other hand, the circle of poets developing who made it their object to mystify themselves mutually and the public with the dawning products of the new poetic poetry with a cometlike world out of scent and tone without a core. For this ironic sublimation towards meaninglessness and longing, the lyrical form is natural and creates itself almost out of itself because the playing in unreal tones of the hollow mind is not, for verse and rhyme, embarrassed by content. In the dramatic branch, reality, character, and

* Figures in the *Merry Wives of Windsor*.

plot cannot be dispensed with. The inner void, which is demanded by the theory of irony, leads here to what mediocrity hits upon by itself—lack of character, inconsistency and accidentality, boastful dryness. The theory adds only this, that mediocrity, even with the maxim of unprincipledness and superficiality, produces. With this point of view, criticism gave itself a new, bold, not seldomly also insolent impetus and impressed a group who wanted to be at the aesthetic apex because a public forms itself, as Solger frequently expresses the experience, around every bold and glossy crookedness. But a nation—for we may certainly also speak of a nation in relation to literature and distinguish it from a mere public—the nation, therefore, has now since then just as little permitted this strange thing, in terms of external form as well as content, to be imposed upon itself as it had formerly achieved indigenous national poetry following the expulsion of French taste through that first crisis in form and feeling.—

A great many literary phenomena and opinions that belong to the spirit of this time pass before our eyes in this correspondence. Yet the most audacious and flourishing period of irony, *Lucinde, Athenäum,* etc., occurs already beyond this.* Soon there were more serious interests, the war and the political conditions, which bound together that point of view hostile to a serious content to an ever more particular circle not only externally but also in the interior of the individuals. Solger's more profound judgment always fell far short of the standpoint of the *Athenäum,* not to speak of a *Lucinde.* Even less could he in more mature years participate in the utmost grotesqueness to which the humor in the Hoffmannesque productions itself intensified. Just to give a few examples of that tendency, Solger, in his youth, finds in the novel begun by Novalis, the *Heinrich of Ofterdingen* (p. 95), a new and extremely daring attempt to depict poetry through life, the idea of a mystical story, a tearing apart of the veil that the finite on this earth holds around the infinite, an appearance of the godhead on earth, of a true myth, which here, however, forms itself in the mind of an individual man. "That this novel is not continued further and ceased exactly at the

---

*Athenäum: The periodical of the early Romantic School in Germany, edited by August Wilhelm and Friedrich Schlegel (1798–1800). *Lucinde:* A novel by Friedrich Schlegel (1799) famous for its emancipatory tendencies in terms of equality for women.

beginning of the most important, that distresses me exceedingly."
The sparkling onset corrupted the young man, but he still did not
realize that a conception of this kind is deficient precisely in not
being able to be continued and brought to a conclusion. The
shallow characters and situations shudder back from the reality
towards which they should move if they are to progress. On p. 124
the *Song of the Nibelungs* is declared, according to its outline, as
greater than the *Iliad*. In a lecture of A. W. Schlegel on Dante, Solger
finds neither the proper solemn awe before this lofty mysticism, nor
sufficient receptivity for the sublime artlessness.

Solger's close friendship with Tieck brings about the frequent
mention of the Tieck productions. This section of the correspondence is especially characteristic with regard to the literary and the
mystical tendency of the period linked with it. We therefore want to
linger here a little longer. First of all, as far as the Tieck products are
concerned, with Solger the friendship has a fair share in their
evaluation, but he occasionally proceeds to open, penetrating criticism. Tieck probably had it printed as a monument to the friendship, when we read on p. 350 that Solger knew of few German
dramas which could stand comparison to *Blaubart*,* or p. 428,
what Solger wrote in the year 1816: "It is my innermost conviction:
upon you (Tieck) rests the salvation of German art; you are the only
one who in the midst of the adulterated era stands forth in pure
poetic clarity! Your work is the true and divine. It has always
emerged ever more pure out of the whole jumble." On p. 294 Solger
indeed still considers it an indication of how strong the reflective
sense has become that criticism has been leveled against the mingling of a fairy-tale world with the real and everyday one in the Tieck
fairy tales. If Solger, as he says, could hardly have imagined this
objection, then we have in more recent times seen Tieck himself give
up that heterogeneity, abandon the fairy-tale ground and proceed to
novellas, where the setting and the external material are taken not
from the often childish and trifling, in any case from what has
disappeared from our belief or rejected by it in the fairy tale, but
from relationships of our world and truth. In later reviews which
Tieck wrings from Solger's friendship, the critical sense of the latter
modifies itself more closely to the insight into deficiencies which he
seeks to point out to the author on the basis of *Zerbino*, p. 388f.,

**Blaubart:* A poetic work by Ludwig Tieck.

and in *Genoveva,** p. 465ff. What is no longer to Solger's taste is the lack of control—remarkable enough—basically, even the mingling, the reproach of which he did not admit earlier, but had understood as higher, namely, as the mingling of the truly poetic with the merely fabricated, capricious, intentional. The two friends talk back and forth throughout several letters about *Genoveva,* and the profoundly developed insight of Solger expresses itself definitively therein as opposed to his earlier manner of criticism and the Tieckean point of view. When Tieck, on the other hand (p. 453), says of this poem that it came to him entirely out of his soul, how it surprised even himself and had not been made, but become, p. 465, that it was epoch making in his disposition, that he had been entirely dispassionate with it, then Solger feels that as much as it is in many places and scenes completely permeated by inwardness and love, nevertheless, this disposition was not the state of the poet, but rather a deep longing for it. Otherwise it would penetrate us as more immediately present, indeed, as the only true and possible. The inwardness appears in an opposition against something different, whereby consciousness is made at odds with itself and is brought to reflection. There is a lack of inner and actual necessity. Furthermore (p. 501), Tieck admits to the criticism that the poem appears unharmonious even to him; but this only leads to this, that the tones, accords, feelings, presentiment, forest, air, etc., rise up into harmony and music. What concerns design, coloring, style, there he is dissatisfied and finds the disharmony. The religion, the wilderness, the apparitions are for him the all-encompassing tone of the painting, and this he would not like to have called mannered. One sees that in Tieck's consciousness, the tone, the lyrical and subjective, not the content and inner solidity, is brought to contemplation.

Even more definitively, however, there arises in Solger the feeling about that fundamental evil of the Kleistian products, which are often mentioned in the correspondence. The character of the Kleistian works is just as profound as ingenious as has been analyzed and proven earlier in these yearbooks.† As much as Solger respected Kleist's talent, and on p. 558 where he is discussed at length especially appreciated the energetic and plastic power of the external

Zerbino, Genoveva: Poetic works by Ludwig Tieck.
†Vol. I, May 1827, pp. 686–724 by H. G. Hotho.

depiction that is very well documented in his stories too, so does the great emphasis this poet placed upon farfetched situations and effects, the intentional endeavor to go beyond the given and real and transport the actual plot into a foreign spiritual and wondrous world, in short, a certain bent towards a capricious mysticism, strike him nevertheless. The self-deception with which the poetic talent shifted is pertinently mentioned here. Kleist suffers from the common, unhappy inability to place the central interest in nature and truth and from the drive to seek it in distortions. The capricious mysticism suppresses the truth of the human psyche through miracles of the psyche, through the fairy tales of a supposedly higher inner spiritual life. Solger justifiably elevates the *Prince of Homburg* by the same author above his other pieces because here everything lies in the character and develops itself from it. With this deserved praise, it is not taken into account that the prince is made into a somnambulistic sick person like Käthchen of Heilbronn, and this motif is not only fused with his being in love, but also with his position as a general and in a historical battle. With this, the principle of the character just like the entire situation and entanglement becomes something tasteless, one could say ghoulishly tasteless.

Tieck gives us in his letters he had published in this collection a great deal of the best that belongs to this circle. One might be curious as to the realization of the character which was supposed to have been a self-reflected quintessence of those tendencies (p. 597)—the character "of a despiser of everything basic and good emerging from *Zerbino, Sternbald, Tom-cat,* and his other writings, with that hypercriticism which equals nought." That Shakespeare is a frequent subject of conversation in these letters was to be expected. A good many of the idiosyncrasies and profundities of the Tieckean way of looking at things is already spooking around here. "In Germany there is no study, truly no genuine one of the poet, and in England, an erroneous one," Tieck says after his return from England on p. 565. "Since Wieland, we Germans have remained in quite dilatory and complacent admiration." "One would think that in Germany there never lacked for a genuine study and understanding of Shakespeare, and specifically as a poet (see above), just as little as for well-known and famous fruits of this study, which Goethe and A. W. Schlegel, for example, have given us." Even the Englishmen, one would surmise, understand their Shakespeare. They would at least strongly deride the philistine arrogance of the Continent if because of a few of their critics going astray and their scholarly mistakes in the most trifling details, we sought to extol our study above their evaluation of the poet. For this, the historical-scholarly study is usually superfluous. That on this side of the channel too it is easy to be led astray and to fads, so that in the end something odd eventually results from such extensive and unedifying efforts, for that the letters at hand furnish the example themselves. The specter is already there of Tieck's well-known quirk about the advantage of the external setting that the theater at Shakespeare's time had above the present one. It is supposed to have been an advantage that the stage was only wide and not, like today, deep. The drawback of the frequent scene changes that become necessary with the production of Shakespeare's dramas as well as the uncertainty into which city or location one was now placed, was, as one knows, certainly remedied, and indeed the latter, in that a large placard fastened to a pole in front of the painted gate, city wall, houses, etc., gave the requisite information; that, furthermore, the actors, in order to travel from one city to another, had only to go through the curtain separating the stage in such a way that on its other side the other city, also identified by an inscription, was painted, so that no change of scene was bothersome. Indeed, the further circumstance is not considered to be a disadvantage of today's art, namely, that in today's theaters the audience is protected not only in the loges, but also on the main floor against rain, wind, and sun by means of a roof. But Tieck writes about that old arrangement on p. 693 that he is not disinclined to believe that even the lack of poets and meaning arose, for the most part, from the abandoned stage scaffolding, "and that in Germany, it hindered us in the production of genuine works." But in this correspondence nothing appears yet about the additional peculiar notions which Tieck has since permitted to venture out into the public about the characters in *Hamlet,* even about Lady Macbeth. Otherwise, many a thing is told about which one could be amazed, as on p. 502, that for many years perhaps Tieck excessively admired Shakespeare's *Pericles,* out of which *Zerbino* and *Oktavian* are to have originated, on p. 696, that a play of Calderón he admired ten years ago now appears almost thoroughly bad. Such aberrations of taste can only be understood in terms of the abstract thrust of criticism that does not pay heed to the objective in art. Solger has been saved from going along to the extremes through his classical education and philosophy. But whether at the same time the afore-mentioned contains elements of more solid criticism and is not completely uncanny in many a romantic product (like p. 606, e.g., with *Fortunato*), then this has still not surfaced. And in that very same place (still in the year 1818), one finds the evaluation of Shakespeare's *Love's Labor Lost*, this play as weak in the whole as teeming with platitudes in the specific, that among the comic plays the maturity of poetry in this poet expresses itself most distinctly herein because it is the least determined by a specific tendency (the tendency is indeed only very paltry) and "is based on the purest irony." One can admit the latter in the meaning often linked with it, that it is the purest irony to seek to come across any value in the play, which should be the delusion of any expectation other than just the humor of the matter.

In comparison, Solger's judgment proves itself especially pertinent, mature, and quick about the manifold additional phenomena lying outside the field of the romantic, which aroused undeserved atten-tion during the period of this correspondence. One sees with satis-faction how Solger deals with them right at their first appearance while they arouse the greatest sensation with a broad public and permit the public to expect the most significant results, until these matters and all their expectations are ruined without even account-ing for it, as through a mere forgetting. Just look at, for example, Solger's early and at the same time mature opinion about the once admired, now completely forgotten nature poetizing of Hiller* (vol. I., p. 128), even more about Pestalozzi† (ibid., p. 135 ff.), which can be instructive even now for many a person as to why the cause of this so noble a man, as an individual, did not produce a revolution in the educational system, nor could itself effect any nuance of progress. One is just as delighted by the profound views about many such literary productions that have appeared with great pretentiousness

---

*Philipp Friedrich Hiller (1699–1769). Author of spiritual and religious songs.
†Johann Heinrich Pestalozzi (1746–1827). A famous representative in the field of theory and practice of education.

and with even greater admiration, for example, about the *Ancestress* p. 636, about *Sappho* p. 653, etc.*

One can still emphasize in Niebuhr's *Roman History* (1811–32) what he, prevented from writing more extensively, only briefly notes on p. 222, since the second edition can now be compared with earlier, more thorough evaluations. Solger states that for him most of the first centuries of Rome, especially the view of old poems from which Livy is supposed to have drawn, appears quite chimeric. Schlegel's review in the *Heidelberger Yearbooks*† is recognized on p. 222 as one that is seldom found and again renews the highest respect for Schlegel among all the impartial. "Virtually nothing is left standing of Niebuhr's hypotheses up to Romulus, and everything is refuted with very convincing reasons." Schlegel, from Romulus on, also gets into conjectures to which Solger could not subscribe, but not in imaginary saturnalian heroic poems, the invention of which, for him [Solger] belongs to the most incomprehensible aberrations. The reproach has been made to the philosophers in recent times of writing history à priori. Solger's philosophical sense could allow the specialized historians and the philologists this right just as little as the others.

Equally interesting are opinions about many events of the times, about conditions and their spirit. Solger's utterances, for example, about the Sandian murder and the related mind-set are remarkable enough.‡ Just to emphasize some of that now, he writes about it on p. 722ff.: "It makes me shudder whenever one gains insight into such a disposition as this Sandian one. He has certainly been raised as a well-disposed young person for whom one must feel pity. But now, the idiotic stupidity to want to save the fatherland through the murder of the old milk-sop! The cold, insolent arrogance to pass judgment upon the supposed evil one like a petty world judge! The vain hypocrisy with religion, or rather their fine phrases which are supposed to justify the greatest abominations! It is enough to drive one to despair whenever one thinks of it! Nonetheless, all of that is

---

*The Ancestress, Sappho: *Die Ahufran, Sappho*. Tragedies by Franz Grillparzer (1791–1872).

†*Heidelberger Yearbooks: Heidelberger Jahrbücher der Literatur*: A famous periodical of the time dealing with critical and philosophical topics.

‡K. L. Sand was murdered in 1819 by August von Kotzebue.

not in the least new to me. I know exactly where everything is coming from. For ten years one has preached to them sufficiently that they were the wise and splendid ones from whom the rebirth of the state and the church must proceed. Stupidity, futility, arrogance—these are the spirits which propel them, and those are true spirits of Hell."—p. 725 on the Sandian history. "It affords us a sad glimpse into the condition of so many young souls. Here is shown a mixture of original good-naturedness with a narrow-mindedness, stupidity, I would like to call it, an arrogance, an unconscious religious hypocrisy before oneself and others, that one shudders. Could you believe that there are professors here who admire the inane coquettish bombast which the young person has written to his own people? But one remembers only far too much the idle twaddle of the Wartburg speakers* and so much of that ilk. Yet, as I said, we don't want to blame anyone but the popular spirit of the times. For a long time already, everything has been assuming this ruinous tendency towards wanton world reform and inane arrogance, and many totally different doctrines have constantly promoted them. The unfortunate intellectual enlightenment which so many have under their skin, the malicious doctrine that the so-called better ones must be and do everything and that everyone who believes in nothing but inane world improvement is one of these better ones, is the proper school of inflated stupid arrogance. One should work against this with all one's powers and at least assuage one's conscience."

Regarding the Wartburg scenes, it says on p. 720: "In that very place several professors have held silly, childish speeches in order to propagate their shallow enthusiasm." One should have either forbidden or prevented this early enough or depicted these political-philosophical fools afterwards in such a way that they would have appeared in their complete nakedness. One might have perhaps been able to consider it as something salutary if Solger had taken over this depiction and countermanded that glaring mischief by making his views public. It was, however, probably right to grant him for the rest of his life that which was to last only six more months, to have spared him the anticipated virulent enmity because

---

*The Wartburg festival took place on October 18, 1817, in commemoration of the Reformation and the Leipzig Battle in which Napoléon was defeated. It was a manifestation of German nationalism.

of a servile disposition, etc., and to have kept peace for himself through public silence.

Yet we must set limits to the inventory of the interesting of which so much of a fresh, just as penetrating as cheerful view of art and life is still found in the letters of Solger and also in those of his friends, especially the one by the editor, von Raumer, in order to proceed on to the side which must chiefly claim our attention. The correspondence nevertheless contains fewer data and explanations about Solger's training and advances in philosophy than one would initially surmise. The circle of men who converse here in letters had not chosen one and the same scholarly vocation. Each pursues a specific major interest, indeed takes the interest of an educated man in the work of the other, but does not look into the objects and content further. One can therefore not expect the drama of the development of a philosophy, a reciprocal communication and discussion of philosophical propositions and concepts. The reciprocity is general encouragement or participation, and whenever Solger invites more detailed remarks and criticism about his published writings, it is always the same: one of his friends had not yet had the time to read the text, the other postpones a deeper investigation of the reading to be repeated and, in the time being, limits himself to the criticism of particularities, style, and such. The Tieck letters express a more direct relationship to philosophy. Solger's explications about that are, in contrast to this friend, the most frequent and detailed. He expresses the satisfaction he derives from communicating with Tieck repeatedly and sincerely. "How often (he says, p. 375) does it give me new fortitude and new strength that you recognize my endeavors when everything around me is silent about it. You come to my aid. Even if you are not a philosopher, you are nevertheless acquainted with the philosophies, and what is even more important, you live, through your own profession, in the subject of philosophy. Your approval and evaluation often keep me calm whenever dismay seeks to creep in with me." In these published letters, Tieck shows the public his kind of relationship to philosophy and the course of his disposition and mind. Such a disclosure of an important individual about himself is in itself an interesting portrait of a soul, and all the more, because it represents a type. Tieck's point of view towards philosophy is, in keeping with the times, certainly that negative attitude against it; yet affirmative insofar as it is at the same time linked to the recognition of the affirmative in philosophy on the whole as of that which is identical to the essence of religion and poetry, and to that extent, diverges from the usual understanding of the enlightenment and the theory of faith. But that negative relationship to philosophy simultaneously brings a one-sidedness into that very principle which considers and expresses itself as the mystification of religion and poetry because this principle has remained a product of reflection, not impartial disinterested religiosity and poetry. This mysticism constitutes only a further reflection of the point of view discussed earlier, and as it is the reflex of one part of Solger's philosophical point of view, the illumination of the Tieckian disclosure in its main features shall at the same time serve as an introduction for this.

"The course of all thoughts and ideas shall only confirm to me deep prejudices, i.e., but only with other words: faith and eternal love" (p. 341f.). We see in this the old doctrine which Socrates and Plato have initiated that whatever should be considered as true and good for the human being must reside originally in his mind, but it only becomes faith, in that it has, furthermore, also entered into his consciousness in a more obscurely or clearly felt or suspected manner and can also, to the degree that it is not based on insight, be called prejudice. Like mysticism, that doctrine annuls everything merely positive of external authority. In relation to the innermost genuine content, philosophy does nothing but confirm it as such, but what it simultaneously effects by that is the purification of the same and the segregation of the counterfeit, of the positive of another kind, which is in it as prejudice. In the same context Tieck says, however, that for him it had "never been a matter of thinking as such"; "the mere pleasure, practice and play of ideas, even of the most daring, is uninteresting to me." To obtain for faith the philosophical form, thinking cognition of the content too, naturally depends entirely upon individual need. But precisely this cognition leads to insight into the nature of thinking and shows that thinking produces something other than merely an exercise and play of ideas, and impedes, without simply denying cognition of the same. In the letter of March 24, 1817 (p. 535), Tieck gives a detailed narration, which he calls a confession, about the course of his intellectual direction. Before his acquaintance with Jacobi, with whom he was first able to maintain a dialogue ("from two shores over a chasm, where we probably heard more an echo than our words"), he had not found any dialogical philosophers, and the various systems did not satisfy him (the satisfaction is linked to that which one seeks, and Plato, e.g., was certainly also a dialogical philosopher). "All particularly offended my instinct for religion." So "the love of poetry, of the peculiar and old," led him "at first with almost sacrilegious frivolity" (wherein the sacrilegious is to have consisted, one does not see) "to the mystics, especially to J. Böhme, who had so taken possession of all my vital powers that from this point I sought only to understand Christianity, the most living word in the image of the struggling and self-revealing power of nature, and now all old and newer philosophy became for me merely historical manifestation" (the reverse happens to philosophical perception, for which mysticism and its formations become historical manifestations). "From out of my wonderland I read Fichte and Schelling and found them easy, not deep enough, and only as silhouettes or panes, as it were, out of that eternal globe full of wonder" (easy, because for the mystical requisite, it was only a matter of the general sense, the abstract idea, as stated above, not of thinking in itself; not deep enough, because in the form of thought and its development, the illusion of depth disappears before that of which thought is ignorant, for one usually finds a content deep only in the state of its concentration and often, as it mostly occurs with J. Böhme, of a fantastic confusion and severity, but fails to recognize the depth in its development). With Böhme, Tieck was carried away by the "magic of the most marvelous reverie and the liveliest fantasy." The equally enormous defectiveness in this mysticism becomes obvious, to be sure, only to the requisite of thought. Elsewhere (p. 392), and indeed outside of and following the ebbing away of that condition, the notion of a connection between reason and understanding also occurs with the elevation of the soul. It is said right there, "to elevate oneself up to the illumination of an enthusiastic soul, and here again to come across reason and understanding too, in the spheres of a highly complex interconnection and the harmonious union of all powers, is granted to only a few, to give information and an account of it, to the fewest—until now, it seems, to no one."—If Tieck was not satisfied there in this direction by Franz Baader, Hamann, St. Martin, etc., what would, for example, prevent one from finding with Plato, not to mention others, the desired union of the enthusiastic soul and the reason and understanding that give information and account of it? Obviously, only the ignorance of and unfamiliarity with finding its way in the manner whereby thinking reason depicts the genuine capacity of enthusiasm so as to recognize that capacity in it again—or the mistaken demand for also seeing, along with the philosophical mode of cognition, the incompatible melancholy leavening and phantasmagorism of mysticism. If one is familiar with the nature and manner of thinking, however, then one knows that philosophy only gets its due if one maintains that at least from Plato on—not perhaps none, nor the fewest, but rather the greatest number of philosophies gave information and account with reason and understanding about that genuine capacity, its interlacing within itself and its coherence, and those for whom the mind has made its home in philosophy have possessed this information and account.

Out of that hypochondriacal method Tieck (p. 539) adds that he had "often foolishly tried to give others that feeling of mysticism." What he adds—no one was as steeped in Böhme, yes, he suspects, not even in the philosophers—is probably not the correct reason that he did not succeed, for J. Böhme succeeded in communicating this to Tieck himself; but rather this, that aside from the organ of philosophy, which he misunderstood and scorned, the innate capacity for communication through which he was probably before and after able to communicate feelings of depth did not at that time stand at his disposal. For he indicates about this state of the soul that for him the joy in poetry, in images, had appeared to him as something objectionable, wrong. He adds to this portrait that since he now believes to have found speculation and the inner life, he considered that it was not compatible with worldly pursuits, so there were many hours in which he longed for the seclusion of a monastery to be able to live entirely for his Böhme and Tauler and the wonders of his soul. "My power of production, my poetic talent seemed to me to be shattered forever." These interesting features lead themselves to the observation that in reality, with such a hypochondria, with this state of nonanimation and lack of form and shape of the mind, even if they are already called inner life, marvels of the soul, speculation can be connected just as little as poetic production.

But Tieck emerges again from this state. It is interesting to read what healed him. Just what "frivolity" and "arbitrary act" is supposed to mean in this depiction cannot easily be understood. It was (p. 540) "my old Homer and the Nibelungs and Sophocles" (Homer and Sophocles could certainly be amazed to find the Nibelungs between them) "my dear Shakespeare, a sickness, Italy, a super-saturation of the mystics, probably especially my stirring talent, which in my desperation gave me new frivolity. And almost as frivolously as I had slipped into this field, I again transferred myself, through an act of free will, out and now again stood on the field of poetry and serenity and could again work." This reverted capability for work is probably the most genuine evidence of regained health of the mind out of that unfruitful abstraction of inwardness, for work-ing means to renounce this abstraction and to give what inwardness would have had in content, reality and truth. But in his manner of judgment, Tieck did not fully absorb the significance of his return to work. That split remains in his views, and with that, the one-sided and abstract subjectivity remains yet a more genuine, yes, a higher point of view. For example, to be able to locate the essence of Shakespeare's greatness or poetry in general in its mysticism, about which there is so much talk, it is necessary rather to abstract what makes a poet from the concrete determination and accomplishment of the characters and plots developed. To volatilize the concrete and solidity of his shaping into the abstraction of the mystical and interior is the working of a reflecting mind, not that of criticism promoting and discerning the idea and animation. With inner life as the principle of criticism, with such a view, it is still the same case as before in the state of the subject, that as abstraction is fixed against the developing activity of thought, so it is against the shaping activity of poetry.

Thus even the entire manner of how Tieck's insight into and comprehension of Goethe's poetic nature and production are con-stituted depends upon this point of view. We should mention it here, insofar as it throws a new light on that point of view even from its own perspective, and in that Tieck extracted this relationship from the intimate communication initially intended only for a friend and displayed for the public, the remarks at the same time reveal them-selves not as a momentary mood, but as a permanent judgment. He comes to speak of Goethe frequently, and indeed with ill humor, just to use this word right away, because his evaluation proceeds from this and also towards this. It was cited above from Solger's criticism about *Genoveva* that the intentionality and reflection, the merely longing and not truly present mood of love and inwardness in the poet, had struck him, so that as Tieck correctly expresses it, what Tieck had considered as enthusiasm appeared to Solger as ill humor. Aside from the fact that Tieck otherwise takes offense at Goethe (among other instances, 488, he is annoyed that Goethe did not even once read *Erwin*),* he thinks on p. 485 an author may himself later choose to call what he had earlier called enthusiasm, ill humor. So it appears to him how Goethe did it with his *Werther*,† and p. 487 he asks indignantly: "May he, because his overflowing young spirit first showed us what this world of appearances around us is which until him was uncomprehended—may he, just because he proclaims it, turn away from it with a kind of genteel demeanor and be impious and ungrateful towards himself and towards the most beautiful?" Goethe analyzes in his life just as interestingly as charmingly, how he, ill with his certainly not yet metaphysical, but rather sentimental hypochondria, with a still high-spirited and vital longing not yet entangled in abstraction, but in life, worked himself out of that ill humor and freed himself from it precisely through the production of that novel. Just as with an illness the core of life must still be healthy in order to recover from it, so were heart and head still healthy, and their power became poetry that was able to change the ill-humored feeling into the matter and the object and elaborate it out into an external efflorescence. In that the ill humor now became the content of the work, it ceased to be the mood of the poet. He finished up with himself through the work just as the work itself became something finished in itself, a work of art. But with that alone he had not yet finished with the dear public. He describes the agony he attracted from all sides that pursued him in all places and incessantly. It was that one constantly expected that morbidity of spirit from him, even readily wanted to love and prize it in him. And even now, following what became clear from all his works anyway, right from the next, his *Götz*‡ and after he had even described that crisis and the cure effected by the production, he has to see the reproach made that the sick understanding of the world of appearances was

---

Erwin: Four Conversations about the Beautiful and Art (1815). Main work by Solger.

†*Die Leiden des jungen Werther:* A novel by Goethe.

‡*Götz von Berlichingen:* A drama by Goethe.

the correct understanding and that he had turned away from such a point of view and thereby become "impious and ungrateful towards himself." From the reproach of this impiety and ungratefulness, there follows quite naturally the additional whim, the reproach that "this magnificent soul had thrown itself one-sidedly into antiquity essentially out of ill humor," that Goethe "thereby tears himself away from the fatherland." It would be difficult to say if a poet were more deeply rooted in his fatherland than Goethe. But if others rank the foreign and the older, Shakespeare, Calderon, etc., just as high or higher than the national, then one can hardly fault him for that, even if not all indigenous art, the poetry of poetry, among others, does not agree with him and he finds a higher satisfaction in un-troubled antiquity. Moreover, it is not a matter of contrasting subjec-tive feelings, but about aesthetic insights based on meaning, study, and reflection. Completely unfortunate is the opposition on the following p. 488: "I (Tieck) had also seen antiquity, St. Peter, and could only admire the Straßburg cathedral all the more." Was Goethe then not one of the first to have had a sense for the Straßburg cathedral and had again, as it were, discovered a sense for its evaluation and insight?

In mentioning the manner of depiction of the Hindu religion through Friedrich von Schlegel (p. 709), Solger says quite rightly: "It is a main point to abandon all transmitted terminology of emana-tion, pantheism, dualism etc. No people or a person has ever seri-ously harbored the one-sided and empty concepts which these expressions designate, and they derive from times when one cruelly anatomized the living insight." Thus it would have brought both friends greater success if the expressions of mysticism, inner life, poetry, particularly irony—yes, even religion and philosophy—had themselves remained out of the picture because then one would have had to speak about the matter and about the content. This manner of evaluating is a decidedly negative tendency against objectivity, one of those tendencies that has proceeded from the Fichtean philosophy of subjectivity. Such evaluating does not deal with content, but rather revolves around faded notions that dispose of the matter of religions and philosophies with abstractions of inner life, mysticism, with reflective designations about identity, dualism, pantheism, etc. This style appears at the same time both as a refined disposition that takes care of the matter and stands above it. It is indeed finished with the matter in that sense that it has removed it. It is a step above it because it is indeed outside of this.

The self-conscious frustration of the objective has called itself irony. Since the most excellent ironical individuality is to be found on our path, let us briefly mention this. In the connection cited, Solger notes, first of all, quite appropriately about one part of the elaborators of the Indian religion: "They have drawn out the thread, to which I can fasten everything, completely one-sidedly theoretically and dogmatically extracted, so that it is no longer what it was as a living band, and this especially Friedrich Schlegel has done." Throughout his entire public career, the father of irony has given himself the same relation noted here to philosophy. He has, namely, always behaved judgmentally towards it without ever articulating content, philosophical sentences, or even a developed sequence of them, not to speak of having proven or even refuted the like. Refuting requires the assertion of a basis, and with this an engagement in the matter. This would mean, however, condescending from the genteel position or (to use one of his earlier inventions of categories) from the divine insolence and from the heights of irony (one can just as easily say: from the satanical or diabolical insolence of evaluating and disputing, from the position above the matter to condescending to the ground of philosophizing itself and to the matter). Mr. Friedrich von Schlegel has constantly pointed out that he stood on the highest peak of philosophy without ever proving that he has penetrated this science and understood it in a merely ordinary fashion. His discernment and reading have certainly acquainted him with problems that philosophy has in common with religion and that even get in the way of philological criticism and literary history. But the kind of solution he intimates everywhere and only ostentatiously gives one to understand instead of simply stating it or indeed justifying it philosophically, is partly a subjective solution, which may convenience him as an individual this way or that, but partly demonstrates the entire demeanor of his remarks, that the requisite of thinking reason, and with that, the basic problem of that and a science of philosophy conscious and honest towards itself has remained foreign to him.

Tieck's irony remains free of charlatanry in its relationship to philosophy and on the whole limits itself to setting aside the objective formation of content through thinking, that is, of the characteristic of philosophy to deduce the abstract universal, that called mystical, and in relation to Solger's philosophy, to have a sincere interest and occasionally acknowledge its content, usually to formulate the response to the explicated Solgerian depictions and explanations with a general agreement enclosing the same with the often-repeated good-natured assurance of understanding Solger, of understanding him completely, of having finally understood him. In the year 1814 (p. 322) he had written that after reading a few dialogues of *Erwin,* he only now believed that he understood Solger fully, just as on p. 320 Solger expresses his satisfaction that in an oral conversation Tieck admitted to him that the drive of enthusiasm for which he had strived in art had only been brought to full consciousness for him through Solger's revelation which will also be repeated elsewhere. Thus Tieck writes still in the same manner in the year 1819 (p. 711) in response to the announcement of philosophical letters which can be found published for the first time in the second volume of this posthumous work: "I believe that I understand you more with every word, and it becomes ever more clear to me that it is this which I have sought."

Second Article

What ultimately has been presented in the foregoing article as a reference to the philosophy of Solger may indeed be taken for a reflex of the same in Tieck's friendship. It illuminates, however, in and of itself, that the manner of this reflex can only have significance for one side, that of Solger's ideas. For the content we must now turn to Solger's expositions that are offered to us in the collection at hand. These expositions are of such a kind that they provide a much more definitive representation of Solger's basic views than the writings that appeared during his lifetime. In these posthumous writings we see him frequently striving to make his ideas press forward, partly for his friends, partly for his public, in several essays he worked out for an edition in the last year of his life. Nevertheless, these are not systematic expositions, but intended only for the preparation of the public and for the prospectus as a "manifesto," as Solger calls the main essay (I, 688ff., 726), in order to explain there for the larger public too what he takes philosophy to mean and how he stands opposed to present endeavors. They go so far with this ulterior purpose, however, in order to make the profundity of his idea and his speculative capacity in philosophy clear and to authenticate it. With Solger it is not a matter of what is usually otherwise also termed philosophy. With him we find rather the speculative requisite of reason active, not to put aside with complaint and meekness the interest and consciousness of the highest oppositions and contradictions that arise, like courage, but to look them straight in the eye in their entire definitiveness and severity, and in their disintegration to seek and gain only the satisfaction of the mind. Solger does not shy away from the obvious forms that lend themselves to expressing the reconciliation of oppositions, which is then the case when these oppositions are left alone in a concrete manner as they exist in representation and are not reduced to their simple thought determination.

I shall first cite the familiar form in which he expresses the idea, in the letters as well as frequently in the others essays (I, 603), namely, that when we have grasped our absolute and eternal relationship to God, we "clearly and without any vacillation recognize that everything which is true and good in our doings and life can only be God himself. In that God now exists or reveals himself in our finiteness, He sacrifices Himself up and destroys Himself in us because we are nothing." The following additional determinations should be cited here. In the context (I, 511) that not our own essential being constitutes our truth, it is stated: "We are for this reason insignificant manifestations because God has assumed existence in us ourselves and has thereby separated Himself from Himself. And is this not the highest love that He has placed himself into nothingness, so that we might exist, and that He even sacrificed Himself and annihilates His nothingness, has killed His death, so that we do not remain a mere nothing but return to Him and may exist in Him?" Then further: "The nothingness in us is itself the divine, inasmuch as we perceive it as nothingness and us ourselves as such." I notice, first of all in general, that the logical concept, which constitutes the foundation for all speculative knowing, is found in this idea, the "sole genuine affirmation, namely" (it is the eternal divine activity which is represented) comprised as the negation of negation. Furthermore, one sees this abstract form in its most concrete shape taken in its highest reality, namely, as the revealing of God, and indeed, this not in the formal superficial sense that God reveals Himself in nature, history, in the fate of the individual human being, etc., but in the absolute sense that the unity of the divine and human nature existing in Christ as primordial and divine is brought to consciousness for the human being, and precisely with that, what the nature of God and what the human in truth is, together with the further developing inferences. In connection with the initially cited, this is certainly expressed thus on p. 603ff. (as elsewhere p. 511): "So" (in that God exists in our finiteness and sacrifices Himself) "our entire relationship to Him is continuously the same which is established for us in Christ as a type. We should not only remember it, not therefore merely derive reasons for our behavior, but we should experience and realize this event of the divine self-sacrifice in us, what takes place in each and every one of us that has happened for the whole human race in Christ. It is not merely a reflex of our thoughts, what we have of it, but the most real reality" (cf. p. 632). One sees that this doctrine of Christianity (including the Trinity, which according to its basic definition is contained in what is cited), having been set aside by the theology in the Protestant church reigning almost exclusively through exegesis and reasoning, having reduced the manifestation of Christ to a mere object of remembrance and moral foundations and exiled God into an intrinsically indefinite void hereafter as an unknowable and thus unrevealed being outside of reality, found its refuge in speculative philosophy. It illuminates, however, that when the negation of negation as genuine affirmation (which is the entire abstract concept) receives the completely concrete shape contained in the cited expressions, which it has in the doctrine of Christianity, a detailed scientific explication is required to show the transition from that abstraction to this abundance of content, to gain a concrete shape for the idea of reason just as much as to vindicate the Christian doctrine again for the thinking mind and restore it again to its rights against the void of that so-called reason and the pietistic piety which formed a common cause.

In that transition which, philosophically carried out, will be a long pathway, many difficulties and contradictions result to be resolved. Already in the lecture cited such things become manifest. One time, we are postulated in it as nothingness (which is the evil), then again, the harsh, abstract expression about God is used that He annihilates Himself, that He is thus the one who postulates Himself as nothingness, and this furthermore, so that we may exist, and thereupon the nullity in us ourselves is called the divine, insofar as we, namely, perceive it as nullity. This opposition of determinations, that we are originally nothing and arrive at existence only in relationship to God, and again, that only through this connection do we become nothing, would have required an additional exposition to be balanced out. The asserted, which can be seen as the process of eternal love, furthermore already immediately contains the presupposition of God, on the one hand, and of us, on the other, and the difficulty is the same whether we are presupposed as existences or as nothingness. With this, the moment of creation in general and of the human being in God's image specifically is missing, and from there, that of the transition from this merely primordial, merely abstractly existent, not yet fully existing unity of human nature with the divine to what is expressed as appearance and nothingness. Appearance determines itself towards the more concrete, which is consciousness and freedom, and the difficulty is that this appearance contains not only the wellspring of evil, that eating of the tree of knowledge of good and evil falling away from being in God's image, but also the principle of the return to the image, so that God Himself is introduced saying: Look, Adam has become like us and knows what good and evil is (Gen. 3: 22)—the passage which constitutes the other side of the earlier meaning of knowing and is usually regarded far too little in its depth, or hardly even noticed.

The lack of that presupposition noted here does not disappear in the following depiction which occurs in vol. 1, p. 703: The true and eternal: "exists simply as that which is, as God, as the good. For us creatures thrown into reality, both" (the true and the appearance) "are inseparable.* For the good would not exist for us if it did not have an appearance it kills, for which sake it embodies itself, becomes flesh, because it must annihilate it according to its eternal

---

*This exposition is made in a context in which Solger speaks of contemporary philosophy and as it might appear according to the initial letter H., perhaps of a reviewer. There the view is mentioned in which higher speculative thinking in its lawfulness and generality was explained as the only real, and everything else, even the knowledge of experience, insofar as it cannot be referred back to these laws, as a disappointing and in every respect void futile splintering of this. Without analyzing to what degree this depiction contains distortions, I wish to note only what Solger opposes as his opinion. This is that false perceiving and its object both exist, but both exist too much. It immediately makes clear that this determination would already not be opposed to the above, where it is not a matter of a denial of existence by the knowledge of experience, which can hardly have occurred to anyone, but only of the possibility of reducing this to the concept and testing it against it. If, however, in the sequel to the above-mentioned, what is called false perception here is expressed more abstractly than the moment of appearance essential for the revelation of the good itself, as that which the destruction of nothingness is, then this concept has already been mentioned before, and the superficial view of each of my writings, already in the *Phenomenology of the Mind*, which appeared in the year 1807, even more in my *Logic*, which appeared in the year 1811ff., would demonstrate that all forms, be they taken as forms of existence or of thought, disintegrate in the same concept, which has not only long been explained there as the center of everything, but proven as well. In this most abstract speculative apex, no difference opposed to the philosophy cited would therefore result. But the development of this concept and the necessity for it is yet another matter, and that Solger did not see his way clear about insight into this lies in what has already been cited from his ideas and will reveal itself even more in what is to follow.—*Hegel's note*

good nature and thus reconcile existence with itself. The higher mode of existing is to reveal oneself, and to reveal oneself means to annihilate one's nothingness, i.e., to exist through oneself; both are completely the same."

It might appear that the process of creation is also contained in what has been said, but the same is only mixed, at least more with the process of reconciliation in which finite existence appears presupposed. It means that the inseparability of the good and the appearance or negation is only for us, just as much as that the eternal nature of the good creates its own appearance for itself in order to annihilate it, and that it thus exists only through itself, whereby this inseparability, this existing only relatively for us, would be taken away. But everywhere it remains a significant, insoluble basic determination, as p. 579, that since we are not capable of thinking and knowing other than in oppositions, "within us contradictory beings the completely void appearance, the true positive nothingness must stand in opposition to the reality or the revelation of the eternal." It is Solger's expressed determination of philosophy not to be caught up in a dualism (e.g., I, p. 510). Because indeed, every drive for truth is already this, to tear oneself away from the dualism of our consciousness, our appearance, or Manichaeanism, because all dualism has Manichaeanism as its basis. The ending in higher reality and in reconciliation must, however, complete itself into that direction, not begin with the presupposition of a dualism.

This, then, is essentially linked to the fact that in the cited expositions even the representation of God as a presupposition is present. If as in the above ideas it is assumed as known what God is, how He is that, then one could not at all imagine what philosophizing were still for, because philosophy can have no ultimate purpose other than to perceive God. Were that acquaintance not satisfactory, however, and were more than mere acquaintance required, namely, knowledge, then this means that the justification is not there of itself to say of God He does this or that, embodies Himself, etc. Because all such determinations could only attain their foundation through the knowledge of its nature, that manner of expressing oneself has, first of all, the advantage of being popular and laying claim to general religiosity, even with being able to come forward with a certain confidence because of the imposing effect which the word *God* has. But in philosophical respect, this manner has disadvantages, particularly this, that the link between that which is attributed to God, to his nature, i.e., the insight into the necessity of that determination or actions, does not reveal itself, indeed not even the demand of this necessity about which it can only be a matter of going beyond believing to philosophizing. Just as disadvantageous as for philosphizing itself as for the discourse and understanding is that admixture of such concrete representations as God, sacrificing oneself, we human beings, knowing, evil, etc., with the abstractions of being, nothingness, appearance, and the like. One is uncomfortably thrown back and forth from one of these heterogeneous grounds to the other. The feeling of the unsuitability of the abstract forms of thought to the abundance that lies in the representations is in itself disturbing, even if one does not possess the closer insight into the unrelated which brings that admixture into the thought process.

In the first treatise of the second volume—*Letters Concerning the Misconceptions about Philosophy and Their Relationship to Religion* (p. 1–53), and in the second, *On the True Meaning and Determination of Philosophy, Especially in Our Time* (p. 54–199)—the additional main interest is to determine the relationship of the basic idea indicated to philosophical cognition and to uncover and pursue the errors of cognition and the false surrogates. First of all, one should select out from this the determination also expressed everywhere else by Solger that philosophy and religion have the same content, that philosophy is nothing but thinking about the presence of being in our knowledge and existence or, in other words, about divine revelation (II, 116), that thinking which is philosophizing is entirely the same as knowledge through revelation, just observed from another side (p. 174).

Philosophy has previously been given a bad reputation about its relationship to religion. After reason had indeed been opposed to what was once called religion, the reconciliation of both is finally achieved in such a way that so-called reason was drawn over by theology to its side, and through it, the religious content was made ever more thin and empty. This empty conviction, which continually assumes the name of Christianity, presumes the shriveling up of the objective content into the subjective, into feeling, and henceforth declares itself against philosophy for the entirely opposite reason, as opposed to the earlier one, for this reason, namely, that the fundamental doctrines of Christianity with which the new theology believes to have just finished up, rather find their defense in philosophy and that from there, the maintenance or reawakening of this threatens this Christianity of feeling, the death of which it believes to be already able to enjoy in peace. Among the plans with which Solger dealt, he also mentions I, 349 the development of how Christianity can be understood and brought to insight from purely speculative reasons.

In general, this essential definition is given for philosophical cognition: "The idea is the positive content of higher knowledge, the true unity of the materials merely related to one another through reason ([I], p. 92f.). The organ of philosophy is thinking. It originates from this, that the essence and the inner unity of our knowledge is activity, that activity involves a transition from one to the other and accordingly, an opposition, but the cognition of the opposites in their relationship to each other and their suspension into the original unity wherein they simultaneously become opposites of the same thing (of thinking) with themselves, is thinking." The progression of thinking is mentioned there and its one-sidednesses made evident. Solger has not continued on to the higher task, however, this progression for itself, that is, to comprehend the inner necessity in cognition, to the actual nature of the dialectic.

On the other hand, he expresses his opinion about the necessity of philosophical cognition emanating from reflection with definite insight and emphatically: "Our entire life is divine revelation, every satisfaction through the true, every pleasure in beauty, every reassurance in the good, comes to us from this essential, insofar as it is present for us in the given moment. But the same is always only the essential of the given condition, of the relative linkage for the specific moment, and thus itself falls among the relationships of existence. Pure consciousness cannot reassure itself with these relative forms. It is through philosophy, which faith itself is, but comprehended in its form as insight whenever it occurred in the other as experience, that the idea becomes known how it is in all moments of its revelation the same, how it is capable of joining itself to existence and absorbing it in itself through the oppositions that it contains as complete unity in itself." So the idea comes to consciousness only in its entire significance, since it is otherwise always clouded by special conditions and relationships. That consciousness cannot find itself satisfied in these, therein lies the necessity that it be driven to philosophy. Philosophizing is therefore by no means an arbitrary undertaking, but a necessary and inevitable one. Whoever does not want to decide to philosophize must nevertheless try his luck at it and will now be driven to be satisfied with an unfortunate substitute and thereby degrade faith itself (II, 116ff.). "The human being must philosophize whether he wants to or not" (it is expressed II, 112), "and if he doesn't decide to do it in the correct scientific manner, then philosophy will take revenge upon him through the most groundless and pernicious sophistries." Solger is well familiar with the false surrogates for philosophy, with the shirkings and evasions of finding satisfaction with economizing of thinking. He develops these errors and attacks them behind all the multifarious formations that they assume with warmth and with thorough insight. The pious (it says II, 37) who want to maintain only the essential and simple in religion about which one need not think, should probably beware of what this essential is; faith without insight loses itself in external facts, miracles, and superstition. Solger points out the one-sidednesses of ordinary understanding and the orthodoxy and pietism no less caught up in the same things (II, 37ff.). He shows the desolation into which this understanding has deteriorated as enlightening, out of which again another illusory philosophy has emerged, the kingdom of opinions (p. 58), which is especially well characterized as a thinking that models itself according to every form of experience, according to every drifting of time [that] has invented theories, especially in history, for the moment and for every special purpose, in that it still always needs the recollection of the essential. No one believes it, and everyone plays the hypocrite before himself and others. As with this superficiality of consciousness with which they circumvent truth, so can one find on p. 192 serious pictures of a fantasizing playing around about the depths of the human soul and about other charlatanries elsewhere drawn from profound experience and sketched with a secure hand. These sophistries maintain the rapturous approval of the masses because they are easy to comprehend and make the effort of thinking unnecessary, even impossible.

The Series of Letters mentioned engages further in the uncovering and combating of the misconceptions about philosophy and its relationship to religion. As much as they contain important and instructive things, so do such corrections nevertheless tend not to have as much of an impact as one would stand to expect from their content. One has in general become weary of the philosophers' explanation that one has misunderstood them. The intelligibility in the discourse of abstract ideas on the one hand, and the capacity to reflect upon philosophical thoughts, on the other, are conditions about which it would at least require a great deal to come to a clear understanding. Yet there is a kind of misunderstanding from which it can be directly demanded that it not occur, namely, the inaccuracies in what is the factual. If it leads to nothing or indeed only to greater confusion to polemicize against other kinds of misconceptions, then philosophy can at least justifiably complain about the false statements of facts, and if one looks more closely, this kind is, contrary to expectation, the most common and extends in part to the unbelievable.

The chief interest of the second treatise is to demonstrate partly that relationship which takes place in the relative manner of cognition, that, namely, the eternal is merely a presupposition, with this, however, merely an abstract universal, so that the original identity could become a mere form of unity and linkage, not the divine fact itself, but partly the true relationship of this divine fact to cognition. According to the aforementioned, this fact is that God is real and present in our existence, creates Himself in us to existence within us, and we must experience and recognize this existence of the same in us. The true relationship of this fact to cognition should be this: in that thinking concludes itself in its progress, the idea itself as the eternal act of unity comes forward freely in the points of juncture to which it brings and thereby suspends its oppositions and relative determinations and restores itself again as a present entity, so should the presence of God be experienced immediately within us ourselves.

But because it is not the intention of the author in the above-mentioned purpose of "a manifesto" to prove the fundamental ideas, but only to exponentiate them with the polemical consideration of imperfect ways of knowing, the advantage then arises for the essay of giving more a series of repetitive assertions and assurances than a development of reasons that could generate a persuasion. Neither with thinking itself is the necessity that it relinquish its reflection, that it proceed to the relinquishing of its oppositions and to their union shown, and even less the necessity of the transition from a conceived unity to a so-called divine fact and the actual experience of this. It was still too much the author's concern to make his point of view impressive and to secure it against errors for it to have been able to be a concern for his philosophical formation to take the direction towards the interior and reach the logical development of these thoughts and thereby come to a clear understanding for himself and his readers without concern for those external considerations. It is therefore not surprising that the exposition of such deep thoughts still offers unclarified difficulties and contradictions of determinations that make the understanding much more difficult than that the nonmethodical manner of discourse could alleviate it. The two determinations, the relationship of which is completely at stake, are, as cited, the development of thinking and the eternal itself. The nature of knowing is (p. 141) contained in the important determination that it is the conclusion and perfection of thinking, and indeed thus, that this perfection never be possible through thinking alone, but that at the same time it require that the substances of thinking in their oppositions be intrinsically one, so there may be linked simultaneously with each and every such conclusion (actually in that thinking brings back those oppositions to their first intrinsically existing unity) an observation or experience of this essential unity of the substance, and there arise complete knowledge only from both sides of cognition. One sees, first of all, that thinking is distinguished from its perfection. In consideration of those who present it as self-deception, presumption, rapture and such, of wanting to know divine things, or who even say (p. 141ff.) that the human being may probably once again come so far, but we have not yet reached that point, the relationship of the existence of the eternal and of knowledge will be maintained in such a way that "in full consciousness the eternal being makes itself into substance, establishes itself as its ground, and exists prior to its externalization and revelation." The manner in which we know this, its existing beforehand, is what is called faith, the absolutely certain direct knowledge itself upon which, for us, absolutely everything rests. What is now there for us through faith, revelation, and its branching out into the oppositions of existence, we can and should in truth know.

This presence, reality of the true, the impossibility of knowing and doing anything without this foundation and presupposition, is the one fundamental point. It can be seen as an insignificant discrepancy that in the last lecture the immediacy of the eternal in consciousness is distinguished from knowing, in the first, however, only from thinking, which is taken with that merely as one of both moments of knowing, as this was determined there. The other fundamental point, however, outside of the relationship of the foundation and presupposition, is the separating of what is called the experience of the eternal from this knowing or self-concluding thinking. The lecture remains in this assertion with the categories of reality, fact, faith, experience, on the one hand, and of thinking on the other, and with the assertion of its essential maintenance of separation, without analyzing these categories further. The eagerness to make the assertion emphatic hinders looking back upon itself. Most, however, indeed all controversies and contradictions must allow themselves to be harmonized through the apparently simple means of taking up only what expresses itself in asserting, simply to observe and compare it to the additional that one likewise asserts. To know what one says is much rarer than one thinks, and it is with the greatest injustice that the accusation of not knowing what one says is considered the harshest. With this, let us now look at Solger's assertion carefully.

First of all, the correct and important determination of philosophical knowing is always presented that it is the thinking of the eternal, insofar as the eternal is contained in the oppositions of its revelation as one and the same (p. 124). It is repeatedly recognized as the true manner of knowing that philosophical thinking dissects the inner unity of knowledge as its substance, but that is just that kind of dissection "through which it engenders itself again as true, essential, and present substance in every true point of linkage" (p. 149 and everywhere). Is not, I ask, just in this determination of the presence and reality of the eternal, the divine of the original unity itself unmistakably accepted and recognized? Is the fact of the eternal and the animation and the experience of the fact not assumed as existent in this, that the dissection of the inner unity through thinking is such that this unity remains simultaneously present in that as something undissected, as substance, as one and the same in thinking? What is used from the eternal as fact, presence, or whatever popular representations are otherwise used, or should be especially attributed for a differentiation, cannot be foreseen, all the less, since Solger just as often sufficiently contradicts the position through which the original unity would turn into a mere generality, to an intrinsically indefinite and abstract. It is the constant assertion that the original unity reveal itself, that it, activity, is in itself a transition from one to the other, the dissection in itself, and therefore contains within itself an opposition (see above), that through this alone the eternal joins itself to existence, is present in it, etc. What should be attributed to that faith, the experiencing of the eternal prior to the unity where philosophical knowing should indeed continue itself outside of itself for its suspension, in and to what it essentially moves and continues itself within itself according to the above, can, according to the matter, no longer be something characteristic and different. For that, there remains nothing but the empty form of immediacy that should be attributed to what is called fact, experience, faith, in popular representation (in the popular imagination) exclusively against cognition as that which is caught up only in mediations. Solger is not caught up in this last bad notion, however. For him, philosophical knowing is itself expressly the suspension of the opposites, and with that, what exists only through another, and just as much the suspension of the merely relative perceiving that does not go beyond the standpoint of mediation. The immediacy is itself only the determination of an opposition, the one side of the same. True thinking, like suspending oppositions in general, does not permit determination to remain outside of itself, by itself. In that it grasps the opposites in their original unity, as mentioned, so it has equally well in this unity the reference to itself, which is immediacy, in fact, immanent within itself. This exposition is to have made it clear that it, as has been said, only requires the simple reflection upon that which Solger asserts as the essential nature of philosophical thinking in order to find expressed therein even that which he wants to distinguish from it.

When it is now said further, in the sense of the assumed disparity of the determinations cited on p. 125 "that there is an experience of revelation, i.e., a divine existence that creates as well as annuls existence and a philosophy in justaposition that only follows as a consequence of our not ourselves being the eternal; in this both are the same for us in an inconceivable manner," so according to the content, there is nothing to contradict that a deficiency is expressed about philosophy in which the acknowledgment lies that "we are not the eternal." Yet if such things are said, then there is a distortion there, as if this were not everywhere self-evident. Otherwise it would be superfluous to say such things. If in the cognition of revelation the experiencing of revelation is itself also contained, then for that reason it would be a far cry from "our being the eternal," even according to Solger's own determination that the revealing of the eternal and the experiencing of revelation are a particular existence.

As far as incomprehensibility is concerned, however, this is also one of the many words used indiscriminately without any concept. To be sure, it is present in that the experiencing of a divine existence is always transferred to outside of knowing. As is shown, this contains in it even what is supposed to be something distinct from it. Comprehensibility and true comprehending, however, are nothing other than just the stated reflection that in the thinking of the eternal as one and the same in the oppositions, even the unity of the experiencing and knowing is contained, even expressed. One could surmise that the assertion of incomprehensibility is revoked by the manner in which thinking is comprised. It is determined there that it must represent the essential and nothingness at the same time, which would only be possible if it behaved indifferently towards both or thought them in their relationship of transition. This indifference would not be that of mere form, such as that which can attach itself to infinitely different substances, but would lie in the complete unity of the substances with one another, and through such a thinking the entire substance would become directly determined, so that this thinking, which is philosophizing, would be the same as knowledge through revealing. One sees that here the grasping of just such a unity, which earlier was called the incomprehensible, is attributed to thinking. The determinations of our consciousness given in the immediately preceding determinations lead to the same thing if they are analyzed more closely. Consciousness consists precisely in that something contrary to itself attaches itself through its knowing to itself. Since consciousness is certainly not to be taken for a complete flowing over of nature and the mind into each other talked about there, but binds itself to itself expressly through its knowing, that is how it comes to the unity in it which converges with experiencing.

The inconsistency in the observation of this highest point of view obviously derives, as earlier, from this, that what comprehending, thinking, knowing is, is presupposed only in a vague manner, that these notions have not themselves been analyzed and recognized. The same can be noticed about another expression, of "being in and of itself." In this connection, on p. 171 and p. 172 where the most profound expositions are to be found, there is mention of the eternal in and of itself, of existence in and of itself. It is immediately apparent that this in and of itself is nothing other than the abstract, untrue; the eternal is of itself unattainable for our knowledge. In that the same is grasped as revealing itself, as activity, then there remains left for that eternal without attainability for knowing, i.e., without revealing and activity, nothing concrete, but only the determination of an abstraction. Similarly, in that existence in and of itself is only determined as that which being is not, the nothingness of being, so it is said itself with this that only the abstract, appearing nothingness is designated by that in-and-of-itself, existence taken merely alone, without the link to that in which its in-and-of-itself first consists. I do not want to go into that any further, that first the eternal appears as the underlying fact which is revealed, and then revelation itself as this fact. Only the analysis of what is fact would be capable of truly determining its relationship to revealing as to being and to comprehensibility. If, moreover, with respect to knowability, it should be a matter of avoiding not only immodesty, but also the appearance of that, then it would probably have been advantageous, in this as in philosophical respect, to leave out the expressions of God's existence in us, the existence of God as penetrating our entire presence, etc. To bring God into immediate connection with the finite carries too large an incongruity with it as not to be striking. But whether God "brings Himself to existence" in us at all or also in our knowing, can, with respect to modesty, make no difference. That in those immediate connections with the finite, God is taken not in His abundance, but in a more abstract understanding, announces itself through another disadvantage, that instead of God, also the expressions "the eternal," "the true," "being," or "essential unity" are used alternately. With God, however, we understand still more than merely the eternal, the true, being, etc.

The reviewer believed to have had to reproduce the comments about the use of undeveloped categories because this usage is of itself present in popular depictions where it has its disadvantages or not, according to whether a healthy sense and mind delivers the content, is predominant and maintains the upper hand above the categories of reflection. But it is another matter if the depiction is to be philosophical and with this, depends on determinations of thought. Even the expositions of as thorough a thinker as Solger have not escaped the seduction of making presuppositions of notions and not analyzing the final categories at stake and with that, the disadvantages resulting from that. Moreover, with other philosophizing writers, the basic wrong, especially of presupposing as known the categories upon which the validity of everything depends, like immediacy, thinking, knowing, understanding, comprehensibility, etc., is completely predominant. Against this manner, there is no means of reaching an agreement because it is the opposite of wanting to understand its basic determinations. For just that reason it is not even possible to have anything to do with it because it allows nothing but assertions, and naturally only its own, and is ignorant about this, that what it gives as reasons are themselves assertions.

But with this depiction of Solger's highest determination of the idea and of the highest rung of his philosophical development, one perhaps misses finding the irony touched upon preliminarily in the previous article mentioned, which because it otherwise occurs as labeled the highest, one can especially expect to meet here, to find its sense and determination exponentiated and safeguarded against misunderstandings. As it usually occurs, it is to be regarded as more than simply a famous, supposedly refined apparition. In relation to Solger, however, it can never be treated as a principle, and in this sense we want to consider it more closely here. For this purpose we distinguish the speculative moment lying in one side of irony and certainly finds itself in the speculative determinations observed. This is, namely, that negativity in general, which in the elevating to its abstract apex constitutes the basic determination of Fichtean philosophy. In the ego = ego not only all finiteness, but also all content in general has disappeared. The highest starting point for the problem of philosophy has indeed been brought to consciousness with this elevating, to develop the specific from the unconditional, the general—a principle containing the possibility for that because it is itself simply the impulse of development. But this principle is, first of all, itself a presupposition and only in its abstract and therefore itself not in its true, one-sided purity. A principle must also prove, not be required that it be accepted from intuition, immediate certainty, inner revelation, or as one may call it in a word, in good faith. The demand for proof, however, has become something obsolete for the very many and at the same time such monochromatic so-called philosophies of the time. The difficulty with this is to unite the mediation of the proving with that unconditional of the general in the idea. Through what appears as proving, the abstraction of the general is at the same time determined as a concrete, in which alone the possibility of development lies. In the cited form, that negativity has remained only in the one-sided, finite affirmation that it has as ego. In this exclusively subjective affirmation, it has been taken up from Fichtean philosophy by Friedrich Schlegel with a lack of understanding of the speculative and setting aside of the same, and so torn out of the field of thought, that turned directly toward reality, it has flourished into irony, to the negation of the animation of reason and truth and to the degradation of the same to the appearance in the subject and to the appearing for others. Fichte himself in the end corrected the one-sidedness of his principle through inconsequence, and with that preserved morality and truth in their rights. For that perversion, innocent Socratic irony had to allow its name to be perverted. It deserved all the less to be drawn into this, since if we leave out the page entirely according to which it was only the charming sophistry of cheerful, well-meaning conversation of Attic urbanity in which Plato and Aristophanes are these great masters, if we take them according to the sense in which they are attributed to Socrates in relation to his scholarly manner of teaching, it can appear to have been attributed to Socrates unjustly, were it accused or as praise. If it is mainly assumed thereby that Socrates began his introduction in conversation with the assurance of not knowing anything and caused the others, sophists, the learned, and whoever else there was, rather to display their wisdom and scholarship that then was brought to confusion and shame by him through his dialectic, so this success is certainly well-known, but is at the same time usually of such a kind that it remains something negative and without a scholarly result, so that the peculiarity and the great effect of Socrates should be placed in the stimulation of reflection and in the leading back of the human being to his innermost, to his moral and intellectual freedom. The truths that Socrates did not really teach and his students gained from him, that which is considered true and right for the human being, what he must draw and confirm from his own interior through reflection, refer entirely alone to that free self-assurance of the mind in general.

Accordingly, that preamble in Socrates considered as untrue, that he asserted to know nothing, to possess no knowledge, should, on the contrary, be considered by us as stated completely in earnest, as completely correct and by no means ironic. We do not find it contradicted by his actual teaching and activity.

If for Solger irony is now, according to his own explanations, by no means the "scornful disregard for everything which essentially and seriously interests the human being, for the entire discord in his nature" (II, 514 in the review of A.W. Schlegel's dramatic lectures),* but he instead expressly rejects this meaning of it, just as it is in other respects contrary to all his principles, his definition nevertheless remains not without the admixture of something crooked, as I have already noted elsewhere (*Outlines of the Philosophy of Law*, p. 150), and which emerges in connection with the speculative ideas explained above in an even more definitive light. What is to be differentiated from the purely abstract attitude of the speculative category of negativity discussed is the reflex of this upon the specific, upon the field where duties, truth, principles begin. It is in this transition where irony appears. "When it looks towards reality," it states in vol. I, p. 689, "mysticism is the mother of irony, when towards the eternal world, the child of enthusiasm or inspiration." We have seen before what is expressed right there (vol. III, p. 515ff.), that it is an immediate presence of the divine that reveals itself precisely in the disappearance of our reality. The mood that makes this directly manifest to human events is tragic irony. The comic shows us equally well "the best, yes, the divine in human nature, as it has unfolded completely in this life of dismemberment, of contradictions, of futility, and we recover from it for just that reason, because it has thereby become completely familiar to us and completely transplanted into our sphere. For that reason the highest and holiest, as it takes shape with the human being, must also be the

---

*August Wilhelm von Schlegel, "On Dramatic Art and Literature." Lectures, 3 volumes, Heidelberg, 1809–11.

object of comedy, and the comic, for its part, carries its seriousness, even its harshness, with itself again precisely in irony." Immediately before, it had been said that the highest for our behavior was there only in limited, finite formation, that for that reason it was as insignificant with us as the least and necessarily goes down with us and our insignificant meaning because, in truth, it is only there in God, in whose going down it then transfigures itself as divine. If we first take this elevation and its sentiment which is called tragic irony here, then what is necessary has already been mentioned with regard to the relationship of both definitions that relate here to each other, for which philosophical knowledge was the one definition, the point of departure. This elevation itself, in itself, whatever its point of departure may be, is nothing other than devotion, and if it is only a matter of popular depiction, then it does not require a large circumlocution in order to make one acknowledge it. In relation to ancient tragedy too, we may use the term devotion because that depiction of art was part and parcel of the cult, and as pure and enhanced devotion may be, it is nevertheless in general an elevation to God out of the occupation of the mind with temporal interests and cares and out of the impurity of the soul. But it is only the Sunday of life, the workdays follow. Out of the cabinet of the interior, the human being steps out of the specific present and work, and the question is: how does the reflex of the divine, which is present in devotion, look in this world? Solger is far removed from the view that the workday and activity in this world are and could only be a godless life; his theology is also morality (see the previous article), his philosophy for this reason at the same time worldly wisdom. But in the connection cited, the reflex of the divine in the world, "the unfolding of the same into the world of dismemberment, of nothingness." etc., through which the divine becomes familiar to us and transplanted completely into our sphere, appears only as comic irony, "the highest and holiest" as the object of comedy. Without wanting to go further into the dissection of "the highest and holiest," so much is clear that between the worldly presence of this kind and that elevation above the finite, the middle in which the "highest and holiest" as morality, law, love, and in every virtue has worldly presence, is missing, as Solger himself views everywhere the state, the entire moral life, as the revelation of God. Here affirmation must receive an entirely different determination than merely that of a subjective affirmation persisting negatively against the concrete. Whenever devotion returns out of its spiritual abode to worldly reality, it carries along the acknowledgment of duties, strengthening, and hearty earnestness to these and to life's profession, and by these, by these fruits, must essentially recognize itself if it is itself of a true, penetrating kind. It may have occurred to others to bring along for this domain too the viewpoint of irony. Certainly the moral laws, deeds, attitudes, etc., must also be considered in the aspect of the finite, "even the highest is for our behavior only there in limited finite formation," and devotion, although elevation in a higher region, is, if it is, as has been said, of the proper kind, far removed from making that formation merely trivial or contemptible with the abstract category of "finite" and behaving ironically or comically against it.

It is rather comical, an unconscious irony, that it is very obvious to Solger in the review of A. W. Schlegel's dramatic lectures cited (II, 514) to find irony, "in which he perceives the true central focus of dramatic art, so that even in philosophical dialogue" (more of this later) "it is not to be dispensed with, mentioned only once." But irony is also supposed to be the opposite of that view of life in which earnestness and jest, as Schlegel takes them, are rooted. Solger has met up with the same: in the speculative expositions of the highest idea, which he presents in the above-mentioned treatise with the innermost mental seriousness, not to mention irony at all, that which joins itself most intimately with enthusiasm and in which depths art, religion, and philosophy are to be identical. There especially, one would have believed, must be the place where one would find cleared up what the philosophical case might be with the noble secret, the great unknown—irony. If Solger says about the view of life that Schlegel takes, that it is the opposite of irony, it is then completely comprehensible that this has not occurred to Schlegel there, even if he had made "approximating remarks" earlier, just as much as the category of irony did not occur to Solger with his speculative and serious expositions, also not in the additional treatises contained in this second volume about the idea of the state and morality, and how these, his basic views of life, are the opposite of this. Where it seriously and truly deals with the concrete, serious, and true, this principle remains of itself far away. With Tieck, whose attachment to irony has been noted in the former article, we see the same thing happening. Several times (e.g., in the novella *The Poet's Life*) he gives a depiction of the excellence of Shakespeare's drama *Romeo and Juliet* written with true enthusiasm. Here, where philosophical discussions were not to be expected anyway, one could hope to find the point that constitutes irony in this love and its harsh fate shown by one example, but even there one does not find irony mentioned, just as little as it would easily occur to anyone else.

If we now see that with Solger the kind of subjectivity which irony is leaves the highest speculative principles as well as the axioms of concrete truth unharmed, so it nevertheless has to occur, for the sake of the imperfection of form in the highest determinations, that a subjective side comes out in another way—which should already reveal itself from the overview of the whole of the moments cited above. The first determination is (II, 144, 175, and otherwise) that the Godhead create itself directly to a present reality, which moment is for us only among the determinations and relationships of existence in which we are constrained. This relative fact should, however, raise itself in us into the experience and reality of God. With that the omnipresence of the same is expressed in everything finite, but with this obligation to experience, we are, first of all, no farther than what Spinoza expressed, that everything must be observed sub specie aeternitatis, or it is furthermore the same that the pious soul does to be devout in all natural things and changes, as in the occurrences of the circle of human things, to acknowledge and to experience in that the higher, God's finger and presence. The indefinite of this attitude becomes a definite content only through cognition. That this is true, for that not only the relative manner of cognition is enough for Solger, the so-called explaining out of natural causes that proceeds along the finite and stops within the circle of the limited, but also the manner of cognition that makes the eternal merely a presupposition and with that an abstract universal. Furthermore, Solger very nicely distinguishes these modes of cognition from philosophical knowledge as that which, within itself, by recognizing the progress of self-limiting determinations, at the same time sees itself in thought going beyond its finiteness and its original unity necessarily emerging out of that. Since Solger, however, separates from this objective being in truth, from the knowledge of opposites, what he calls the experiencing of divine reality, it still remains again for this only to make the "subjective sensation and devotion" a demand and bring about the elevating to the consciousness of divine presence in the same way it is produced through the religious excitement of the soul. It should be essential only in relation to itself, or also, that it be produced in the relation to philosophizing. It is only in such a superficial manner, therefore, that Solger can now seek to bring about this experiencing of the divine, since he has not recognized that for philosophical cognition, it is immanent as affirmative result as much as foundation and in the activity of progressing.

In the last chapter of the treatise considered, Solger comes to speak about the form of the discourse in which philosophy "should be able to satisfy its established meaning and determination best," which is supposed to be the dialogical form,—a blunder that pursued him throughout his entire career, which in spite of the experience of being thereby standing rather in the way of the effect of his expounded ideas, we see him stubbornly retaining and only reaping discord out of it. That form is entirely connected with that meaning of philosophy of being able to produce the animation of the idea in the subjective only outside of itself. If the exhibited hiatus between scholarly thinking and the existence of truth in the subject becomes a stoppage in knowledge, then a stoppage results in the direction taken towards the empirical quantity in the most pressing interest of efficacy, and out of that a false evaluation of the public and a discord in the relationship of the author to it. This gloomier feature permeates the entire letter collection and appends itself conspicuously to the characterization of the philosophical and individual position of Solger. There are times in which religion is a public condition acknowledged and attested to daily by all. Here it cannot occur to philosophy to want to create this firm ground for life and science first, but it will immediately set about acquiring the religious content only for thinking reason and, similarly, procuring satisfaction for its characteristic need. Other situations, however, can appear as if interest and faith in higher as well as sensual and temporal truth of daily life were acknowledged as expelled or falsified by the vanity of understanding and the dullness of self-conceit, and philosophy were, above all, to have the business of just producing again a demand and a pure, not deceitful, interest in supernatural objects and then in philosophy too.

We see such a gloomy representation of his time recurring only too often with Solger in the correspondence, and the little attention with which his endeavors for the animation of the sense for divine things seen to be received increases the bad feeling of his judgment about the public, which he sees only beneath the image he makes for himself out of the closer or more distant environment that touches his society. In the year 1815 he writes (I, p. 345ff.) to the wife of Gröben: "This manner of disparaging everything which is only quite pure and truly beautiful is very well known to me, and I am so sick of it that I often find it among people with whom one otherwise admires the sublime zeal for the most magnificent. In order to be considered something legitimate in the eyes of the present world and even of the so-called better ones, one must be at least in one direction quite thoroughly close-minded, flatter (compliment) any weak inclination, and see the true and the good always only in a falsified form." And on p. 359 to his brother: "You can't believe how things are in our societies, even among scholars. One prefers to bore oneself and talks about the silliest things rather than telling the others one's opinion." Earlier it was said: "You should be careful of expressing yourself thoroughly about anything because with that you run the risk of the appearance of omniscience." Such complaints occur too often elsewhere (p. 410, 421, 462) not to feel that this ill humor is more than a passing mood. Still from the year 1818 (p. 607) we read the following result of his experiences about his acquaintances: "I am living in this large city almost as if on a desert island. Even of those whom a limited private interest motivates, there are nevertheless only a few. Everything else is, where it doesn't depend on one's daily bread and one's daily oysters, a further standing swamp. That is how it looks in this "great" era. . . . What this race perhaps still likes, those are things like Müllner's Ravenstone tragedies,* hypocritical mindless collections of examples about this, that there is a God, etc. And if they were only delighted and excited, then there would still be a kernel there. . . . But no! These things have in truth as little an effect as our good things. One has arbitrarily resolved that they should have an effect. It stands written above it, after all, that there are excellent virtuous fashion-

---

*Müllner's Ravenstone tragedies: Amadeus Gottfried Adolf Müllner (1774–1829). Writer and dramatist known for his dark tragedies of blind fate.

able sentiments in it. One should certainly also want these, and that is the only reason why one foolishly talks oneself into being enthusiastic about it! That is the way it looks in this 'promising era.'" When Solger has the opportunity to speak of the reviewer (p. 686), he expresses his opinion: "I was curious about what kind of an impression Mr. H.[egel] would make here. No one talks about him. Only the dumbest blind adherent of the type they would only too gladly have would have to come, then a great alarm would be sounded and the students would be directed into his lectures for the salvation and rescue of their souls. I occasionally make a great joke of plopping into it quite impudently, and that works all the better as they no longer expect anything noble or virtuous from me. What always makes me the most apprehensive about my success, that is that I have no new foolishness to propose."

One cannot look at such a depiction of the farthest reaching ill humor and boredom with the mind, the image of which he has made from his experience, without a painful sensation. If, to be sure, one wants to adhere to what is often the most favorite and celebrated in public commerce, in literary newspapers or even in the theater, etc., then one will perhaps find such depictions not too glaring and such sentiments not unjust. Whatever the case may be with the peculiar spirit of the city in whose aspect Solger lived, who was always considered distinguished by them, so one might have wished Solger that the appearances of acquaintances and the social activity and talk had struck him less and that he had held them back from his imagination and sentiment more, even if it certainly will not do to avoid all situations and meetings in which the dullness or crudeness of such appearances happen or bluntly obtrude. For the lessening of the sensitivity to it, however, the observation would have to add that the manner of superficial social life and literary activity that makes itself most audible is not only for itself, but also often in relation to the individuals themselves who move within it, a superficiality within which they can probably still have a nonapparent seriousness and the need to settle unobtrusively and satisfy thoroughly, but without displaying or laying it out. Where such a need is not present, however, and the entire condition of scholarly and intellectual interest in general has become a glistening superficiality throughout, as Solger has such an aspect before him, then such a thorough leveling is to be left to its fate, the happiness of its conceit.

In that Solger allows this picture of his experience to be too powerful in itself, he had to fail to recognize the deeper need present in his and in every epoch and allow himself to be hindered in directing his activity and work only towards the place worthy of it, to seek and expect his effect in that place. He indeed also returns to a serene mood now and then, as on p. 413, where he says about it that almost no one takes notice of *Erwin:* "We therefore have to write to us and the muses, and not to forget, our friends." So it begins also on p. 509 with an expression of better conviction, namely, that true philosophy can operate only privately, but, it is added, privately and almost unconsciously, because there "are always very few people who can only be brought to this, that they recognize the simple and pure as the highest. They want verve and pomp and extraordinary unheard-of splendors, which they nevertheless piece together for themselves out of the tatters of the ordinary present." "Therefore," it is then continued, "I always insist on this, that philosophy presents itself best in its entire reality through conversation and that this remains its best means of having a lively effect on people." The initially named privacy, in which philosophy is said to thrive, could more easily have led to the opposite result, of having, with the intention of the effect, rather those in mind, though they be few.

In that mood it cannot be surprising to see Solger making popularity his essential goal. "I especially want, however," it says in vol. I, p. 385, "to move the world's heart about religion. Heaven help me towards a rather exciting depiction, so that I do not speak entirely into the wind," or still in the year 1818 (p. 593): "I cherish one thought with great love. . . . It is that of writing out a popular instructive account about religion, the state, art, and the most general moral relationships from my philosophy, so that the un-learned, females, and the youth growing up could instruct themselves." What he regards as the means for this is cited in the following (p. 316): "I believe to be certain through experience, that in today's world the view towards something higher is still enticed away by art in the first place, and that this first draws them into the interior of things." If such an opinion of desperation were quite correct, that times have come so far that one has to make it one's sole object to entice away from people that view towards the higher, then one would have to despair even more of the efficacy of the means for it, of art or philosophy or whatever it might be. The relationship among thinking, living, art, is thought like this (p. 620): "I would like to have thinking dissolve entirely into life again; that is why I immediately set down the artistic dialogical form as my goal. I now almost believe that I have undertaken something that the times do not want and do not like. One does not want to live, but rather chat about life, for no one who wanted to accomplish something truly lively in our times, like Novalis, Kleist, etc., could come through." It is shown above that Solger misjudged the particular animation which the nature of the thinking idea contains within itself, which Aristotle had already grasped so deeply and intimately as the highest animation. This old man says (*Metaphysics* XI, 7): The activity of thinking is life, but God is the activity. The activity existing for itself, however, is his complete and eternal life. But if it is to be a question of the artistic consciousness of the "truly animated," and a modern and German are to be cited as an example and not Goethe perchance, who indeed accomplished the "quite animated" and was also able to "come through," but Novalis! but Kleist! Then one would perceive from this that only a life destroying itself through reflective thinking, indeed remaining divided within itself, is meant. Because what reveals itself as the individuality of Novalis is that the need for thinking drove this beautiful soul only as far as longing and was neither able to overcome nor even relinquish abstract understanding. This rather struck the noble youth so much into his heart, with such fidelity, one can say, that transcendental longing, this consumption of the spirit, carried itself out through corporeality, and this has consequently determined its destiny. The reflection remaining in the dissension of the Kleistian productions has been touched upon above. With all the animation of the configurations, the characters and situations, there is a lack in the substantial content, which in the last instance decides, and the animation becomes an energy of inner strife, and indeed, one producing itself intentionally, the irony destroying and wanting to destroy life.

Already in the year 1800 there is a passage in Solger's diary (p. 15) in which he expresses the intention of writing a book in dialogues, and still among his unpublished writings (in the second volume of this collection) a speculative essay composed in dialogical form can be found. One cannot seek to deny that the Platonic mastery in dialogue could not in today's times still be capable of being respectably emulated and thereby produce a great effect and acknowledgment. Yet Solger protests expressly against it, that he had wanted to imitate Plato. But the imitation of a method cannot be called anything but carrying out what is useful and correct about it. Only Solger did not take up the plastic form that the dialogue can gain only through the attribute of having dialectics as its soul, but changed it into its opposite, into conversation, through which every advantage of this form for abstract materials that accompanies strict necessity of continuation with an external enlivening has been lost, and only the disadvantage, exhausting breadth of the discourse, a burdensome excess, the form of the fortuitousness of the enunciated, the disturbance or impossibility of retaining and overseeing the thread of *raisonnement*, has been brought in. One of the friends considers the discussions of *Erwin* (vol. I, p. 353) as difficult: "You must, through whatever means there may be, simply make the future ones more understandable." Another says to him later yet (p. 741) and also not in a cheerful context: "Up to now I still understand the Straßburg Cathedral better than your *Erwin*." The best means of making the content of *Erwin* more understandable would have been the straightforward exposition in a coherent discourse. The thoughts of the first part, which deals with the reputation of earlier definitions and points of view about observing the beautiful, could probably be clearly and definitively enunciated on a few pages. Thus it would be easy to grasp what is hardly ever achieved with the arduous difficulty of reading through the conversations. In the same connection, the first of the friends says, in order to impress upon Solger the efforts towards comprehensibility more strongly: Not Plato's *Parmenides, Euthydemus, Timaeus,* have essentially founded his reputation, not through these difficult dialogues did he have a wide impact, not for that received the epithet of the divine, not renewed and given birth again to the soul with what is difficult to fathom; much more through *Phaidon,* the *Symposium,* and that, with its great depth, so very understandable *Republic.*" For a view departing from this, I should like to refer to the story that, namely, Plato's doctrine, as it is mainly enunciated in *Parmenides* and *Timaeus,* became the cornerstones of Alexandrian philosophy, which has essentially promoted the cultivation of the higher Christian system, insofar as it contains the knowledge of the nature of God. The difficulty of those dialogues through which Plato had this great influence lies in the nature of the deep content, but it is this alone that has penetrated into the illumination of Christianity and shown itself so powerfully within it. The manner in which it is enunciated in those dialogues is suitable to it. It is the most abstract, strictest, and farthest removed from all conversational style.

We have masterpieces of dialogical discourse in modern languages (one only has to refer to Galiani's dialogues, Diderot, Cousin, and Rameau). But here the form is at the same time subordinated to the matter, nothing idle. The matter is, however, not a speculative content, but rather a kind that, entirely according to its nature, can be the subject of conversation. In that plastic form of Plato, one of the conversationalists keeps the thread of continuation in his hand, so that all content falls into the questions and only the formal agreement falls into the answers. The instructor remains master and does not give information about questions one addressed to him or answers to objections brought forward.

The position is the opposite of the notion one perhaps has about the Socratic method (as one also calls the organization of the Catechism). It is not the ignorant one who asks, and except for that single and indeed inquiring one, the people of the dialogue do not behave with the autonomy a back-and-forth conversation would provide to assert one's particular views, convictions, with reasons, to refute the opposing views, or to look for one's own advantage on the basis of their reasons. Such a procedure of reasoning which may certainly predominate in conversation has been called sophistry by the ancients. With the opposing dialectic of Plato, the form of the dialogue is an extrinsic one that only produces the animation not merely to direct attention towards the result or total representation, but to become stimulated towards agreement for every detail of the continuation. The episodic charm likewise brought about with this form is only too often too seductive for many not to stop at the introductions, at the so contrasting dryness of the logical abstractions and the development of it, not to go wearily into these and still think to have read Plato and mastered his philosophy. So that the agreeing is not something stark and a lame formalism, however, that relationship carries with it the compulsion that every individual determination and sentence be explained simply and in the strictest connection. Such a plastic form of continuation is only possible, however, through the analysis of the concepts penetrating to the most simple. According to this essential determination of speculative discourse, Aristotle is just as plastic in his developments, so that if one took the form of questioning away from the more solid dialogues of Plato and put the sentences all in a row in direct elocution, one could just as well believe one were reading Aristotelian writings, as one would be able to make Aristotelian writings or chapters into sections of Platonic dialogues through transformation of the sequence of sentences into the form of questions.

I shall be satisfied with these general comments about the dialogue. It would be tedious to prove them with examples from the philosophical conversations contained in these posthumous writings or to go back for that to *Erwin* and the *Philosophical Conversations* published by Solger in the year 1817. Of that dialogue *On Being, Non-Being, and Knowing* (II, 199–262), it may only be mentioned, as is already evident from the title, that Solger's philosophical career brings itself to a close there in an elevation to the observation of purely speculative objects. With this attempt, there also occurs, aside from the annoyance of the conversational form, the drawback noticed earlier, that the abstractions of being and nonbeing are mingled with the more concrete determinations like knowing. The main points are such inappropriate connections as these, that nonbeing is knowing, that knowing is a nonbeing of that specific being into the infinite, but with that, is also the general, etc. But otherwise, the general concept of the evolution of the idea is that it is in every point a synthesizing, a return to itself, as the speculative character of the concept is on the whole predominant in it. Solger does not shrink back from expressing the unity of being and nonbeing. It occurs that knowing is completely one with being, only that the one is that which the other is not, and p. 224, that the general and the particular are necessarily completely one, since precisely the general is nothing other than the nonbeing of the entire particular (p. 245). One sees it: to think of the speculative boldness, the contradiction that according to traditional logic is not conceivable and should probably be existing even less, was not lacking, just as the speculative insight that the idea essentially contains the contradiction was not. Only this is retained in the cited expressions in its entire crudeness, so that it appears as something enduring, and its just as immediately essential disappearance, which is its disintegration and at the same time makes it tolerable for representation as for thinking, is not linked to it. But even those crude expressions of contradiction are important in themselves, so that if one hears about the solving of the contradiction and the reconciling of thinking out of and within itself, one would be far removed from thinking that such a solving and reconciling and anything affirmative, reason and truth in general, could take place without immanence.

In addition to the range of Solger's philosohical meditations, the Philosophy of Law and the State, about which three previously printed essays are given in the second volume, must still be cited. Although they are aphoristic and not completed, probably intended to serve as the guide for his lectures about this material, one can nevertheless recognize the depth of the ideas sufficiently enough from them, and the basic view is drawn definitively enough to differentiate them completely according to the general idea as well as to particular categories that are important for law, state, constitution, from that which constitutes current principles about these materials. The reviewer was pleased to find himself in such positive agreement with their contents while reading through these essays.

There follow yet a few unpublished essays and speeches held on the occasion of the king's birthday, among them a Latin one. Solger's skill in round, clear, and at the same time thoughtful diction gives these essays their particular value. One should be grateful to the editors that they have had published the substantial preface of Solger's translation of Sophocles and the just as important review of the A. W. Schlegelian *Lectures on Dramatic Art and Literature*, even more interesting in what is occasionally treated there as in the refutations that appeared in the Viennese Yearbooks. Ingenious essays from the field of classical studies to which Solger at an early time turned his inclination and diligence, for himself as well as in relation to philosophy, and maintained throughout his entire career, form the conclusion. The "Mythological Views" is an essay revised by Herr Professor Müller in Göttingen from Solger's notebooks and handwritten collections and, as rich as it is, still could contain only little of that for which Solger had worked and made manifold preparations. One of the treatises worked out by Solger himself, *On the Oldest View of the Greeks of the Formation of the World*, examines Voss's well-known essay on this subject, where we see how this passionate hobgoblin in his presumption about history and exactness of dates took the liberty of equipping his in-and-of-themselves stark representations with self-made fabrications. The many materials collected by Solger for the history of religions from reading and meditation were meant for a comprehensive work about this subject. His interest reaches deeply into the various disputed views and methods of dealing with mythology in recent times. Letters from the last months of his life (see vol. I), in which he encounters his friend von der Hagen* somewhat sharply, still have to do with this subject. Yet among the richness and variety of materials, this, has, like much else, interesting things in terms of its general content or even personality, like the letters to his wife full of pure and delicate sentiments, that must be overlooked in this report, which has been brought before the public from the intimate circle of personal acquaintance and exhibited for evaluation through publication, and could only take up that which could serve not only to characterize more closely the personal individuality with which the reviewer has had the gratification of coming into contact, but also the scholarly one.

Translated by Diana I. Behler

---

*Friedrich Heinrich von der Hagen (1780–1856). Scholar of Germanics known for his work of the minnesingers.

THE GERMAN LIBRARY
in 100 Volumes

Gottfried von Strassburg
Tristan and Isolde
Edited and Revised by Francis G. Gentry
Foreword by C. Stephen Jaeger

German Medieval Tales
Edited by Francis G. Gentry
Foreword by Thomas Berger

German Humanism and Reformation
Edited by Reinhard P. Becker
Foreword by Roland Bainton

Immanuel Kant
Philosophical Writings
Edited by Ernst Behler
Foreword by René Wellek

Friederich Schiller
Plays: Intrigue and Love and Don Carlos
Edited by Walter Hinderer
Foreword by Gordon Craig

Johann Wolfgang von Goethe
The Sufferings of Young Werther
and *Elective Affinities*
Edited by Victor Lange
Forewords by Thomas Mann

German Romantic Criticism
Edited by A. Leslie Willson
Foreword by Ernst Behler

Philosophy of German Idealism
Edited by Ernst Behler

Heinrich von Kleist
Plays
Edited by Walter Hinderer
Foreword by E. L. Doctorow

E.T.A. Hoffman
Tales
Edited by Victor Lange

Georg Büchner
Complete Works and Letters
Edited by Walter Hinderer and Henry J. Schmidt

German Fairy Tales
Edited by Helmut Brachert and Volkmar Sander
Foreword by Bruno Bettelheim

German Literary Fairy Tales
Edited by Frank G. Ryder and Robert M. Browning
Introduction by Gordon Birrell
Foreword by John Gardner

Heinrich Heine
Poetry and Prose
Edited by Jost Hermand and Robert C. Holub
Foreword by Alfred Kazin

Heinrich von Kleist and Jean Paul
German Romantic Novellas
Edited by Frank G. Ryder and Robert M. Browning
Foreword by John Simon

German Romantic Stories
Edited by Frank Ryder
Introduction by Gordon Birrell

German Poetry from 1750 to 1900
Edited by Robert M. Browning
Foreword by Michael Hamburger

Gottfried Keller
Stories
Edited by Frank G. Ryder
Foreword by Max Frisch

Wilhelm Raabe
Novels
Edited by Volkmar Sander
Foreword by Joel Agee

Theodor Fontane
Short Novels and Other Writings
Edited by Peter Demetz
Foreword by Peter Gay

Theodor Fontane
Delusions, Confusions and The Poggenpuhl Family
Edited by Peter Demetz
Foreword by J. P. Stern
Introduction by William L. Zwiebel

Wilhelm Busch and Others
German Satirical Writings
Edited by Dieter P. Lotze and Volkmar Sander
Foreword by John Simon

Writings of German Composers
Edited by Jost Hermand and James Steakley

German Lieder
Edited by Philip Lieson Miller
Foreword by Hermann Hesse

Arthur Schnitzler
Plays and Stories
Edited by Egon Schwarz
Foreword by Stanley Elkin

Rainer Maria Rilke
Prose and Poetry
Edited by Egon Schwarz
Foreword by Howard Nemerov

Robert Musil
Selected Writings
Edited by Burton Pike
Foreword by Joel Agee

Essays on German Theater
Edited by Margaret Herzfeld-Sander
Foreword by Martin Esslin

German Novellas of Realism I and II
Edited by Jeffrey L. Sammons

Friedrich Dürrenmatt
Plays and Essays
Edited by Volkmar Sander
Foreword by Martin Esslin

Hans Magnus Enzensberger
Critical Essays
Edited by Reinhold Grimm and Bruce Armstrong
Foreword by John Simon

Gottfried Benn
Prose, Essays, Poems
Edited by Volkmar Sander
Foreword by E. B. Ashton
Introduction by Reinhard Paul Becker

German Essays on Art History
Edited by Gert Schiff

Max Frisch
Novels, Plays, Essays
Edited by Rolf Kieser
Foreword by Peter Demetz

All volumes available in hardcover and paperback editions at your bookstore or from the publisher. For more information on The German Library write to: The Continuum Publishing Company, 370 Lexington Avenue, New York, NY 10017.